GLOBALIZATION OF EDUCATION

Continuing Joel Spring's reportage and analysis of the intersection of global forces and education, this text offers a comprehensive overview and synthesis of current research, theories, and models related to the topic. Written in his trademark clear, narrative style, Spring introduces the processes, institutions, and forces by which schooling has been globalized and examines the impact of these forces on schooling in local contexts.

Significant conceptual frameworks are added to this second edition, specifically the "economization of education," "corporatization of education," and the "audit state." These concepts are embedded in the global educational plans of major organizations such as the World Bank, the Organization for Economic Development and Cooperation (OECD), the World Economic Forum, and multinational corporations. *Globalization of Education, Second Edition* features the following new and updated information:

- The World Bank
- OECD and the United Nations
- The World Trade Organization and the global culture of higher education
- Corporatization of global education
- Religious and Indigenous education models
- The global workforce: migration and the talent auction
- Globalization and complex thought

Each chapter includes "Key Points" that summarize the content and suggest issues and questions for critical analysis, discussion, and debate. Engaging and informative, the text is designed for courses on globalization and education, international and comparative education, educational foundations, multicultural education, and educational policy.

Joel Spring is Professor at Queens College/City University of New York and the Graduate Center of the City University of New York, USA.

Sociocultural, Political, and Historical Studies in Education
Joel Spring, Editor

For additional information on titles in the Sociocultural, Political, and Historical Studies in Education series, visit **www.routledge.com/education**.

GLOBALIZATION OF EDUCATION

An Introduction

Second Edition

Joel Spring

Routledge
Taylor & Francis Group

NEW YORK AND LONDON

First published 2015
by Routledge
711 Third Avenue, New York, NY 10017

and by Routledge
2 Park Square, Milton Park, Abingdon, Oxon, OX14 4RN

Routledge is an imprint of the Taylor & Francis Group, an informa business

© 2015 Taylor & Francis

Library of Congress Cataloging-in-Publication Data

Spring, Joel H.
    Globalization of education : an introduction / by Joel Spring. — Second edition.
        pages cm
    Includes bibliographical references and index.
    1. Education—Economic aspects.   2. Education and globalization.   I. Title.
    LC65.S67 2014
    370—dc23
    2014002885

ISBN: 978-0-415-74984-8 (hbk)
ISBN: 978-0-415-74986-2 (pbk)
ISBN: 978-1-315-79584-3 (ebk)

Typeset in Bembo
by Apex CoVantage, LLC

CONTENTS

PREFACE

There are significant conceptual frameworks added to this second edition of *Globalization of Education: An Introduction*. These concepts include the "economization of education," "corporatization of education," and the "audit state." These concepts are embedded in the global educational plans of major organizations, including the World Bank, the Organization for Economic Development and Cooperation (OECD), the World Economic Forum, and multinational corporations.

The concept of the "economization of education" is discussed in Chapter 1 and elaborated on in different contexts in Chapters 2 and 3. By "economization of education," I mean the increasing influence of economists on educational research and judging school outcomes in economic terms. The economization of education shifts concerns from schooling for such things as civic participation, protecting human rights, and environmentalism to economic growth and employment. In Chapters 2 and 3, I show how the economization of education places economic value on knowledge, personality traits, and family life.

In Chapters 1 and 5, I utilize the concept of the "corporatization of education," which refers to multinational corporations influencing global school policies to educate and shape human behaviors for the corporate workplace. In addition, global education corporations want national school policies that enhance the sale of their products, such as texts, software, hardware, and online instruction. These multinational corporations network through international organizations, such as OECD, the World Economic Forum, the World Trade Organization (WTO), and regional trade organizations. As part of the discussion of the corporatization of education, I have added a section in Chapter 5 on the work of British sociologist Stephen J. Ball who has studied the networks linking corporations to school policies.

In Chapter 2, I introduce the idea of the "audit state" in the context of the work of the World Bank and the OECD. The "audit state" refers to the use of performance standards to assess government programs, including the use of standardized assessments to evaluate educational performance. OECD's global assessments Programme for International Student Assessment (PISA) and Trends in International Mathematics and Science Study (TIMSS) are key elements of the audit state, along with national standardized testing.

All chapters are updated with current information on global education trends. I have updated Chapter 2 using recent World Bank reports, such as the World Bank's 2013 annual report, recent criticisms of the work of the World Bank, and its proposed educational strategy for the year 2020. Also in Chapter 2, I update the work on the United Nations' millennium development goals. In Chapter 3, I utilize the most recent reports by OECD arguing for a skills-based global curriculum to meet the needs of corporations and help reduce unemployment. As part of the audit state, I review recent materials on the global tests PISA and TIMSS.

In the revised Chapter 4, I add material on the types of educational trade sanctioned by the WTO and the role of global higher education rankings in promoting global uniformity of educational systems. In Chapter 5, besides the previously mentioned discussion on the corporatization of global education, I add material on the corporatization of global English and the radical environmental education rejection of global corporatization. In Chapter 7, I update global migration, or, as it is called, "brain circulation," with recent materials from the United Nations Population Division and by reports from its Commissioner for Refugees.

1

GLOBALIZATION OF EDUCATION

Globalization of education refers to worldwide networks, processes, and institutions affecting local educational practices and policies. The key word is "worldwide." Events happen on a global scale that affect national and local school systems. Global educational policies and practices exist in a superstructure above national and local schools. Nothing is static in this superstructure. Nations continue to independently control their school systems while being influenced by this superstructure of global education processes. Today, many nations choose to adopt policies from this global superstructure in order to compete in the global economy.

What constitutes this global education superstructure? There are international organizational networks that directly and indirectly influence national school systems along with multinational education corporations and schools. In the first issue of the journal *Globalisation, Societies and Education* (2003), the editors stated that globalization of education would be considered as an intertwined set of global processes affecting education, such as worldwide discourses on human capital, economic development, and multiculturalism; intergovernmental organizations (IGOs); information and communication technology; nongovernmental organizations (NGOs); and multinational corporations.[1] Each of these aspects of the educational global superstructure is discussed in later chapters. For example, global discourses exist about the knowledge economy, lifelong learning, global migration, and brain circulation.

The major global institutions affecting worldwide educational policies are the Organization for Economic Cooperation and Development (OECD); the World Bank; the United Nations Educational, Scientific, and Cultural Organization (UNESCO); the World Trade Organization (WTO) and its General Agreement on Trade in Services (GATS); and other IGOs and NGOs, such as human rights, environmental, and women's organizations. English, as the global language of business and tourism, also impacts local schools often resulting in English being made part of the curriculum. Explanations and analyses of the previously discussed aspects of educational globalization and their impact on national school systems constitute the major part of this book.

Global Corporatization of Education

I will use "global corporatization" and the "economization of education" as important concepts, but not the only concepts, in describing some trends in global education. Multinational corporations, including global education corporations, are currently influencing global school policies with the goal of educating and shaping human behaviors for the corporate workplace. I call this the "global corporatization of education" with multinational corporations pressuring national school systems to adopt favorable education policies. These multinational corporations network through international organizations, such as the OECD, the World Economic Forum, and the WTO, and through regional trade groups.

Global corporatization of education involves schooling for a global labor market using human capital economic theories. These theories, as I explain in more detail later in this chapter, focus on shaping human behavior and knowledge to meet corporate needs. Simply stated, human capital economists claim that investment in education to produce better workers will result in economic growth, reduction of inequality of incomes, and increased employment.

In this book, I consider human capital education as part of the ongoing "economization of education." What I mean by the economization of education is the increasing influence of educational research conducted by economists and judging school outcomes in economic terms. The economization of education shifts concerns from schooling for such things as civic participation, protecting human rights, and environmentalism to economic growth and employment.

The global economization of education emphasizes teaching skills for the workplace. Human capital education emphasizes teaching two types of skills. One type is the cognitive skills and knowledge needed to succeed in the workplace. The other type, which is referred to as "soft skills," is the behavior needed to function in the corporate world. Human capital economists argue that preschool is necessary for the development of soft skills or character traits to succeed in the workplace.[2]

Corporatization, in the context of teaching soft skills, means shaping human behavior to meet business needs. This fits another economic paradigm referred to as "nudge" based on the work of University of Chicago economist Richard Thaler and Cass Sunstein, a regulatory official in the U.S. government, in their book *Nudge: Improving Decisions about Health, Wealth, and Happiness*.[3] *Nudge* involves the application by governments of behavioral economics and social psychology to shape public behavior. Sometimes called "libertarian paternalism," behavioral control of the population is considered in the interest of those wanting to reduce government spending and taxes, while solving problems of unemployment and government dependency by changing public behaviors.[4] In an article on the use of nudge in the United Kingdom, *New York Times* reporter Katrin Bennhold stated, "Every civil servant in Britain is now being trained in behavioral science. The nudge unit has a waiting list of government departments eager to work with it, and other countries, from Denmark to Australia, have expressed interest."[5]

In summary, the corporatization of global education refers to corporate influence over national school policies, enlisting economists to judge the work of school systems, teaching cognitive skills and knowledge needed in the workplace, and shaping behavior in schools and by government to meet the needs of corporations and to sustain free market economics. While the corporatization of education is the main trend in global education, there are other voices competing to be heard, as I will describe subsequently, such as education for civic activism, human rights, the environment, and religious and Indigenous forms of schooling.

An example of complete corporatization of human life can be found in *Fallen Land* by novelist Patrick Flanery. The heads of his imaginary company called EKK envision a global corporation that is "active everywhere, touching all aspects of a person's life, from conception . . . to death and disposal (cremation, organ and tissue recycling, human remains management)."[6]

The EKK's corporate divisions include fertility and biotech, health care and medical subcontracting, charter school administration, curriculum development, profit-making universities, employment, employee relations, financial and assets management, security and incarceration, immigration and detention centers, entertainment, travel, hotel and resort management, and old-age care. In other words, all parts of a citizen's life are corporatized.

Paralleling human capital concerns with teaching soft skills or character traits needed for corporate life, EKK provides its employees with a home protection system that monitors not only for fire and burglary, but also family behaviors. In other words, family members are to be protected against family interactions or behavior traits that might harm their ability to be efficient corporate workers. The home protection system will report back to EKK any household or individual behaviors detrimental to the good of corporate life. Of course, EKK operates its own schools designed to educate obedient workers.

Will, as Patrick Flanery suggests, every aspect of human life be brought under global corporate control for either profit or to ensure the education and behavioral control of workers to meet corporate needs? Is this a future direction of global education?

Globalization of Education

In 1985, the economist Theodore Levitt coined the term "globalization" to describe changes in global economics.[7] The term was quickly applied to political and cultural changes that affect in common ways large segments of the world's peoples. One of these common global phenomena is schooling. As the opening editorial in the first edition of *Globalisation, Societies and Education*—the very founding of this journal indicates the growing importance of globalization and education as a field of study—states, "Formal education is the most commonly found institution and most commonly shared experience of all in the contemporary world."[8] However, globalization of education does not mean that all schools are the same as indicated by studies of differences between the local and the global.[9]

The European Commission's document *Teaching and Learning: On Route to the Learning Society* describes three basic causes of globalization: "the advent of the information society, scientific and technical civilisation and the globalisation of the economy. All three contribute to the development of a learning society."[10]

The growth of worldwide educational institutions, networks, and discourses has led to similar national educational agendas, particularly the concept of education as an economic investment. Consequently, educational discourses around the world often refer to economic growth, teaching work-related skills, and lifelong learning for work. Also, the global economy is sparking a mass migration of workers resulting in global discussions about multicultural education.

IGOs, such as the United Nations, OECD, and the World Bank, are promoting global educational agendas that reflect discourses about job preparation, economic development, and multiculturalism. Information and communication technology is speeding the global flow of information and creating a library of world knowledges. Global NGOs, particularly those concerned with human rights and environmentalism, are influencing school curricula throughout the world. Multinational corporations, particularly those involved in publishing, information, testing, for-profit schooling, and computers, are marketing their products to governments, schools, and parents around the world.

Global and Comparative Education

How is the study of globalization and education different from the traditional field of comparative education? First, researchers on globalization and education are not drawn exclusively from comparative education though many of those studying globalization are identified with that field. As a new field of study, researchers into the processes and effects of globalization on educational practices and policies come from a variety of education disciplines, including anthropology, curriculum studies, economics, history, sociology, educational policy, comparative education, psychology, and instructional methodologies. For instance, the book *Globalizing Education: Policies, Pedagogies, & Politics* is edited by Michael Apple, a curriculum researcher; Jane Kenway, a sociology of education researcher; and Michael Singh, an educational policy researcher.[11] Consequently, at least in its initial stages, research in this new field is interdisciplinary.

Second, comparative education has traditionally focused on comparing the education systems of nations. Referring to the "new world for comparative education," Roger Dale wrote that with globalization the world "can no longer unproblematically be apprehended as made up of autonomous states, an assumption that had been fairly fundamental to much work in comparative education, indeed, the basis of the comparisons it undertook."[12] Or, as Carnoy and Rhoten asserted, "Before the 1950s, comparative education focused mainly on the philosophical and cultural origins of national education systems."[13] In an editorial in *Comparative Education*, Broadfoot wrote about the value of globalization to the field of comparative education: "At the present time we find ourselves at the latter extreme, with governments around the world anxious to learn about educational practices in other countries, as they scan the latest international league tables of school performance."[14]

KEY POINTS: THE COMPONENTS OF EDUCATIONAL GLOBALIZATION

1. The adoption by nations of similar educational practices, including curricula, school organizations, and pedagogies
2. Global discourses that are influencing local and national educational policymakers, school administrators, college faculties, and teachers
3. IGOs and NGOs that influence national and local educational practices
4. Global networks and flow of ideas and practices
5. Multinational corporations that market educational products, such as tests, curricula, and school materials
6. Global marketing of higher education and educational services
7. Global information technology, e-learning, and communications
8. The effect of the world migration of peoples on national and local school policies and practices regarding multiculturalism
9. The current effect of English as the global language of commerce on local school curricula and cultures
10. Global models of religious and Indigenous education

Global Flows and Networks

Global education flows in education refer to the worldwide movement of people, ideas, policies, money, and education companies. Global networks link people, IGOs and NGOs, professional societies, and corporations. Arjun Appadurai introduced the image of global flows of ideas, practices, institutions, and people interacting with local populations.[15] He calls the global flow of the world's peoples "ethnoscapes." The global movement of people includes those relocating to other nations, tourists, and workers, particularly those working for multinational corporations. Obviously, this flow of people involves a global flow of cultures that interact and change.

Of particular importance for education is the flow of ideas and practices regarding government and other institutional policies, which Appadurai calls "ideoscapes." This global flow of ideas interacts with national and local ideas about government and institutional practices. This interaction results in changing the ideas in the global flow and ideas at the local level. Nothing is static in this image: global ideas change at the same time as they affect local school practices.

Using Appadurai's imagery, the educational superstructure consists of global flows of ideas, institutions, and people with dynamic interactions with local organizations and people. These global flows are speeded up by advances in transportation, and communication and information technology. Advances in new technology in Appadurai's image are also part of the global flow that he calls "technoscapes." It is new transportation technology that makes possible the quicker movement of global migrants, workers, and tourists and makes it possible for educational and government leaders to easily meet almost any place on the globe. Communication and information technologies allow for the global exchange of ideas about educational practices and create a world library of information. Of course, new educational technologies have an impact on local pedagogies.

Another image is that of global networks. These networks are composed of people, IGOs NGOs, and multinational organizations. Communications and information technology enhances the possibility of building and sustaining global networks. Global education networks link educational institutions, educational policymakers, professional educational organizations, and IGOs. Because of the Internet, networks can compress time and space so that communication becomes almost instantaneous. Also, networks continue to expand and attract members. Being in a network increases the possibilities of success in most endeavors. Larger networks can encompass smaller networks. For instance, there might exist a global network of educational scholars whose members participate in other networks that link intergovernmental agencies and multinational educational corporations.[16]

In *Global Education Inc.: New Policy Networks and the Neo-Liberal Imaginary*, sociologist Stephen J. Ball contends that global networks now govern national school policies. He writes, "I contend that policy networks do constitute a new form of governance, albeit not in a single and coherent form, and bring into play in the policy process new sources of authority and indeed a 'market of authorities'."[17] In other words, the global connection of people and institutions results in global decisions that can exercise authority over local schools.

Flow and network images of globalization have been criticized for portraying individuals as being passive participants or subjects.[18] In the imagery of flows and networks, there is a danger of thinking that a teacher's educational practices are simply a product of the influences of global ideoscapes, technoscapes, and ethnoscapes, and global networks linking education policymakers and intergovernmental and nongovernmental institutions. In reality, local school officials and teachers do not simply dance to the tune of global flows and networks. First, they might give meaning to the influence of global educational policies and practices through the lens of their own cultural perspectives. Second, they might adapt global educational practices to local conditions. Lastly, they might reject or resist global influences.

In summary, the globalization of educational institutions and practices can be envisioned as a superstructure composed of global flows and networks within with their influence being determined by the interpretation, adaptation, or rejection by local educators.

KEY POINTS: GLOBAL FLOWS AND NETWORKS IN EDUCATION

1. The global flow of ideas or ideoscapes contributes to global similarity in national education policies.
2. Networks of educational policymakers working for IGOs, such as UNESCO, OECD, and the World Bank, engage in global educational discourses and contribute to the global glow of educational practices.
3. Networks of educational policymakers and scholars who through e-mail and other forms of communication, scholarly publications, and international meetings contribute to a global flow of educational ideas and discourses.
4. Global flow of capital and trade or financescapes includes multinational corporations marketing educational products and services.
5. Global networks include those belonging to other global networks of educational policymakers and scholars, members of IGOs, and multinational corporations that contribute to the flow of educational discourses and practices.
6. Global networks linking global educational networks with local educational policymakers, administrators, and teachers that contribute to the flow of educational discourses and practices.
7. Global migration or ethnoscapes contribute to the formation of global communities that extend beyond the boundaries of a nation-state.

World Education Culture: The Work of World Culture Theorists

The premise of world culture scholars is that all cultures are slowly integrating into a single global culture. Often called "neo-institutionalist," proponents of this school of thought believe that national policymakers draw on this world culture in planning their school systems.[19]

Two classic works by world culture theorists are John Meyer, David Kamens, and Aaron Benavot's *School Knowledge for the Masses: World Models and National Primary Curricular Categories in the Twentieth Century* and David Baker and Gerald

LeTendre's *National Differences, Global Similarities: World Culture and the Future of Schooling*.[20]

The authors of *School Knowledge for the Masses* contend that local education policymakers rely on a world education culture to make their policy decisions. As a result, the "general outlines of mass education and its curriculum often show surprising degrees of homogeneity around the world."[21] For instance, most of the world's government school systems are structured around an educational ladder leading from primary grades to some form of middle school to secondary education to higher education or some form of postsecondary school. This educational structure is so common that global educational reports can combine national statistics under common headings such as primary or secondary. As an example, the statistical table on education in the UNICEF report *The State of the World's Children 2006: Excluded and Invisible* simply reports enrollment and attendance figures for the world's nations under columns labeled "primary school" and "secondary school."[22] Most readers of this and similar reports probably don't consider it unusual that the world's nations utilize the same educational ladder.

Regarding curricula, the authors of *School Knowledge for the Masses* found a significant worldwide similarity in organization and course labels for primary education. They concluded from an examination of national curricular outlines that there was "more homogeneity and standardization among the curricula prescribed by nation-states, than might have been expected . . . The labels, at least, of mass curricula are so closely tied to great and standardized worldwide visions of social and educational progress, they tend to be patterned in quite consistent ways around the world."[23]

The global homogeneity of the curriculum is the result of national policy elites, particularly in developing countries, selecting from a world education culture of education. In other words, local school people select from a global best educational practices agenda. While the authors of *School Knowledge for the Masses* do not use the language of global flows, the image they create is of a global flow of best educational practices that national policymakers choose from. National policymakers then align global practices with local needs and practices.

How was the world education culture created? According to the authors of *School Knowledge for the Masses*, it was a result of worldwide spread of the Western concept of the nation-state, which included a belief in educating the citizenry to ensure political stability and economic growth. By the late nineteenth century, the authors argue, "the gradual rationalization of the Western polity, the modern curricular structure became a taken-for-granted 'model' by the turn of the twentieth century."[24] As the Western concept of the nation-state spread, "the standard model of the curriculum has also diffused throughout the world, creating a worldwide homogeneity in the over-all categorical [curriculum categories] system."[25]

Because of this global flow of Western ideas, Baker and LeTendre declare: "In spite of the fact that nations . . . have immediate political and fiduciary control over schooling, education as an institution has become a global enterprise."[26]

One reason they assert is the growing importance of educational credentials for employment in the global marketplace. Some standardization of the educational ladder and curricula is necessary for educational credentials to be of value in the global economy. University degrees from institutions in India and China should be similar to degrees from universities in the European Union and the United States so that the degree can be used as a credential for global employment.

Baker and LeTendre believe that a world culture of schooling has developed that will lead to homogeneity between global school systems. They argue, "Mass schooling is the predominant model of education in the world today. It pervades every part of people's lives in modern society and creates a cultural education unparalleled in human existence."[27]

In response to critics of an evolving single global model of schooling, Francisco Ramirez explained the origins of the concept of a world education culture. Working with other Stanford University sociologists in the 1970s and 1980s on the evolution of world culture theory, Ramirez wrote, "The [world] culture at work, we later asserted, was articulated and transmitted through nation-states, organizations, and experts who themselves embodied the triumph of a schooled world 'credential society'."[28] A "credential society" is one in which an educational credential is necessary for acquiring employment. He claims that a world culture of education developed as part of an increasing emphasis on global identities and goals. Schooling provides entrance to the global economy. In Ramirez's words, "Schooling arises as a favored technology for identity affirmation and goal attainment; its intense pursuit by individuals and by states makes sense only in a world that strongly privileges schooling."[29]

Ramirez locates the origins of world cultural theorists in the work of John Boli, Frank Lechner, George Thomas, and Immanuel Wallerstein.[30] These theorists argue that a world culture began with the spread of Western Christian ideas in the late nineteenth century and escalated after the end of World War II. Boli and Thomas claim:

> Arising out of Western Christendom and propagated via the processes and mechanisms analyzed so well in world-system ... research, this transcendent level of social reality began to crystallize organizationally in the second half of the nineteenth century. After the vicissitudes of the two world wars, it has played an astonishing authoritative role in shaping global development for the last fifty years.[31]

Therefore, world education culture is nested in a more general world culture. One group of world cultural theorists concludes, "A considerable body of evidence supports our proposition that world-society models shape nation-state identities, structures, and behavior via worldwide cultural and associational processes."[32] From this perspective, as stated previously, world education culture developed alongside the worldwide spread of Western models of government and nation.

In summary, world education culture theorists believe that the striking similarity between the world's school systems, particularly regarding educational ladders (primary, middle, secondary schools, and higher education) and similar curricula, is a result of the following:

- The worldwide spread of Western concepts of government and nation in which a component is mass schooling;
- National elites and others drawing on world models of schooling when planning school systems;
- The spread of credential societies where educational credentials are necessary for employment;
- The existence of globally available educational research indicating the best educational practices.

World System and Postcolonial/Critical Theories

World system theorists, in contrast to world culture theorists, argue that ideas and policies from the global flow are imposed on nations by the economic power of multinational corporations and institutions like the World Bank.[33] The world system theorists see the world divided between three unequal economic groups. One economic group contains rich nations like the United States, the European Union, and Japan. A second economic group contains emerging economic powers, such as China, Russia, India, and Brazil. The third economic group includes the world's poorer nations.

World system theorists argue that the richest nations legitimize their power by imposing their educational values on other nations. These educational values include schooling for economic growth and developing workers for a free market economy.[34] The forms of knowledge favored by rich nations are imposed and legitimized global organizations, such as publishing corporations, research organizations, higher education institutions, professional organizations, and testing services.[35]

From this perspective, educational globalization is part of an effort to impose particular economic and political agendas that benefit wealthy and rich nations at the expense of the world's poor.[36] Supporting the arguments of world system theorists is postcolonial/critical analysis that stresses that Western schooling dominates the world scene as the result of its imposition by European imperialism and Christian missionary allies. Simply stated, Western-style schools spread around the globe as a result of European cultural imperialism.[37]

These theorists argue that after the breakup of British, French, and Portuguese colonial empires in the twentieth century, these countries, along with the United States, continued to exert new forms of power. Previous colonizers' power reemerged in new forms through the work of IGOs, multinational corporations, and trade agreements. In their current manifestation, postcolonial powers benefit, it is argued, by the promotion of market economies, education for economic growth, and free trade. In the framework of postcolonial/critical theory, education is viewed as an economic investment designed to produce better workers to serve multinational corporations.[38]

In describing what they consider to be the negative effects of global IGOs and trade agreements on Latin American education, Schugurensky and Davidson-Harden state, "We take a postcolonial perspective in considering the historical inequalities . . . mark the region's relations with the world's richer countries . . . [WTO/GATS] has the potential to continue the cycles of imperialism which have subdued Latin American countries' development since the time of colonisation."[39]

In general, postcolonial/critical analysis "includes issues of slavery, migration and diaspora formation; the effects of race, culture, class and gender in postcolonial settings; histories of resistance and struggle against colonial and neo-colonial domination; the complexities of identity formation and hybridity; language and language rights; the ongoing struggles of Indigenous peoples for recognition of their rights."[40]

Culturist: Educational Borrowing and Lending

Culturalists stress the existence of different "knowledges" or different ways of seeing and knowing the world and the lending and borrowing of educational ideas.[41] As implied in the term culturist, these theorists recognize the importance of cultural difference in interpreting global education policies. They reject world theorist arguments that globalization is resulting in a uniformity of educational policies and institutions and the world system argument that postcolonial powers are simply imposing their views on other nations. This group of theorists believes that local actors borrow and adapt multiple models from the global flow of educational ideas. I will discuss the arguments of culturalists in more detail in Chapter 5.

One example of educational borrowing is that of U.S. policymakers in the 1980s, who became enthralled with the Japanese and other educational systems after concluding that the U.S. economy was declining in world markets as a result of its school system. The 1983 federal government report *A Nation at Risk* blamed the allegedly poor academic quality of American public schools for causing lower rates of productivity and slowing technological development as compared to Japan and West Germany. The report states, "If only to keep and improve on the slim competitive edge we still retain in world markets, we must rededicate ourselves to the reform of the educational system for the benefit of all."[42] Not only was this argument almost impossible to prove, but some have claimed it was based on false data and assumptions as captured in the title of David Berliner and Bruce Biddle's *The Manufactured Crisis: Myths, Fraud and the Attack on America's Public Schools.*[43]

While the analysis may have been wrong, U.S. educators rushed to study Japanese schools as a means of improving U.S. schools. This represented an interesting example of borrowing and lending of educational ideas because the current organization of Japanese schools was imposed on Japan by the United States after conquest during World War II. Against the backdrop of Japan's highly test-oriented school system, the *A Nation at Risk* report recommended that the American school system be tightly governed by "standardized tests of achievement."[44] The result was a push by U.S. policymakers to mimic the Japanese schools.[45]

In developing a theory of policy attraction, David Phillips suggested a study of transnational movement of education reforms, which include the borrowing and lending of ideas.

> Analysis of the attraction of aspects of educational provision in Japan to American observers over a long period, for example would be of considerable interest. So too would detailed examination of the foreign models used in the policy discussions in the countries of Eastern Europe following the dramatic changes of 1989, or of the influence of child-centered primary education in Britain on policy and practice in other parts of Europe.[46]

Besides the transnational borrowing and lending, culturalists argue that global educational ideas are often adapted to local conditions. Kathryn Anderson-Levitt contends that the colonial imposition of Western education "into new areas ... for example, [by] England versus France, have looked different from the beginning."[47] She argues that while there is an appearance of homogenization of global schooling, in reality teachers and other local school officials resist and transform global models of schooling.

Also, culturalists reject the idea that all global organizations are working in unison to promote the same educational agenda. The World Bank and UNESCO, it is argued, sometimes offer different advice to local schools. For instance, the U.S. Agency for International Development (USAID) and France's international development agency offered different advice to school people in Guinea.[48] In Brazil, the religious education model supported by the Catholic Church differed from the model offered by the World Bank and USAID. As described by Lesley Bartlett, nonpublic educational institutions in Brazil supported an education model that emphasized themes of human development and social justice. Within the South American Catholic Church, as I describe in a later section, this humanitarian education model was influenced by liberation theology. On the other hand, Brazilian public schools under the influence of the World Bank and USAID adopted an economic growth model. The result was a striking difference in the teaching of literacy. Many Catholic schools, those influenced by liberation theology, taught literacy in a social and political context. In contrast, Bartlett wrote, the economic growth model used in the public schools "studiously avoided the political aspects of schooling, utilize[d] phonics-based instruction, and aver[red] that education can and should contribute to economic development."[49]

Culturalists also argue that there is not one world education model but that there are competing models. In her criticism of world education culture theorists,

Kathryn Anderson-Levitt argues that there are two competing world models for education. World culture theorists, she argues, consider the goal of the world education model to be preparing students to be workers in the global economy. She identifies two competing world education models, which I will label "Economic Education World Model" and "Progressive Education World Model." I propose the existence of two other competing global models, which I label "Religious Education World Models" and "Indigenous Education World Models." These last two global models openly reject world models of schooling based on Western education.

KEY POINTS: INTERPRETATIONS BY THEORISTS— WORLD EDUCATION CULTURE, WORLD SYSTEM AND POSTCOLONIAL/CRITICAL, AND CULTURALIST

World Education Culture

1. Development of a uniform global education culture sharing similar goals, educational practices, and organizations
2. Similarity of national school systems a result of adoption of Western model of the nation-state, which requires mass education
3. Most national schools systems share a common educational ladder and curriculum organization
4. Global uniformity of schooling provides entrance into the global economy

World System and Postcolonial/Critical

1. Educational ideas and practices imposed on other nations that favor the economic advantages of rich nations
2. The creation of global educational uniformity will be used to legitimize the power of rich nations
3. Global organizations supporting policies that will benefit rich nations and people such as educating students as workers for the global economy and privatization of schooling

Culturalist

1. Rejects the claim of growing uniformity of global policies and goals
2. Emphasizes how local communities change ideas borrowed from the global flow of educational ideas and practices
3. Recognizes the existence of different knowledges and global education models
4. Does not believe that global organizations are working in unison to create global educational uniformity

The Economic Education Model, Economization of Education, and the Audit State

The concepts of "economization of education" and "audit state" and are now embedded in global school policies. As stated earlier in the chapter, economization of education refers to making the primary goal of schooling to be economic and income growth and to rely on economic research to guide school policies. This makes education an economic function that includes analyzing the education through the lenses of an economist. Looking through the lens of economization, funding schools becomes investing in human capital, namely students, for the purpose improving the workforce. In this conceptual model, investment in education should yield an improved workforce.

But how do you measure a return on investment in schools? From an economic perspective this requires some form of accounting, or in the language of education, it requires "accountability." The economic concept of accounting requires something to be measured, which in business enterprises is profit and loss in money. In education, an economist view seeks to measure output in skills needed by the workforce. For instance, in the United States, accountability of student learning is the measurement or testing of skills embodied in the Common Core State Standards. The Common Core State Standards are supposed to contain skills required by the new global economy.

Skills, in economic jargon, become the "new currency" of the global education system. International and national student testing, in the framework of the economization of education, is supposed to measure the contribution of national school systems to economic growth. This measurement is part of the "audit state," which continually monitors performance, including educational performance, by standardized assessments. National education systems in most countries now use standardized assessments for secondary school graduation and college admissions. Many use standardized testing to measure performance at different grade levels.

The economization of education includes global measurements to compare national school systems. Global assessment standards are reported by OECD, which has been called the "World Ministry of Education." OECD audits national school systems and compares them using scores from the Programme for International Student Assessment (PISA) and Trends in International Mathematics and Science Study (TIMSS).[50] Education officials often compare the results of their nation's performance to that of other countries. These international tests will be discussed more extensively in Chapter 3.

OECD's auditing of national school systems with PISA and TIMSS is based on the economist view that developing work skills is the primary purpose of schooling. The concern with skills education is reflected in the title of OECD's 2012 publication *Better Skills, Better Jobs, Better Lives: A Strategic Approach to Skills Policies*.[51] This publication claims,

Skills have become the global currency of the 21st century [author's emphasis]. Without proper investment in skills, people languish on the margins of society, technological progress does not translate into economic growth, and countries can no longer compete in an increasingly knowledge-based global society. But this "currency" depreciates as the requirements of labour markets evolve and individuals lose the skills they do not use. Skills do not automatically convert into jobs and growth.[52]

The World Bank's educational investments provide a good example of the economization of education (I will discuss the functioning of the World Bank in more detail in Chapter 2). The World Bank is the greatest global financier of education lending money to developing countries. The *World Bank Group Education Strategy 2020* contains a banker's view of the importance and functioning of school systems and contains a clear example of the economization of education.[53] In the foreword to *Education Strategy 2020*, Tamar Manuelyan Atinc, vice president of Human Development Network, The World Bank, uses economic terms to state the three pillars of its education plan: "Invest early. Invest smartly. Invest for all."[54]

The World Bank's economist view of schooling is also tied to measuring outputs. *Education Strategy 2020* states that "getting value for the education dollar requires smart investments—that is, investments that have proven to contribute to learning. Quality needs to be the focus of education investments, with learning gains as a key metric of quality."[55] To determine the "value" of educational investments requires assessment of students. Assessments become the method for determining the "value" of educational reform:

> By investing in system assessments, impact evaluations, and assessments of learning and skills, the Bank will help its partner countries answer the key questions that shape educational reform: Where are the strengths of our system? Where are the weaknesses? What interventions have proven most effective in addressing them? Are learning opportunities reaching the most disadvantaged groups? What are the key roles of public and private sector in service delivery? Are children and youth acquiring the knowledge and skills that they need?[56]

The World Bank admits that there is no conclusive evidence that expanding educational opportunities result in economic growth. The World Bank refers to evidence as being "encouraging but somewhat mixed."[57] Rather than dismissing investment in schools as a source of economic growth, the World Bank qualifies it by claiming that it is what students learn and not the time spent in school. This justifies assessment measures of learning in contrast to time spent in school as the best determiner of returns on educational investments: "By measuring education levels based on what students have learned . . . an increase of one standard deviation in student scores on international assessments of literacy and mathematics is associated with a 2 percent increase in annual GDP per capita growth."[58]

The economist view of education considers social and economic problems as soluble by teaching skills needed by the labor market. For instance, there is a global problem of youth unemployment. Youth unemployment might be a result of the lack of jobs. However, the World Bank sees it as an education problem: "Youth are leaving school and entering the workforce without the knowledge, skills, or competencies necessary to adapt to a competitive and increasingly globalized economy."[59] Maybe the problem is general unemployment, or, as in the case of the United States, it might be caused by the lack of well-paying entry level jobs, which disappeared as manufacturing companies moved their operations overseas to find cheaper workers. In other words, complex economic problems cannot be simply explained as youth lacking the right skills.

The World Bank uses OECD's PISA and TIMSS tests to evaluate the effect of education loans to developing nations. Research sociologist Marlaine Lockheed in "Causes and Consequences of International Assessments in Developing Countries" writes, "Developing nations generally joined international large-scale assessments with the encouragement of, and when supported by international donor agencies."[60] She identifies the World Bank as the key agency in spreading the use of PISA and TIMSS in developing countries.

The economization of education and human capital will be discussed in more detail in Chapters 2 and 3. In general, this economic approach is supported by many national leaders because it promises growth and development. According to world education culture theorists, it is the one relied upon by national elites. The primary goal of the economic model is educating workers for jobs in the global economy. This Economic Education World Model contains the following components including the teaching of English as the language of global business. Language issues will be discussed in more detail in Chapter 7.

Economic Education World Model

- Education considered as an investment in the workforce;
- Students are considered as human capital to be educated for work;
- Skills-based instruction;
- Accountability of school programs using student test scores;
- Performance evaluation of administrators, teachers, and school programs based on standardized testing of students;
- National tests benchmarked with PISA and TIMSS;
- Teaching English as language of global business;
- The goal of education is educating workers to compete in the global economy;
- The value of education is measured by economic growth and development.

The Economic Education World Model can be criticized for not educating citizens to be politically active in bringing about economic and social change. It can also be criticized for not preparing students to work actively for social justice and for environmental protection. In addition, the Economic Education World Model imposes the culture of the global economic system on local cultures and attempts to change them, including those of Indigenous peoples, to meet the requirements of the global economy.

Progressive Education World Model

The Progressive Education World Model will be discussed in more detail in Chapter 5. This model provides more teacher and student control of curriculum and instruction. In contrast to the economization of education model, the goal of the progressive model is to educate citizens who are conscious of social injustices and actively work to correct them.

Progressive Education World Model

- Learning how to change political, social, and economic institutions;
- Preparing students to participate in issues of social justice, human rights, and environmental protection;
- Learning based on students' interests and participation;
- Active learning;
- Teacher-determined assessment;
- Protection of local languages;
- Education for ensuring social justice;
- Education for active participation in determining social and political change.

Progressive education theories were born in the work of John Dewey in the late nineteenth and early twentieth centuries. Today, progressive methods of instruction are embedded in human rights, peace, social justice, liberation, and environmental education. Dewey wanted to develop methods that would demonstrate to the student the social value of knowledge and the interdependence of society. One method Dewey hoped would achieve these objectives was the development of social imagination through cooperative group activities. Dewey defined social imagination as "the habit of mentally constructing some actual scene of human interaction, and of consulting that for instruction as to what to do." One of his early educational experiments took place in the 1890s in a high school ethics class. Dewey wanted the students to view ethics in relation to real problems as opposed to abstract principles. Dewey presented the students with an actual case of human misery and asked them to use social imagination to work out the problem of charity. Social imagination is the ability to relate isolated ideas to the actual conditions that have given them their original meaning. Dewey argued that this method aided a student in forming "the habit of realizing for himself and in himself the nature of the practical situations in which he will find himself placed."[61]

This method of teaching ethics is based on another important principle. Progressive education as advocated by Dewey was to prepare students to participate in fighting for social justice by teaching the historical and social origins of ideas, values, and social institutions. He believed that if students understood that ideas and institutions originated from human actions, they would realize that they also could participate in changing these ideas and institutions. Dewey worried that civilizations become trapped by ideas and institutions that are no longer practical and may support elite domination of the rest of society. According to Dewey, ideas, values, and institutions should change as the needs of society change.

Dewey believed it was unnecessary for students to become aware of the relationship between knowledge and social experience and to be given an opportunity to act on ideas. When acted on, it becomes judgment. "The child," Dewey stated, "cannot get power of judgment excepting as he is continually exercised in forming and testing judgment." Therefore, as Dewey saw it, the school must avoid the teaching of abstract ideas; rather, it must provide actual conditions out of which ideas grow, and the child must be given an opportunity within the school to test moral and social judgments. According to Dewey, the school should be a community of real social relationships.[62]

An often quoted statement by Dewey is that the school is a community with a real social life. Dewey wanted to utilize this community and make it a part of the learning process. He believed that the learning process should be part of an active solution to a social problem because this provides the best basis for helping the student to see the social value of knowledge.

Dewey's ideas on active learning and preparing students to solve social problems are now part of many different educational programs seeking social justice, peace, human rights, and environmental protection, as well as liberation from authoritarian governments. We will be discussing these programs throughout this book.

There is a major difference between the Economic Education World Model and the Progressive Education World Model. In schools, the Economic Education World Model controls teachers' behaviors through a prescribed national curriculum and reliance on standardized testing with the goal of educating workers for the global economy. In the Progressive Education World Model, students are actively educated to change the world in the name of social justice.

Religious Education World Models

Both the economic and progressive education models are part of Western education traditions that have entered the global flow of educational ideas. A criticism of both education models is that they support a secular society whose goals are either economic development or economic equity. Missing, for some, are spiritual and religious goals and values. I will discuss religious models of education in more detail in Chapter 6. Globally, there are large numbers of religious schools serving Christian, Buddhist, Islamic, Hindu, and other religious communities. Some provide religious instruction after school hours or on religious days, while others operate full-time schools. Religious schools offer instruction that emphasizes spirituality in contrast to the economic and secular emphasis of economization of education and progressive education world models.

Some religious education organizations support interfaith toleration. The Religious Education Association (REA) founded in 1903 states its global mission as creating "opportunities for exploring and advancing the interconnected practices of scholarship, research, teaching, and leadership in faith communities, academic institutions, and the wider world community."[63] The organization's mission statement stresses international networks for religious educators:

> Through creation of international networks of communication, cooperation and support in order to strengthen leaders in religious education, and religious education as a distinctive and vital field; and through interpreting the nature, purposes, and value of the field of religious education to the wider society and those preparing to become professors, researchers, or other leaders in religious education.[64]

Also, the REA, and this might not be true of other religious organizations, promotes interfaith dialogue. A 2003 editorial for *Religious Education* stressed, "At the turn of the century [nineteenth to twentieth] there was optimism among REA founders that religious education might nurture inter-religious tolerance and understanding as well as informed belief and commitment."[65]

Religious Education World Models

- Study of traditional religious texts;
- Study and practice of religious rites;
- Emphasis on spirituality;
- Emphasis on instilling moral and ethical standards;
- Rejection of secularism.

Indigenous Education World Models

In its September 13, 2007, news release announcing ratification of the Declaration on Rights of Indigenous Peoples, the United Nations estimated that there were 370 million Indigenous peoples existing around the globe in areas of the South Pacific, Asia, and Europe and, of course, including the numerous Indigenous nations of Africa and North and South America.[66] Who are the Indigenous peoples of the world? One definition emphasizes long-term occupancy of a particular geographical area.[67] For instance, the Indigenous nations of Canada emphasize "long-term occupancy" by choosing the self-identifier "First Nations." Today, some groups that identify themselves as Indigenous were previously imperialistic powers with empires that dominated other peoples and lands, such as the Aztecs, Mayans, and Incas of the Americas. Are these nations or the peoples they dominated the long-term occupiers? One resolution of who is Indigenous can be through self-identification. The World Bank includes in its definition of Indigenous "self-identification" and "subsistence-oriented production." The World Bank's definition is as follows:

> The term Indigenous Peoples (also often referred to as "Indigenous ethnic minorities," "tribal groups" and "scheduled tribes") describes social groups with a social and cultural identity distinct from the dominant society which makes them vulnerable to being disadvantaged in the development process.[68]

Characteristics of Indigenous Peoples

- Close attachment to ancestral territories and their natural resources;
- Self-identification and identification by others as members of a distinct cultural group;
- An Indigenous language, often different from the national language;
- Presence of customary social and political institutions;
- Primarily subsistence-oriented production.[69]

However, "subsistence-oriented production" does not realistically describe the work of some self-identified Indigenous peoples who hold jobs in modern factories, corporate agriculture, or other professional and business occupations.

Indigenous peoples struggled to restore traditional education methods after Western forms of schooling attempted to eradicate their cultures. In some cases, Indigenous peoples were denied schooling as a method for excluding them from entrance into dominant economic and political organizations. Consequently, many Indigenous nations are trying to restore their control over education and ensure recognition of traditional educational methods.

I will discuss Indigenous models of education in more detail in Chapter 6. Indigenous Education World Models include the following:

Indigenous Education World Models

- Indigenous nations control their own educational institutions;
- Traditional Indigenous education serves as a guide for the curriculum and instructional methods;
- Education is provided in the language of the Indigenous nation;
- Education reflects the culture of the Indigenous nation.

Examples of the Diffusion of Global Educational Models

World culture theorists present a benign image of national elites and local groups choosing from a world education culture, while world system theorists and post-colonial/critical theorists stress the use of power to impose educational models. Culturalists stress the importance of the borrowing and lending of educational ideas and their local adaptation. However, the story of the global spread of this model is much more complicated and involves choice and imposition. Initially, as postcolonial/critical theorists argue, Western forms of schooling were spread around the globe as the result of European imperialism. Besides a quest for wealth, European colonialists were also motivated by a belief in the superiority of Western civilization and a desire to convert the world's peoples to Christianity. I have called this process "white love."[70] Convinced of the inferiority of other civilizations and that Christianity was the only true religion, colonialists believed they were helping others by trying to change local religions and cultures.

The early diffusion of Western schooling did not include, though the process laid the groundwork for its later adoption, the current economization of education world model. The global diffusion of the economization of education model occurred after World War II. The work of Christian missionaries does represent one global religious model. In the Americas, the Spanish established an extensive network of churches and schools to convert Native Americans. In North America, the British encouraged Protestant missionaries and school people to convert and educate Indigenous peoples. In both South and North America, physical force was sometimes used to save souls for a Christian God. In Africa, Europeans established schools and sent church people to win the hearts and minds of those being subjugated. In India, the British made English and education in English-style schools the path for locals into the colonial administration. While the French did not encourage the expansion of European-style schooling for colonized peoples in Cambodia and Indochina, they did establish schools for the education of the children of colonial administrators and supported the efforts of religious groups to convert and educate the local population. The Dutch followed a similar pattern in Indonesia.[71]

On the other hand, some countries chose Western-style schooling for defensive reasons while trying to protect local ethical systems. In the nineteenth century, Japanese leaders urged the establishment of Western-style schools to learn Western technology and science to build a war machine that could resist European expansionism in Asia. The Charter Oath issued by the newly created Japanese Education Department in 1868 reflected a global view in organizing a new educational system: "Knowledge shall be sought from throughout the world."[72] Adopting a Western-style school structure, Japan's 1872 Fundamental Code of Education mandated the building of 54,760 primary schools, middle school districts, and university districts.[73] A similar development pattern occurred in Arab countries when, after Napoleon's army marched into Egypt in 1798 and occupied the country for three years, Egyptian leaders decided that their citizens needed to study European technology, science, and military organization. In *Putting Islam to Work: Politics and Religious Transformation in Egypt*, Gregory Starrett summarizes these efforts to "gain military parity with Europe that motivated the initial importation of the European-style school to Egypt."[74]

China's educational history supports the claim by world education culture theorists that the spread of mass schooling accompanied the adoption of the Western model of the nation-state. In 1912, the Chinese emperor was replaced by a Western-style republic supported by the followers of revolutionary leader Sun Yat-sen. The future leader of the Chinese Communist Party, Mao Zedong, recalled that after the 1912 abdication of the Emperor, "Modern schools sprang up like bamboo shoots after a summer rain."[75] Modern or Western-style schools were considered essential for maintaining a republican form of government. The new minister of education, Cai Yuanpei, issued an edict eliminating Chinese classic texts from the primary school curriculum and banned all textbooks not in agreement with republican ideals.[76] It is important to note that both China and Japan adopted Western school models while attempting to retain traditional values as exemplified by the following educational slogans: *Japanese Spirit, Western Skills*; *Western Science, Eastern Morals*; and *Western Function, Chinese Essence.*[77]

The progressive education model was part of this global flow of educational practices and ideas.[78] It is associated with movements for social justice and political and economic change. In 1919, the icon of progressivism education John Dewey made a two-year lecture tour of China. In China, he was hailed as the "Second Confucius."[79] The Chinese who invited him were part of the growing transnational movement of students. In 1908, the U.S. Congress agreed to return funds owed by China to the United States, which were then to be used to support Chinese students to study in the United States. Between 1921 and 1924, it was estimated that the United States was hosting the largest number of Chinese students studying abroad.[80]

After 1917 Bolshevik revolution, Soviet educators were attracted to American progressive education when the People's Commissariat of Education created an experimental educational system. The People's Commissariat of Education encouraged active learning through class discussion and aesthetic education along with an integrated curriculum in which reading, writing, arithmetic, history, geography, literature, chemistry, and other subjects were studied together. The Commissariat recommended the use of the Dalton plan developed by U.S. progressive educator Helen Parkhurst in 1918. In the Dalton plan, students signed monthly contracts in which all subjects were to be studied in the context of a single theme. Students fulfilled their contracts working at their own pace.[81] American progressive educational ideas received further support in 1929 when the People's Commissariat of Education ordered all schools to adopt the project method as the system of instruction.[82] The project method was first proposed in 1918 by American progressive educator William Heard

Kilpatrick who was a friend and colleague of John Dewey at Teachers College, Columbia University.[83] All of this changed when Stalin rose to power. In 1931, the Commissar of Education Andrei Bubnov condemned the project method at the meeting of the All-Russian Conference of Heads of Regional Departments of Education. He asserted that teachers were inadequately prepared to use the project method and activity-based instruction. He demanded that schools provide systematic instruction in mathematics, chemistry, and physics. The Central Committee of the Communist Party declared, "It is necessary to wage a decisive struggle against thoughtless scheming with methods . . . especially against the so-called project method."[84] In 1932, the Central Committee condemned the Dalton plan.

The global spread of educational ideas and institutions is not a one-way road from Europe and the United States to the rest of the world. The next section of educational borrowing and lending demonstrates how global ideas are changed and then influence global education discourses.

Examples of Educational Borrowing and Lending: The Case of South America

South America exemplifies the borrowing and lending of global educational ideas and their adaptation to local conditions. South American countries have been influenced by Spanish colonialism and U.S. economic education models.[85] The South American example demonstrates how the global flow of educational ideas and institutions is not one way. It involves, as captured in the title of a book edited by comparative educationist Gita Steiner-Khamsi, *The Global Politics of Educational Borrowing and Lending.*[86]

Peruvian Jose Mariátegui was a pioneer in progressive educational thought in South America. His writings influenced the educational philosopher Paulo Freire, the literacy crusade following the Cuban revolution, and the literacy campaigns led by liberation religious leaders. Mariátegui called for mass political education of peasants and Indigenous peoples as a necessary condition for economic justice in South America. He became a Marxist when, after receiving an eighth grade education, he took a job at the Peruvian newspaper *La Prensa* and began writing political articles. The radicalism of his articles caused the Peruvian government to exile him to Europe in 1919. In Europe he moved in Communist circles in France and Italy and became acquainted with progressive ideas about freeing human thought from ideological subjugation by the state and economic elites.[87]

Mass political education, Mariátegui believed, was necessary for achieving economic justice in the context of South America, particularly for the recruitment of peasants and Indigenous peoples. Mariátegui argued, "The problem of Indian illiteracy goes beyond the pedagogical sphere. It becomes increasingly evident that *to teach a man to read and write is not to educate him* [my emphasis]."[88]

It was the global flow of educational ideas and institutions that Mariátegui partially blamed for the destruction of Indigenous cultures and for creating a life of abject poverty in Peru. Regarding the effect of Spanish colonialism, he stated:

> The Spanish heritage was not only psychological and intellectual but above all economic and social. Education continued to be a privilege because the privileges of wealth and class continued. The aristocratic and literary concept of education was typical of a feudal system and economy. Not having abolished feudalism in Peru, independence would not abolish its ideas about education.[89]

The economic education borrowed from the United States, he argued, perpetuated Peru's social class divisions. In the early twentieth century, Peruvian education leaders called for the adoption of the U.S. economic education model to aid in industrial development by linking education to economic planning. The leading advocate of the U.S. model was Manuel Villarán, who argued that "education in Peru . . . suffers from its failure to meet the needs of the developing national economy and from its indifference to the Indigenous element."[90] He argued that the economic future of Peru depended on its educational system preparing workers rather than scribes to enter government bureaucracies and the legal profession. Villarán claimed, "The great nations of Europe today are remodeling their educational programs, largely along North American lines, because they understand that this century requires men of enterprise rather than men of letters . . . we should also correct our mistakes and educate practical, industrious, and energetic men, the ones the country needs in order to become wealthy and by the same token powerful."[91]

The 1920 Organic Law of Education converted Peruvian schools to the U.S. model with primary and secondary schooling preparing students for jobs needed for economic development. However, Mariátegui argued that adoption of the U.S. model did not undercut the economic and political power of the descendants of colonial rule. He wrote, "The educational movement was sabotaged by the continued and widespread existence of a feudal regime. It is not possible to democratize the education of a country without democratizing its economy and its political superstructure."[92] The school reforms based on the American model failed to undercut the power of the established upper class of Peru, which therefore proved, Mariátegui argued, that countries must develop their own educational reforms based on national needs. Similar to other progressive and Marxist educators, Mariátegui advocated the abandoning idealist forms of education that never linked knowledge to its origins in economic and social conditions. He called for education to be linked to the real world of work. He quoted Mexican educational reformer Pedro Ureña: "To learn is not only to learn to know but also to learn to do."[93]

A progressive education model in Latin American evolved that encompassed concerns about the culture and power of Indigenous peoples and control by elite economic groups. In summarizing these traditions, Sheldon Liss writes, "Latin American radicals believe that genuine education—the process of critical evaluation and questioning, not merely the dissemination of information—is a marvelous instrument of progress that will eventually help negate the 'truths' of the prevailing system."[94] Liss concludes, "Almost all the *pensadores* [Latin American progressive intellectuals] agree that the power of the oppressors exists only as long as the masses obey them."[95]

One of the people influenced by Mariátegui's writings was Che Guevara. Following the completion of the Cuban revolution in 1959, Cuba engaged in a mass literacy program. Guevara declared that society must become a "gigantic" school. Referring to the literacy crusade, he wrote in 1965 that the state should give direct political instruction to the people: "Education takes hold among the masses and the foreseen new attitude tends to become a habit. The masses continue to make it their own and to influence those who have not yet educated themselves. This is the indirect form of educating the masses, as powerful, as the other, structured, one."[96] "What is needed," he asserted, "is the development of an ideological-cultural mechanism that permits both free inquiry and the uprooting of the weeds that multiply so easily in the fertilized soil of state subsidies."[97]

Out of this milieu of South American progressivism emerged the great progressive educator Paulo Freire, who might be considered the successor to John Dewey. Freire's model of progressive education embodied many of the cultural and economic concerns of other progressive South Americans. His work had a major influence on the literacy campaigns led by liberation theologians.

Born in 1921 in Recife, Brazil, Freire abandoned a law career in 1947 because he thought law served the oppressor while education could serve the oppressed. In 1964, Freire went to Chile after being exiled following a coup d'état by the Brazilian military elite. During his exile, Freire's socialist philosophy and instructional methods crystallized, and he wrote *Pedagogy of the Oppressed*. In the charged atmosphere of Chilean politics, Freire met socialists from many Latin American countries, including Cuba.[98] During his exile in Chile, Freire made several trips to New York City where he experienced "thematic" lessons conducted by Catholic priests. In one session, which Freire later reports in *Pedagogy of the Oppressed*, an educator presented to a group of African Americans and Puerto Ricans a photo of the street in front of the building in which they were meeting. The photo showed garbage on the sidewalk. Using a pedagogical method that would become central in Freire's work, the group leader asked the participants what they saw in the photo. The responses ranged from a street in Latin America to Africa. Participants refused to believe it was a street in the United States until one of them commented, "Might as well admit it's our street. Where we live."[99]

Pedagogy of the Oppressed answered the central problem facing Latin American progressives about how to include peasants and Indigenous peoples in a revolutionary movement. Freire attributed the apparent backwardness of these groups to their living in a culture of silence. Freire's educational methodology promised to educate peasants and Indigenous peoples to improve their lives.

Another example of the global flow of educational ideas was Freire's recognition of the influence of Chinese leader Mao Zedong's educational ideas on Freire's greatest work, *Pedagogy of the Oppressed* (1968). He referred to the "fundamental aspect of Mao's Cultural Revolution" to support his assertion:

> The pedagogy of the oppressed, as a humanist and libertarian pedagogy, has two distinct stages. In the first, the oppressed unveil the world of oppression and through the praxis commit themselves to its transformation. In the second stage, in which the reality of oppression has already been transformed, this pedagogy ceases to belong to the oppressed and becomes a pedagogy of all men in the process of permanent liberation. In both stages, it is always through action in depth that the culture of domination is culturally confronted.[100]

Ivan Illich's Center for Intercultural Documentation (CIDOC) in Cuernavaca, Mexico, helped to spread both liberation theology and Freirian educational ideas.[101] Liberation theologists, such as Gustavo Gutiérrez, and North and South American educators, including Paulo Freire, John Holt, and Clarence Karier, gathered at CIDOC to exchange ideas on radical change and education. Illich, a former priest and supporter of liberation theology, advocated abolishing formal schooling because it had become a method of oppression. Priests and educators provided a variety of descriptions of CIDOC's influence, ranging from "shock treatment" to "jolt[ing] . . . foreigners into questioning what they were doing." I first met Paulo Freire at CIDOC in 1970 and for the first time learned about his educational theories. I was one of those who carried his ideas back to North America. At CIDOC, I coedited books with liberation theologist Father Jordan Bishop and American educational historians Clarence Karier and Paul Violas. These books contributed to discussions of radical school reform in the United States.[102] By the end of the 1970s, wars of liberation in Nicaragua and El Salvador sparked literacy crusades that reflected the influence of liberation theology and Paulo Freire's pedagogical methods. These literacy crusades will be discussed in more detail in Chapter 6.

Today, both John Dewey and Paulo Freire are considered icons of progressive education. The global influence of their education models exemplifies the global diffusion of educational ideas. Their educational methods were to bring about social justice and change in contrast to the economization of education, the study of religious texts, and Indigenous education models.

Conclusion: Different Lenses for Interpreting Global Education

The remaining chapters will analyze the intertwined set of global processes affecting education. These analyzes will be in the context of world education culture theory, world systems and postcolonial/critical theories, and the work of

culturalists. These theories provide different lenses for examining global education discourses, the educational work of IGOs and NGOs, the influence of multinational learning and testing organizations, global migration, and English as a
global language. In this global arena, there are competing global education models:
economization of education, progressive, religious, and Indigenous.

In the next chapter, I will analyze global education discourses, particularly
those involving the knowledge economy and economization of education. Of
course, these discourses flow through global networks of government and nongovernment organizations, policy elites, local communities, and multinational
corporations. The story of how these networks operate will be discussed after a
consideration of the main global education discourses.

Notes

1 Roger Dale and Susan Robertson, "Editorial: Introduction," *Globalisation, Societies and Education* 1(1) 2003, pp. 3–11.
2 For instance, see James J. Heckman and Alan Krueger, editors, *Inequality in America: What Role Human Capital Policies?* (Cambridge, MA: MIT Press, 2005).
3 Richard Thaler and Cass Sunstein, *Nudge: Improving Decisions about Health, Wealth, and Happiness* (New York: Penguin Books, 2008).
4 See Katrin Bennhold, "Britain's Ministry of Nudges," *New York Times* (December 7, 2013). Retrieved from http://www.nytimes.com/2013/12/08/business/interna tional/britains-ministry-of-nudges.html?ref=business&_r=0&pagewanted=print on December 8, 2013.
5 Ibid.
6 Patrick Flanery, *Fallen Land* (New York: Riverhead Books, 2013), p. 142.
7 Nelly P. Stromquist, *Education in a Globalized World: The Connectivity of Economic Power, Technology, and Knowledge* (Lanham, MD: Rowan & Littlefield, 2003).
8 Dale and Robertson, "Editorial: Introduction," p. 7.
9 For examples, see Kathryn Anderson-Levitt, "A World Culture of Schooling?" in *Local Meanings, Global Schooling: Anthropology and World Culture Theory*, edited by Kathryn Anderson-Levitt (New York: Palgrave Macmillan, 2003), pp. 1–26.
10 European Commission, *Teaching and Learning: On Route to the Learning Society* (Luxemburg: SEPO-CE, 1998), p. 21.
11 Michael Apple, Jane Kenway, and Michael Singh, eds., *Globalizing Education: Policies, Pedagogies, & Politics* (New York: Peter Lang, 2005).
12 Roger Dale, "Globalisation, Knowledge Economy and Comparative Education," *Comparative Education* 41(2) 2005, p. 123.
13 Martin Carnoy and Diane Rhoten, "What Does Globalization Mean for Education Change? A Comparative Approach," *Comparative Education* 46(1) 2002, p. 1.
14 Patricia Broadfoot, "Editorial. Globalisation in Comparative Perspective: Macro and Micro," *Comparative Education* 39(4) 2003, p. 411.
15 Arjun Appadurai, *Modernity at Large: Cultural Dimensions of Globalisation* (Minneapolis: University of Minnesota Press, 1996).
16 Manuel Castells, *The Rise of the Network Society* (Oxford: Blackwell, 2000).
17 Stephen J. Ball, *Global Education Inc.: New Policy Networks and the Neo-Liberal Imaginary* (London: Routledge, 2012), p. 9.

18 Simon Marginson and Erlenwatin Sawir, "Interrogating Global Flows in Higher Education," *Globalisation, Societies and Education* 3(3) 2005, pp. 281–309.

19 See John Boli and George Thomas, editors, *Constructing World Culture: International Non-government Organizations since 1875* (Palo Alto: Stanford University Press 1999); Frank Lechner and John Boli, *World Culture: Origins and Consequences* (Malden, MA: Blackwell, 2005); Francisco O. Ramirez, "The Global Model and National Legacies" in *Local Meanings, Global Schooling: Anthropology and World Culture Theory*, edited by Kathryn Anderson-Levitt (New York: Palgrave Macmillan, 2003), pp. 239–255; and Francisco Ramirez and John Boli, "The Political Construction of Mass Schooling: European Origins and Worldwide Institutionalization," *Sociology of Education* 60 (1) 1987, pp. 2–17.

20 John Meyer, David Kamens, and Aaron Benavot, *School Knowledge for the Masses: World Models and National Primary Curricular Categories in the Twentieth Century* (Bristol, PA: Falmer Press, 1992); and David Baker and Gerald LeTendre, *National Differences, Global Similarities: World Culture and the Future of Schooling.* (Palo Alto, CA: Stanford University Press, 2005).

21 Meyer, Kamens, and Benavot, *School Knowledge for the Masses*, p. 2.

22 UNICEF, *The State of the World's Children 2006: Excluded and Invisible* (New York: UNICEF, 2005), pp. 114–117.

23 Meyer, Kamens, and Benavot, *School Knowledge for the Masses*, p. 2.

24 Ibid., p. 72.

25 Ibid.

26 Baker and LeTendre, *National Differences, Global Similarities*, p. 3.

27 Ibid., p. 12.

28 Ramirez, "The Global Model and National Legacies" in *Local Meanings, Global Schooling*, p. 242.

29 Ibid.

30 See Boli and Thomas, *Constructing World Culture*; Lechner and Boli, *World Culture*; Immanuel Wallerstein, *The Politics of the World-Economy: The States, the Movements, and the Civilizations* (Cambridge: Cambridge University Press, 1984); and Immanuel Wallerstein, *World-Systems Analysis: An Introduction* (Durham, NC: Duke University Press, 2004).

31 Boli and Thomas, "Introduction," in *Constructing World Culture*, p. 3.

32 Ibid.

33 Ibid.

34 Richard Tabulawa, "International Aid Agencies, Learner-Centred Pedagogy and Political Democratization: A Critique," *Comparative Education* 39(1) 2003, pp. 7–26; Wallerstein, *The Politics of the World-Economy*; and Wallerstein, *World-Systems Analysis*.

35 Hans Weiler, "Knowledge, Politics, and the Future of Higher Education: Critical Observations on a World Wide Transformation" in *Knowledge across Cultures*, edited by Ruth Hayhoe and Julie Pan, (Hong Kong: University of Hong Kong, 2001), pp. 25–45.

36 Michael Apple, "Are New Markets in Education Democratic" in *Globalizing Education: Policies, Pedagogies, & Politics*, edited by Michael Apple, Jane Kenway, and Michael Singh (New York: Peter Lang, 2005), pp. 209–230; Phillip Brown and Hugh Lauder, "Globalization, Knowledge and the Myth of the Magnet Economy," *Globalisation, Societies and Education* 4(1) 2006, pp. 25–57; David Gabbard, "Introduction," in *Knowledge and Power in the Global Economy: Politics and the Rhetoric of School Reform*, edited by David Gabbard (Mahwah, NJ: Lawrence Erlbaum, 2000), pp. xiii–xxiii; Mark Olssen, "Neoliberalism, Globalization, Democracy: Challenges for Education," *Globalisation, Societies*

and Education 2(2) 2004, pp. 231–275; and Weiler, " Knowledge, Politics, and the Future of Higher Education," pp. 25–45.

37 Martin Carnoy, *Education as a Form of Cultural Imperialism* (New York: David McKay, 1974); Joel Spring, *Education and the Rise of the Global Economy* (Mahwah, NJ: Lawrence Erlbaum, 1998); Joel Spring, *Pedagogies of Globalization: The Rise of the Educational Security State* (Mahwah, NJ: Lawrence Erlbaum, 2006); and John Willinsky, *Learning to Divide the World: Education at Empire's End* (Minneapolis: University of Minnesota Press, 1998).

38 Gary Becker, "The Age of Human Capital," in *Education, Globalization & Social Change* (Oxford: Oxford University Press, 2006), pp. 292–295; Michael Crossley and Leon Tikly, "Postcolonial Perspectives and Comparative and International Research in Education: A Critical Introduction," *Comparative Education* 40(2) 2004, pp. 147–156; Robert Rhoads and Carlos Torres, editors, *The University, State, and Market: The Political Economy of Globalization in the Americas* (Palo Alto, CA: Stanford University Press, 2006); Spring, *Education and the Rise of the Global Economy*; Stromquist, *Education in a Globalized World*; Nelly Stromquist and Karen Monkman, "Defining Globalization and Assessing Its Implications on Knowledge and Education," in *Globalization and Education: Integration and Contestation Across Cultures*, edited by Nelly Stromquist and Karen Monkman (Lanham, MD: Rowman & Littlefield, 2000), pp. 3–25.

39 Daniel Schugurensky and Adam Davidson-Harden, "From Córdoba to Washington: WTO/GATS and Latin American Education," *Globalization, Societies and Education* 1(3) 2003, p. 333.

40 Crossley and Tikly, "Postcolonial Perspectives ," p. 148.

41 See Hayhoe and Pan, *Knowledge across Cultures*; Angela W. Little, "Extended Review. Clash of Civilisations: Threat or Opportunity?" *Comparative Education* 39(3) 2003, pp. 391–394; Majid Rahnema, "Science, Universities and Subjugated Knowledges: A Third World Perspective," in *Knowledge across Cultures*, edited by Hayhoe and Pan, pp. 45–54; Zahra Zeera, "Paradigm Shifts in the Social Sciences in the East and West," in *Knowledge across Cultures*, Hayhoe and Pan, pp. 55–92.

42 National Commission on Excellence in Education, *A Nation at Risk* (Washington, DC: U.S. Government Printing Office, 2003), p. 9.

43 David Berliner and Bruce Biddle, *The Manufactured Crisis: Myths, Fraud and the Attack on America's Public Schools* (New York: Perseus Books, 1995).

44 National Commission on Excellence in Education, *A Nation at Risk*, p. 70.

45 See Spring, *Pedagogies of Globalization*, pp. 207–244.

46 David Phillips, "Toward a Theory of Policy Attraction in Education," in *The Global Politics of Educational Borrowing and Lending*, edited by Gita Steiner-Khamsi (New York: Teachers College Press, 2004), pp. 54–65.

47 Anderson-Levitt, "A World Culture of Schooling?" p. 2.

48 Ibid., p. 15.

49 Lesley Bartlett, "World Culture or Transnational Project? Competing Educational Projects in Brazil," in *Local Meanings, Global Schooling*, edited by Anderson-Levitt, p. 196.

50 David H. Kamens, "Globalization and the Emergence of an Audit Culture: PISA and the Search for 'Best Practices' and Magic Bullets," in *PISA, Power, and Policy: The Emergence of Global Educational Governance*, edited by Heinz-Dieter Meyer and Aaron Benavot (Oxford: Symposium Books, 2013), p. 123.

51 OECD, *Better Skills, Better Jobs, Better Lives: A Strategic Approach to Skills Policies* (Paris: OECD, 2012). Retrieved from http://dx.doi.org/10.1787/9789264177338-en on September 10, 2013.

52 Ibid., p. 3.

53 The International Bank for Reconstruction and Development/The World Bank, *Learning for All: Investing in People's Knowledge and Skills to Promote Development—World Bank Group Education Strategy 2020* (Washington, DC: International Bank for Reconstruction and Development/The World Bank, 2011).

54 Ibid., p. v.

55 Ibid., p. 4.

56 Ibid., p. 6.

57 Ibid., p. 12

58 Ibid.

59 Ibid., p. 17.

60 Marlaine Lockheed, "Causes and Consequences of International Assessments in Developing Countries" in *PISA, Power, and Policy: The Emergence of Global Educational Governance*, edited by Heinz-Dieter Meyer and Aaron Benavot (Oxford: Symposium Books, 2013), p. 166.

61 John Dewey, "Teaching Ethics in the High School," *Educational Review* (November 1893), p. 316.

62 John Dewey, "Ethical Principles Underlying Education," *The Third Yearbook of the National Herbart Society* (Chicago: National Herbartian Society, 1897), p. 31.

63 "The REA Mission," The Religious Education Association. Retrieved from http://www.religiouseducation.net/mission on September 25, 2013.

64 Ibid.

65 Theodore Brelsford, editor, "Editorial," *Religious Education* (Fall 2003). Retrieved from http://old.religiouseducation.net/journal/historical/brelsford_v_98_4.pdf on September 21, 2013.

66 UN News Service, "United Nations Adopts Declaration on Rights of Indigenous Peoples." Retrieved from http//www.un.org/news/printnews.asp?nid=23794 on September 14, 2007.

67 George Dei, Budd Hall, and Dorothy Rosenberg, "Introduction," in *Indigenous Knowledges in Global Contexts: Multiple Readings of Our World*, edited by George Dei, Budd Hall, and Dorothy Rosenberg (Toronto: University of Toronto Press, 2000), pp. 1–7.

68 The World Bank–Indigenous Peoples, "Key Concepts." Retrieved from http://web.worldbank.org/WBSITE/EXTERNAL/TOPICS/EXTSOCIALDEVELOPMENT/EXTINDPEOPLE/0,,contentMDK:20436173~menuPK:906311~pagePK:148956~piPK:216618~theSitePK:407802,00.html on April 18, 2006.

69 Ibid.

70 Spring, *Education and the Rise of the Global Economy*.

71 Carnoy, *Education as a Form of Cultural Imperialism*; Spring, *Education and the Rise of the Global Economy*; Spring, *Pedagogies of Globalization*; and Willinsky, *Learning to Divide the World*.

72 "Preamble to the Fundamental Code of Education, 1872," in *Society and Education in Japan*, edited by Herbert Passin (New York: Teachers College Press, 1965), p. 210.

73 Ibid.

74 Gregory Starrett, *Putting Islam to Work: Politics and Religious Transformation in Egypt* (Berkeley: University of California Press, 1998), p. 26.

75 Philip Short, *Mao: A Life* (New York: Henry Holt and Company, 1999), p. 52.

76 Paul Bailey, *Reform the People: Changing Attitudes towards Popular Education in Early 20th Century China* (Vancouver: University of British Columbia Press, 1990), pp. 139–142.

77 Spring, *Education and the Rise of the Global Economy*, pp. 37–69; and Joel Spring, *Globalization and Educational Rights* (Mahwah, NJ: Lawrence Erlbaum, 2001), pp. 20–56.

78 I trace the global diffusion of progressive education ideas in Spring, *Pedagogies of Globalization.*

79 See Barry Keenan, *The Dewey Experiment in China: Educational Reform and Political Power in the Early Republic* (Cambridge, MA: Harvard University Press, 1977); and David Hall and Roger Ames, *The Democracy of the Dead: Dewey Confucius, and the Hope for Democracy in China* (Chicago: Open Court, 1999).

80 Keenan, *The Dewey Experiment in China*, pp. 14–15.

81 Larry Holmes, *Stalin's School: Moscow's Model School No. 25, 1931–1937* (Pittsburgh: University of Pittsburgh Press, 1999), pp. 8–9. Also see Maurice Shore, *Soviet Education: Its Psychology and Philosophy* (New York: Philosophical Library, 1999).

82 Holmes, *Stalin's School*, p. 10.

83 William Kilpatrick, *The Project Method* (New York: Teachers College Press, 1918).

84 Holmes, *Stalin's School*, p. 28.

85 For a more detailed account of the evolution of the South American progressive education model, see Spring, *Pedagogies of Globalization*, pp. 114–151.

86 Steiner-Khamsi, *The Global Politics of Educational Borrowing and Lending.*

87 Sheldon Liss, *Marxist Thought in Latin America* (Berkeley: University of California Press, 1984), pp. 1–30.

88 José Mariátegui, *Seven Interpretive Essays on Peruvian Reality* (Austin: University of Texas Press, 1971), p. 122.

89 Ibid., p. 79.

90 Quoted in Ibid., p. 86.

91 Quoted in Ibid., p. 87.

92 Ibid., p. 88.

93 Ibid., p. 119.

94 Liss, *Marxist Thought in Latin America*, pp. 272–273.

95 Ibid., p. 272.

96 Che Guevara, "Socialism and Man in Cuba," in *Global Justice: Liberation and Socialism*, edited by Maria Del Carmen (Melbourne, Australia: Ocean Press, 2002), p. 35. This book was published in cooperation with Che Guevara Studies Center in Havana, Cuba.

97 Ibid., p. 41.

98 For an intellectual autobiography of his writing of *Pedagogy of the Oppressed*, see Paulo Freire, *Pedagogy of Hope: Reliving Pedagogy of the Oppressed* (New York: Continuum, 2004).

99 Ibid., p. 55.

100 Paulo Freire, *Pedagogy of the Oppressed* (New York: Herder and Herder, 1970), p. 40.

101 The influences of CIDOC, Ivan Illich, and Paulo Freire are represented in my book, Joel Spring, *A Primer of Libertarian Education* (New York: Free Life Editions, 1975).

102 The books coedited at CIDOC are Joel Spring and Jordan Bishop, *Formative Undercurrents in Compulsory Knowledge* (Cuernavaca, Mexico: CIDOC, 1970); and Clarence Karier, Paul Violas, and Joel Spring, editors, *Roots of Crisis* (Chicago: Rand McNally, 1973).

2

THE WORLD BANK

Economic Education Model, the Economization of Education, and the Audit State -

The World Bank is a leading global investor in education and is linked through extensive networks to other worldwide organizations. Comparative education professor Steven Klees asserts that "the World Bank is the architect of what has become a truly global education policy."[1] The Bank describes the extent of its activities as follows: "The World Bank is one of the largest external education financiers for developing countries, managing a portfolio of $8.9 billion, with operations in 70 countries as of August 2013."[2] Through these networks, the Bank is a major participant in global discourses about education.[3]

World Bank networks spread an economization of education viewpoint stressing the contribution of schooling to economic growth through investment in human capital. One reason is that the Bank uses economists with doctoral degrees to do educational research.[4] The Economics of Education Division of the World Bank explains: "Education economists analyze both what determines or creates education and what impact education has on individuals and the societies and economies in which they live."[5] It further explains this as a traditional role of the World Bank: "Historically at the World Bank a great deal of emphasis has been placed on determining outcomes to educational investment and the creation of human capital."[6] In spreading the economization of education focus, a stated Bank goal is "to build and support a network of education economists and build bridges to all those who are interested in their work."[7]

The World Bank also supports the development of the audit state, which uses performance standards to assess government programs, including the use of standardized assessments to evaluate educational performance. The World Bank uses assessments to influence local education systems. The World Bank collects, analyzes, and distributes this assessment data through SABER, which stands for "Systems Approach for Better Education Results," with the slogan: "Strengthening

Education Systems to Achieve Learning for All."[8] The Bank describes its function: "SABER collects and analyses policy data on education systems around the world, using evidence-based frameworks to highlight the policies and institutions that matter most to promote learning for all children and youth. SABER will ultimately cover key domains of the education system—that is, all major areas in which a country makes policy choices that determine how effective its system is."[9]

There are differing interpretations of the World Bank's education policies. World culture theorists consider the World Bank a major contributor to the development of a global culture.[10] Critics see the World Bank's agenda as serving wealthy nations and multinational organizations.[11] The Bank's worldwide networks influence local education practices.[12] Professor Bjorn Nordtveit criticizes the World Bank for not emphasizing education as a human right and creating a global image that "education is unproblematic and overwhelmingly positive as long as its quality is measurable and assessed systematically."[13] In other words, schools are okay if they follow the economic education model and are nested in an audit state.

The World Bank: Knowledge Bank and Networks

The World Bank plays an important role in the globalization of education by serving as a "knowledge bank" for a network of organizations. As a knowledge bank, it attempts to aid local school systems by providing "a high-quality knowledge base for education reforms at the global level."[14] Comparative education specialist Gita Steiner-Khamsi writes that in recent years "the World Bank has reinvented itself . . . as a knowledge bank . . . focusing on the lending of ideas."[15] Professor Steiner-Khamsi asserts that by functioning as a knowledge bank it functions as a "global policy advisor for national governments . . . [using] policy tools to coerce National governments into adopting a particular reform package."[16]

As a knowledge bank, it advocates for particular methods for evaluating local education systems. Through the collection of assessment data on different school systems, the Bank asserts: "Better knowledge of the strengths and weaknesses of particular education systems will enable the Bank Group to respond more effectively to the needs of its partner countries."[17] Building this knowledge base requires, according to the World Bank, "investing in system assessments, impact evaluations, and assessments of learning and skills, the Bank will help its partner countries answer the key questions that shape educational reform."[18]

In other words, the World Bank's education knowledge base can contribute to a homogenization of global schools systems by comparing those countries with the highest international test scores with those with low scores. The assumption is that low-scoring countries can model their education changes on those of high-scoring countries. This modeling process could speed up the homogenization of global school systems. To achieve this knowledge base, the World Bank calls for "investing in system assessments, impact evaluations, and assessments of learning and skills [with which] the Bank will help its partner countries answer the key questions that shape educational reform."[19]

Also aiding the globalization process is the embedding of World Bank education policies in an interrelated network of global and local institutions. These are dynamic relationships with members of the network influencing each other. The economization of education and the audit state are discussed in these networks. While all members of the networks might or might not agree with each other, they are exposed to similar educational ideas. Education and the knowledge economy is one of those important ideas discussed in the Bank's education networks.

World Bank officials have a particular definition and agenda for the "knowledge economy" and "lifelong learning" that is shared by other global players as I will discuss in Chapter 3. Also, the reader should be cautioned that a description of World Bank's global networks does not provide an indication of the degree of mutual influence or the influential power of any particular member of the network. However, few would disagree with the importance of the World Bank in influencing global education policies.

The World Bank Structure

Founded in 1944, the World Bank has provided educational loans to developing nations based on the idea that investment in education is the key to economic development. In 2013, reflecting its commitment to spreading the economic education model, the World Bank declared: "Today, amid a growing urgency prompted by widespread joblessness on the one hand and serious skills shortages on the other, the World Bank is more committed than ever to expanding opportunities for children and youth and nations alike, through education."[20] The Bank consists of the International Bank for Reconstruction and Development (IBRD), which lends money to governments of middle- and low-income countries, and the International Development Association (IDA), which provides interest-free loans and grants to governments of the poorest nations. The World Bank is also part of the World Bank Group, which includes three other organizations that provide technical assistance to developing nations, guarantee against losses for investors in developing nations, and arbitrate investment disputes.[21]

Education as a central method of economic development began in 1968 when the then president of the World Bank Robert McNamara announced, "Our aim here will be to provide assistance where it will contribute most to economic development. This will mean emphasis on educational planning, the starting point for the whole process of educational improvement."[22] McNamara went on explain that it would mean an expansion of the World Bank's educational activities. The World Bank continues to present its educational goals in the framework of economic development: "Education is a powerful driver of development and one of the strongest instruments for reducing poverty and improving health, gender equality, peace, and stability."[23]

Today, education is part of the general strategy of the World Bank to eliminate poverty. The World Bank's *Annual Report 2013* declares: "The World Bank Group has entered a new era by adopting measurable goals to end extreme poverty globally by 2030 and promote shared prosperity, which it will pursue in an environmentally, socially, and economically sustainable way."[24] However, the Bank does warn that eliminating poverty will not solve the economic problem of social tensions caused by inequality of incomes: "Achieving these goals will require acknowledging that economic growth alone will not build sustained and inclusive welfare; increased levels of social unrest around the world have been caused, in part, by a rise in economic inequality and a lack of inclusive opportunities."[25]

Activities for Which the World Bank Provides Loans

- Investing in people, particularly through basic health and education;
- Focusing on social development, inclusion, governance, and institution building as key elements of poverty reduction;
- Strengthening governments' ability to deliver quality services efficiently and transparently;
- Protecting the environment;
- Supporting and encouraging private business development; and
- Promoting reforms to create a stable macroeconomic environment that is conducive to investment and long-term planning.[26]

KEY POINTS: WORLD BANK STRUCTURE AND NETWORKS

World Bank Group

1. IBRD—lends money to *governments* of middle and low income countries
2. IDA—provides interest-free loans and grants to *governments* of the poorest nations
3. International Finance Corporation—loans, equity, and advisory services to *private sector* in developing countries
4. Multilateral Investment Guarantee Agency—encourages and aids *foreign direct investment* to developing countries
5. International Center for Settlement of Investment Disputes—provides facilities for conciliation and arbitration of international investment disputes

Examples of Members of World Bank Education Networks

1. United Nations and its agencies and members, such as United Nations Educational, Scientific, and Cultural Organization (UNESCO) and United Nations Children's Fund (UNICEF)

2. World Economic Forum
3. World Trade Organization
4. U.S. Agency for International Development (USAID)
5. Discovery Channel Global Education Fund
6. Global Development Alliance
7. EdInvest operated by the World Bank Group's International Finance Corporation
8. Human Development Network
9. United Nations Development Program (UNDP)
10. Intergovernmental agencies (IGOs) associated with the World Bank
11. National governments associated with the World Bank
12. Multinational corporations associated with World Bank education efforts
13. Nongovernmental organizations (NGOs) associated with the World Bank

The World Bank and the United Nations' Networks

The World Bank and the United Nations share a common educational network. The World Bank entered into a mutual agreement with the United Nations in 1947, which specified that the Bank would act as an independent specialized agency of the United Nations and as an observer in the United Nations General Assembly.[27]

The World Bank supports the United Nations' Millennium Goals and Targets, which were endorsed by 189 countries at the 2000 United Nations Millennium Assembly. The Millennium Goals directly addressing education issues are as follows:

- Target 2.A: Ensure that, by 2015, children everywhere, boys and girls alike, will be able to complete a full course of primary schooling;[28]
- Target 3.A: Eliminate gender disparity in primary and secondary education, preferably by 2005, and in all levels of education no later than 2015.[29]

These two Millennium Goals were part of the Education for All (EFA) program of UNESCO, which had established as two of its global goals the provision of free and compulsory primary education for all and achieving gender parity by 2005 and gender equality by 2015.[30] Highlighting the intertwined activities of the World Bank and United Nations agencies is the fact that these two goals were a product of the 1990 World Conference on Education for All convened by the World Bank, UNESCO, UNICEF, the United Nations Population Fund (UNFPA), and the UNDP. This world conference was attended by representatives from 155 governments.[31]

The World Bank's support of the UN's Millennium Goals links it to another network of EFA supporters that includes the following:

- International Bureau of Education (IBE), Geneva, Switzerland;
- International Institute for Educational Planning (IIEP), Paris, France and Buenos Aires, Argentina;
- UNESCO Institute for Lifelong Learning (UIL), Hamburg, Germany;
- Institute for Information Technologies in Education (IITE), Moscow, Russian Federation;
- International Institute for Higher Education in Latin America and the Caribbean (IESALC), Caracas, Venezuela;
- International Institute for Capacity-Building in Africa (IICBA), Addis Ababa, Ethiopia;
- European Centre for Higher Education (CEPES), Bucharest, Romania;
- International Centre for Technical and Vocational Education and Training (UNEVOC), Bonn, Germany;
- UNESCO Institute for Statistics (UIS), Montreal, Canada.[32]

These global networks are linked to NGOS through what UNESCO calls the Collective Consultation of Non-Governmental Organizations on EFA (CCNGO/ EFA). UNESCO describes this collective:

> It connects UNESCO and several hundred NGOs, networks and coalitions around the world through a coordination group composed of eight NGO representatives (five regional focal points, two international focal points and one representative of the UNESCO/NGO Liaison Committee), and a list serve for information sharing.[33]

The World Bank *Education Strategy 2020*: Investing in People's Knowledge and Skills

Reinforcing and expanding on the economization of education and the economic education model, the World Bank issued in 2011 its *Education Strategy 2020*, which declared: "Persistently high levels of unemployment, especially among youth, have highlighted the failure of education systems to prepare young people with the right skills for the job market and have fueled calls for greater opportunity and accountability."[34] The economization of education perspective is reflected in the 2020 education strategy's refrain: "Invest early. Invest smartly. Invest for all."[35]

A very important shift in emphasis from school credentials and years of school attendance to learning work skills is contained in the Bank's 2020 strategy: "The new strategy focuses on learning for a simple reason: growth, development, and poverty reduction depend on the *knowledge and skills that people acquire, not the number of years that they sit in a classroom* [author's emphasis]."[36] For the individual, this means there should be less concern about earning a diploma and more concern with acquiring "skills that determine his or her productivity and ability to adapt to new technologies and opportunities." The World Bank claims that Organization for Economic Cooperation and Development's (OECD) assessments measure these skills and can predict economic growth:

> At the societal level, recent research shows that the level of skills in a workforce—as measured by performance on international student assessments such as the Programme for International Student Assessment (PISA) and the Trends in International Mathematics and Science Study (TIMSS)—predicts economic growth rates far better than do average schooling levels.[37]

The World Bank's reasoning reinforces the economic education model by shifting from a concern about everyone attending school to one that students learn work skills. The World Bank claims, "Recent research shows that the level of skills in a workforce predicts economic growth rates far better than do average schooling levels."[38] Even improving health and social conditions to allow for participation in learning work skills is cast in an economization framework. Health is considered instrumental in helping economic growth by making it possible to learn work skills. In contrast, improving health and social conditions could be a simple matter of social justice. The 2020 strategy attributes an economization goal to health and social improvement. In the following quote from *Education Strategy 2020*, health and social protection are linked to education and demands of the labor market:

> Improving education outcomes depends heavily on links with the health and social protection sectors: these sectors influence whether students are healthy enough to learn well, whether the system offers families a strong enough safety net to protect education in times of crisis, and whether schooling reflects adequately the demand for skills in the labor market.[39]

The economization of education viewpoint gives the impression that economic conditions and employment are dependent on students learning work skills. However, unemployment might be a result of crises in the economic system, such as bank failures, corporate greed, or a host of other factors. The World Bank recognizes the potential for economic meltdowns but claims education can help: "Better coping with economic shocks. Households with more education cope better with economic shocks than less educated households, since they tend to have more resources and knowledge about how to cope with income fluctuations."[40] Even adaptation to climate change, which appears to be linked to industrial development, will, according to the World Bank, be enhanced by education: "Adapting to environmental change. Comparing countries with similar income and weather conditions, those countries with better-educated female populations are more capable of coping with extreme weather events than countries with low levels of female education."[41]

The World Bank *Education Strategy 2020*, the Audit State, and Local Autonomy

The use of international assessments is key to the World Bank's *Education Strategy 2020*. But what happens to local control when students are measured by international tests or national tests benchmarked against TIMSS and PISA? Do these tests undercut local autonomy? The World Bank claims that parents and communities armed with test scores can act to change local schools. Using test scores could undercut local autonomy by forcing parents and communities to compare their schools with other global schools, which might persuade them to change local schools to look like those of other communities and nations with high test scores.

The World Bank uses India and Pakistan as examples of local use of accountability information to change school systems. The Bank reports, "In India the school report cards developed by the District Information System for Education summarize school information in an easy-to-read format, giving parents and stakeholders . . . [the power to] hold schools and authorities accountable."[42] Data from these report cards are published on the Internet, which, supposedly, promotes local accountability. Similar report cards are used and disseminated in the Punjab province of Pakistan. The World Bank claims that by increasing knowledge of educational quality and empowering parents with this information resulted in increasing test scores by between 0.10 and 0.15 standard deviations in both government and lower-quality private schools.[43]

Based on this study of assessments in India and Pakistan, the World Bank claims that improved school performance requires local actors to be given greater decision-making power to reform schools based on accountability. Providing test scores to parents and other community members empowers them, according to the World Bank, to engage in school reform. According to the Bank: "Research around the world has found that increased autonomy policies change the dynamics within schools because parents become more involved . . . There is evidence, moreover, that these instruments [assessment] have reduced repetition, failure, and dropout rates."[44]

In summary, the World Bank wants local communities to rely on the Bank's "high-quality global knowledge base on education."[45] In other words, local control is a method for implementing Bank policies and not a call for schools to reflect local educational traditions. In calling for local control of schools, the World Bank emphasizes the audit state and assessment: "According to the expanded definition of an education system, relationships of accountability are the key levers that make a system work. Two powerful mechanisms for improving the accountability of educational providers are availability of information and greater autonomy for providers."[46]

The World Bank and the Economic Value of Knowledge

The economization of education gives knowledge a price tag in what is called the knowledge economy. The question "What knowledge is of most worth?" is answered in economic terms in contrast to those who might focus on religious, Indigenous, social justice, or environmental forms of knowledge. Within the economic education model, the value of knowledge taught in schools is determined by its contribution to economic growth. This can result in trying to force some types of knowledge into an economic mold. For instance, is art education taught for its contribution to the arts, or is arts education shaped and directed toward economic goals? In *Globalization and International Education*, Robin Shields asserts that there has been a fundamental redefinition of knowledge: "Rather than a public good, knowledge becomes a private commodity, 'intellectual property', which can be bought and sold much like any other commodity."[47]

Discussions about the knowledge economy occur on the networks linking the World Bank to governments, global IGOs and NGOs, and multinational corporations. In *Constructing Knowledge Societies*, the World Bank declares, "The ability of a society to produce, select, adapt, commercialize, and use knowledge is critical for sustained economic growth and improved living standards."[48] The book states, "Knowledge has become the most important factor in economic development."[49] The World Bank states that its assistance for education for the knowledge economy is aimed at helping countries adapt their entire education systems to the new challenges of the "learning" economy in "two complementary ways . . . Formation of a strong human capital base . . . [and] Construction of an effective national innovation system."[50] The creation of a national innovation system for assisting schools to adapt to the knowledge economy creates another global network. The World Bank describes this network: "A national innovation system is a well-articulated network of firms, research centers, universities, and think tanks that work together to take advantage of the growing stock of global knowledge, assimilate and adapt it to local needs, and create new technology."[51]

The concept of the knowledge economy can be traced to the work of economists Theodore Shultz and Gary Becker.[52] In 1961, Shultz pointed out that "economists have long known that people are an important part of the wealth of nations."[53] Shultz argued that people invested in themselves through education to improve their jobs opportunities. In a similar fashion, nations could, he argued, increase educational opportunities for people as a stimulus for economic growth.

In his 1964 book *Human Capital*, Gary Becker asserted that economic growth now depended on the knowledge, information, ideas, skills, and health of the workforce. Investments in education, he argued could improve human capital, which would contribute to economic growth.[54] Later, he used the word *knowledge* in relation to the economy: "An economy like that of the United States is called a capitalist economy, but the more accurate term is human capital or *knowledge* capital economy."[55] Becker claimed that human capital represented three-fourths of the wealth of the United States and that investment in education would be the key to further economic growth.[56] Following a similar line of reasoning, Daniel Bell in 1973 coined the term "post-industrial" and predicted that there would be shift from blue-collar to white-collar labor requiring a major increase in educated workers.[57] In the 1990s, Peter Drucker asserted that knowledge rather than ownership of capital generates new wealth and that power was shifting from owners and managers of capital to knowledge workers.[58] During the same decade, Robert Reich claimed that inequality between people and nations was a result of differences in knowledge and skills. Invest in education, he urged, and these inequalities would be reduced. Growing income inequality between individuals and nations, according to Reich, was a result of differences in knowledge and skills.[59]

The knowledge economy is also linked to new forms of communication and networking. Referring to the new economy of the late twentieth century, Manuel Castells wrote in *The Rise of the Network Society*, "I call it informational, global, and networked to identify its fundamental distinctive features and to emphasize their intertwining."[60] By informational, he meant the ability of corporations and governments to "generate, process, and apply efficiently knowledge-based information."[61] It was global because capital, labor, raw materials, management, consumption, and markets were linked through global networks. "It is networked," he contended, because "productivity is generated through and competition is played out in a global network of interaction between business networks."[62] Information or knowledge, he claimed, was now a product that increased productivity and economic growth.

National and global policymakers, including the leadership of the World Bank, uncritically accepted the idea that in a knowledge economy investment in education was a panacea for most of the world's economic problems including growing the economies of poor countries, reducing inequalities between rich and poor people and nations, and ensuring continuing economic development of all countries. In *Constructing Knowledge Societies*, the World Bank worried that "the capacity to generate and harness knowledge in the pursuit of sustainable development and improved living standards is not shared equally among nations."[63]

The World Bank uses the measurement of total factor productivity (TFP) to emphasize the importance of knowledge in economic growth. The Bank contends that postsecondary education "is one of the most influential of the set of complex factors that determine TFP for an economy."[64] In other words, the application of knowledge increases the level of productivity; more goods can be produced using fewer hours of human labor.

Nothing better expresses the World Bank's commitment to the idea of a knowledge economy and the role of education in developing human capital than its publication *Lifelong Learning in the Global Knowledge Economy*.[65] The book offers a roadmap for developing countries on how to prepare their populations for the knowledge economy to increase economic growth. The role of the World Bank is to loan money to ensure the growth of an educated labor force that can apply knowledge to increase productivity. These loans, according to Bank policies, might provide support to both public and private educational institutions.[66] In the framework of public-private partnerships, the World Bank supports private education in developing countries when governments cannot afford to support public schools for all:

> The provision of schooling is largely provided and financed by governments. However, due to unmet demand for education coupled with shrinking government budgets, the public sector in several parts of the world is developing innovative partnerships with the private sector. Private education encompasses a wide range of providers including for-profit schools (that operate as enterprises), religious schools, non-profit schools run by NGOs, publicly funded schools operated by private boards, and community owned schools. In other words, there is a market for education.[67]
>
> The European Union represents one of the many international responses to the idea of education for the knowledge economy. In 2000, the European Commission issued its so-called Lisbon strategy for becoming "the most competitive and dynamic knowledge-based economy in the world, capable of sustainable economic growth with more and better jobs and greater social cohesion."[68] The title of the strategy report for creating a knowledge economy captures the spirit of those advocating education for the knowledge economy, "Mobilizing the Brainpower of Europe: Enabling Universities to Make Their Full Contribution to the Lisbon Strategy."[69] The first strategic objective of the report is "improving the quality and effectiveness of education training systems in the EU, in the light of the new requirements of the knowledge society and the changing patterns of teaching and learning."[70]

In summary, the concept of the knowledge economy contributes to the economization of education. School knowledge is valued for its contribution to economic growth. One possible danger is that cultural traditions will be lost as the value of knowledge is measured by its economic contribution.

The World Bank and the Economic Value of Personality Traits

The economization of education includes giving an economic value to social skills. Cognitive and social skills are valued according to their contribution to economic development. In other words, the goal of the economic education model can be described as producing "homo economicus" or the "economic human" who will fit into the work environment of modern business enterprises or becomes an entrepreneur in the global economy.

A section of the World Bank report *Lifelong Learning in the Global Knowledge Economy* contains a section with the descriptive title: "Equipping Learners with the Skills and Competencies They Need to Succeed in a Knowledge Economy." Two of the three competencies relate to psychological attitudes and dispositions. These competencies could require major changes in some of the world's cultures. For instance, the first listed competency is the following:

> *Acting autonomously:* Building and exercising a sense of self, making choices and acting in the context of a larger picture, being oriented toward the future, being aware of the environment, understanding how one fits in, exercising one's rights and responsibilities, determining and executing a life plan, and planning and carrying out personal projects.[71]

The goal of acting autonomously is echoed in the European Commission's 1998 White Paper on the knowledge economy: "The ultimate aim of education is to develop the autonomy of each person and of his/her professional capacity, to make of the person a privileged element of adaptation and evolution."[72]

Cross-cultural scholars associate "acting autonomously" with individualist societies as contrasted with collectivist societies that emphasize acting in harmony with the group. Acting autonomously does not reflect the values of collectivist communities such as many Asian, Islamic, and Indigenous societies. In fact, the values that the World Bank are recommending be instilled in children are those of a competitive marketplace that emphasizes individual competition.

The World Bank is using a free market model of individual competition in advocating changing the cultural values of many groups of peoples. Cross-cultural psychologist Harry C. Triandis identifies the contrasting character traits of individualist and collectivist societies (see Table 2.1).[73]

Overall, the United States, where the headquarters of the World Bank is located, is ranked as the most individualist nation in the world. Below is a global ranking of nations of the most individualist and collectivist nations.

TABLE 2.1 Individualist and Collectivist Personalities

Individualist	Collectivist
Hedonism, stimulation, self-direction	Tradition and conformity
Good opinion of self (self–enhancing)	Modest
Goals fit personal needs	Goals show concern with needs of others
Desire for individual distinctiveness	Desire for blending harmoniously with the group
Value success and achievement because it makes the individual look good	Value success and achievement because it reflects well on the group
More concerned with knowing one's own feelings	Attuned to feelings of others and striving for interpersonal harmony
Exhibits "social loafing" or "gold bricking"—trying to minimize work in group efforts	No social loafing in group efforts
Less sensitive to social rejection	More sensitive to social rejection
Less modest in social situations	More modest in social situations
Less likely to feel embarrassed	More likely to feel embarrassed

The Ten Most Individualist Nations in Rank Order Beginning with the Most Individualist

1. United States
2. Australia
3. Denmark
4. Germany
5. Finland
6. Norway
7. Italy
8. Austria
9. Hungary
10. South Africa[74]

The Ten Most Collectivist Nations in Rank Order Beginning with the Most Collectivist

1. China
2. Columbia
3. Indonesia
4. Pakistan
5. Korea
6. Peru
7. Ghana
8. Nepal
9. Nigeria
10. Tanzania[75]

The World Bank's report lists a second set of competencies for using technological tools, information, and symbols.

> *Using tools interactively:* Using tools as instruments for an active dialogue; being aware of and responding to the potential of new tools; and being able to use language, text, symbols information and knowledge and technology interactively to accomplish goals.[76]

These competencies would dramatically replace the reliance of Indigenous cultures on traditional tools, ways of knowing, and oral traditions. From a culturalist perspective, local communities would probably adapt these tools to their culture. On the other hand, total acceptance of this package of tools and symbol usages combined with a stress on individualism might result in the transformation of many of the world's cultures.

The final competency implies a world of nomads—workers moving around the global and having to adapt to multicultural workplaces. In this context, the knowledge economy becomes a world of migrant workers including corporate leaders, managers, technical operatives, and professionals to skilled and unskilled laborers.

> *Functioning in socially heterogeneous groups:* Being able to interact effectively with other people, including those from different backgrounds; recognizing the social embeddedness of individuals; creating social capital; and being able to relate well to others, cooperate, and manage and resolve conflict.[77]

Preparation for competencies in multicultural settings is indicated in learning to interact with "those from different backgrounds" and "recognizing the social embeddedness of others." A phrase that at first glance might not be understood is "creating social capital."

The report includes the development of social capital as part of human capital. The World Bank report states:

> By improving people's ability to function as members of their communities, education and training also increases *social capital* (broadly defined as social cohesion or social ties), thereby helping to build human capital, increase economic growth, and stimulate development. *Social capital* also improves education and health outcomes and child welfare, increases tolerance for gender and racial equity, enhances civil liberty and economic and civic equity, and decreases crime and tax evasion [author's emphasis].[78]

As quoted previously, social capital could include ethical or moral values that provide "social cohesion or social ties." A person with proper social capital will not commit criminal acts and will ensure the welfare of children and social justice.

Of course, "crime" and "social justice" are relative concepts depending on the laws and customs of a particular nation or culture. For example, there has been a ban in Saudi Arabia on women driving cars.[79] What about the social capital stated previously that is supposed to lead to "tolerance for gender and racial equity"? In this context, for better or worse, the World Bank's goal would be to change the laws and customs of Saudi Arabia regarding women's driving to enhance gender equity. In other words, the World Bank's concept of social capital is designed to change the cultures and laws of societies and nations.

If the concept of social capital is integrated into the concept of human capital, then the goals of education broaden to fostering individualism, developing technical and language skills, learning to function in multicultural settings, and learning to be ethical or moral in relationship to others.

In summary, the World Bank's ideal social personality for the knowledge economy is a person who acts autonomously and is focused on a sense of self. This concept of individualism, in contrast to personalities in collectivist societies, is a reflection of the values of nations like the United States. It is a personality ideally suited for individual competition in economic markets. In addition, the Bank's concept includes the ability to migrate between cultures and work in multicultural settings. While focusing on him/herself, this type of personality also learns to be obedient to the laws and customs of a nation. The focus on individualism raises the important question: Is the World Bank practicing a form of cultural imperialism? Is the determining factor in what knowledge and social skills are taught in schools a result of a particular cultural view that makes economic growth the most important condition for humans?

The World Bank and Skill Instruction

The World Bank takes an economization of education approach to school instruction through its emphasis on teaching skills needed by the global economy. As a global knowledge bank, its instructional ideas can influence local school leaders. The Bank proposes focusing school instruction on the second competency, using tools interactively, listed in the previous section. [80]

This competency requires learning to use language, text, symbols, information, knowledge, and technology. The World Bank advocates a very specific school curriculum for teaching this competency, which includes literacy, foreign languages, science and math, and civic participation based on the "rule of law." Some might complain about the neglect of instruction in the arts, philosophy, and literature, and, given the emphasis on creating a personality able to function in multicultural workplaces, the neglect of geography, history, and any form of cultural studies.

The World Bank's concept of literacy is a reflection of the economization of education. Literacy is treated as instrumental for completing work related to tasks in the knowledge economy. The Bank's concept of literacy does not include critical literacy skills that would prepare readers to analyze the ideological background and hidden messages in a written communication. It does not include reading for personal enjoyment such as learning to read and appreciate literature. It does not include any idea of being literate for political empowerment. It is, as indicated subsequently, literacy for functioning in the global labor market.

Literacy for the knowledge economy, the World Bank states, requires adults to perform at level 3 of the International Adult Literacy Survey. It should be noted that the survey itself represents the creation of a uniform global standard for literacy. It is a joint project of the OECD, the Educational Testing Service (Princeton, New Jersey), Statistics Canada, and the U.S. Department of Education.[81]

The International Adult Literacy Survey Identifies Five Levels of Literacy

1. Level 1 indicates persons with very poor skills, where the individual may, for example, be unable to determine the correct amount of medicine to give a child from information printed on the package.
2. Level 2 respondents can deal only with material that is simple, clearly laid out, and in which the tasks involved are not too complex. It denotes a weak level of skill, but more than Level 1. It identifies people who can read, but test poorly. They may have developed coping skills to manage everyday literacy demands, but their low level of proficiency makes it difficult for them to face novel demands, such as learning new job skills.
3. Level 3 is considered a suitable minimum for coping with the demands of everyday life and work in a complex, advanced society. It denotes roughly the skill level required for successful secondary school completion and college entry. Like higher levels, it requires the ability to integrate several sources of information and solve more complex problems.
4. Levels 4 and 5 describe respondents who demonstrate command of higher-order information processing skills.[82]

The World Bank's Literacy Targets of Level 3 for the Knowledge Economy

1. *Prose literacy:* Learners should be able to locate information that requires low-level inferences or that meets specified conditions.
2. *Document literacy:* Learners should be able to make literal or synonymous matches. They should be able to take conditional information into account or match up pieces of information that have multiple features.
3. *Quantitative literacy:* Learners should be able to solve some multiplication and division problems.[83]

In summary, the World Bank's plan of global literacy for the knowledge economy focuses strictly on the functional aspects of literacy and not on critical literacy skills and literacy for personal for enjoyment or political empowerment. Level 3 literacy, as stated previously, is for "the demands of everyday life and work in a complex, advanced society." Level 3 encompasses "prose literacy" and "document literacy," which involve low-level inferences and manipulation of information. Also included in this level of literacy is the ability to multiply and divide. The lack of political empowerment associated with this type of literacy will become apparent when I discuss the World Bank's concept of education for participation in civil society.

The World Bank's foreign language instructional goals are directly related to English as the global language. The Bank urges, "Policymakers in developing countries . . . to ensure that young people acquire a language with more than just local use, preferably one used internationally."[84] What is this international language? First, the World Bank mentions that schools of higher education around the world are offering courses in English. In addition, the Bank states, "People seeking access to international store of knowledge through the internet require, principally, English language skills."[85]

Learning math and science is also considered important for the global economy. The World Bank reports that male achievement in science has "a statistically positive effect on economic growth," and male accomplishments in math "positively correlated with growth, although the effect is not as strong as for science."[86] Female achievement in science and math is not correlated with growth, because, the Bank contends, of gender discrimination in the labor market. The positive effect of achievement in science reflects, according to the Bank, a broad-based science literacy and not just the education of highly trained researchers.

The Bank's report does not detail recommended learning for participation in civil society. Using a study conducted for the International Association for Evaluation of Educational Achievement, an organization that through its global testing programs contributes to global education uniformity and is part the World Bank's education network, the Bank concludes that civic education is a good thing because it contributes to economic and social development: "It is linked to good governance and the rule of law, which directly affect economic and social development."[87] Therefore, the World Bank's curricular proposals are directed at increasing economic development through the teaching of functional skills.

KEY POINTS: SCHOOLING FOR THE KNOWLEDGE ECONOMY

The World Bank's Concept of the Knowledge Economy

1. Economic growth is dependent on the knowledge, information, ideas, skills, and health of the workforce
2. Postindustrial shift from blue-collar to white-collar labor
3. Postsecondary education is one of the most influential factors determining economic productivity

The World Bank's Schools of Tomorrow

What type of teaching and school organization will support the World Bank's curriculum for the knowledge economy? First, the World Bank advocates learner-centered instruction. However, it does not mean a progressive model of education where learning is based on the interests of the student and designed for political power. Learner centered for World Bank planners means that instruction is related to what students already know. This requires teachers to learn what students know before introducing new material. The new material is supposed to be related to the prior knowledge of the student. World Bank planners rejected rote learning based on drill. They want students to make connections between the knowledge being presented by the teacher and their own accumulated store of wisdom. From the perspective of the World Bank, learning to make these connections is preparation for making similar connections in the global knowledge economy. "Learner-centered learning," the Bank's report states, "allows new knowledge to become available for use in new situations—that is, it allows knowledge transfer to take place."[88]

A goal of the World Bank is to prepare workers for a knowledge economy that requires manipulation of information. This is the goal of literacy instruction. Consequently, the World Bank education planners advocate knowledge-rich learning involving a few subjects learned in depth. Students are asked to apply their newly gained knowledge in these few subjects to real or simulated problems. This mode of instruction reflects the educational tradition of "learning by doing," which is part of the progressive education tradition. However, progressive educators believe that learning by doing leads to learner participation in the reconstruction of society to achieve social justice. For the World Bank, learning by doing prepares the learner to work in the knowledge economy. Referring to knowledge-rich instruction, the Bank claims, "This kind of learning provides learners with a variety of strategies and tools for retrieving and applying or transferring knowledge to new situations."[89]

Learner-centered and knowledge-rich instruction will be controlled through assessment-driven learning. Standards for learning are created and measured by student progress in attaining these standards. Students are to participate in discussions about these assessments, which are supposed to be "powerful motivators and tools for improved and independent learning."[90] While some might think a test-driven system results in a focus on test preparation and related rote learning, the World Bank claims that assessment-driven instruction promotes "higher-order thinking skills and conceptual understanding."[91]

In addition, Bank planners envision an interconnected learning environment where students learn from each other and from the world outside of school. The Bank refers to this as community-connected learning. Consequently, group work on projects is encouraged as preparation for working with others in the sharing and manipulation of information with group projects involving real-life problems.

Given the goal of preparation for the knowledge economy, the World Bank emphasizes the classroom use of computers and resources from the Internet. Information and communication technology (ICT) allows the adaptation of globally available information to local learning situations. This results in changing the role of the teacher. Based on the experience of teachers in Chile and Costa Rica, Bank officials claim that ICT creates "a more egalitarian relationship between teacher and learner with learners making more decisions about their work, speaking their minds more freely, and receiving consultations rather than lectures from their teachers."[92]

A large percentage of the World Bank's education funds are used for the purchase of educational technology. Critics might complain that this channels large sums of money to be used for education to multinational producers of computers and educational software. On the other hand, ICT is considered vital for education to enter the knowledge economy. According to the Bank's figures, 40 percent of their education budget in 2000 and 27 percent in 2001 was used to purchase technology. It is estimated that between 1997 and 2001 75 percent of the education projects financed by the World Bank included ICT, education technology, and education management information systems along with courses being taught over the Internet as part of distance learning.[93] The World Bank continues to emphasize ICT instruction as evidenced by its 2013 report by Michael Trucano, *Mobile Learning and Textbooks of the Future, E-reading and Edtech Policies: Trends in Technology Use in Education in Developing Countries* (Excerpts from the World Bank's *EduTech* Blog, Volume IV).[94]

How are teachers to be trained for schools that are learner centered, knowledge rich, assessment driven, and community connected? The World Bank identifies the following teacher characteristics needed for education for the knowledge economy:

1. Teachers need an in-depth knowledge of their subject areas including knowledge of facts, concepts, and an understanding of interconnections between knowledge and facts;
2. Teachers need to know methods of instruction related to their subject matter and designed for learner-centered instruction using computers and the Internet;
3. Teachers need training related to the conditions of a classroom that is knowledge rich, assessment driven, and community connected.

Lifelong Learning and the Economization of Education

Economization of education makes lifelong learning an economic necessity in contrast to it being a personal leisure-time activity for pleasure. Lifelong learning is considered essential for individuals to keep pace with the constantly changing global job market and technology.[95] It is preparation for a destabilized life of changing jobs, job requirements, and geographical locations. In this vision of the nomadic worker, people must constantly adapt to new living conditions, technology, and work requirements. This requires learning skills that help the individual to adjust to an ever-changing world.

The World Bank's approach to lifelong learning involves a combination of competencies. Reflecting the previous discussions of the World Bank's vision of the psychological construction of humanity and schooling, the Bank defines the knowledge and competencies needed for lifelong learning as follows:

> These include basic academic skills, such as literacy, foreign language, math, and science skills, and the ability to use information and communication technology. Workers must use these skills effectively, act autonomously and reflectively, and join and function in socially heterogeneous groups.[96]

A lifelong learner should, according to Bank's approach, prepare for working in a multicultural labor force. The lifelong learner is to study new technologies and job skills.

The emphasis on teaching learning skills is the major focus of most discussions of lifelong learning. The European Union's statement on lifelong learning defined it as an "all purposeful learning activity, undertaken on an ongoing basis with the aim of improving knowledge, skills and competence."[97] In discussing the knowledge economy in Hong Kong and Shanghai in a World Bank publication, Kai Ming Cheng and Hak Kwong Yip explain the meaning of lifelong learning among Chinese school officials wanting to prepare students for the knowledge economy as the "ability to learn new things, to work in teams, to communicate effectively, to manage oneself, to question and to innovate, to assume personal responsibility, etc."[98] In one document issued by the European Union, the skills needed for lifelong learning, skills that are to be taught in primary and secondary schools, are described as: "The general elementary and/ or cognitive competencies required for a whole series of jobs, indeed all jobs: mathematics, writing, problem-solving, social communication and interpersonal competencies."[99]

Public-Private Partnership Networks

The World Bank and UNESCO belong to networks linked to multinational corporations. For example, a 2006 workshop organized by the World Economic Forum and UNESCO, "Public-Private Partnerships in Education for All," included Intel, BT (British Telecom), Cisco, SAP, and Hewlett-Packard. These participants represent some of the world's largest manufacturers of computers, software, and information technology who have a stake in selling products to educational systems.[100] Cynics might interpret their involvement as purely a business interest in selling products and educating future consumers. Others might interpret their involvement as an expression of corporate goodwill or a combination of business interests and the desire to do good.

The USAID sponsored the World Economic Forum workshop promoting public-private partnerships in education. Gita Steiner-Khamsi writes, "The strategies of the World Bank . . . and USAID have converged towards the same knowledge-based approach for delivering aid and chosen the same narrow focus on measurable student outcomes, notably literacy and numeracy."[101] USAID had previously participated in a UNESCO-sponsored 2005 study, *Corporate Sector Involvement in Education for All*.[102] This study uncritically accepted the role of multinational corporations: "Closely linked to the fact that corporations consider the value of these programs beyond their short-term returns, their motivations are also clearly economically-oriented."[103] Regarding business interests, the study states, "In the new paradigm of development, education is worth investing in the long run to enhance prosperity of their business activities (better economic and social environment), as well as the firm's own competitiveness (better trained employees)."[104] What can corporations do? The UNESCO study suggests corporations can improve national school systems through "financing, managing, and provision of educational services and/or materials."[105]

The study raised the possibility of a global network linking government education leaders, multinational corporations, UNESCO, and the World Bank. It recommended the establishment of partnerships between national government officials and corporate leaders involving "the creation of a 'mixed' executive board composed of private and public stakeholders who are responsible for making decisions concerning partnership objectives."[106] The World Bank Group's International Finance Corporation encourages private investment in education through EdInvest. According to its website: "EdInvest was initiated in 1998 as an . . . on-line investment information forum on private sector development in education. It began with initial funding from the World Bank Development Marketplace."[107] The International Finance Corporation describes its work as "supporting the development of private educational activities in our member countries . . . we support the start-up or expansion of initiatives in many subsectors of education. These include: post-secondary, primary and secondary schooling with a particular interest in school networks, e-learning initiatives, student financing programs and other ancillary services."[108] These private educational activities include for-profit schools.

In 2007, the World Bank and the Human Development Network hosted a conference on public-private partnerships in education, which included speakers from not only the World Bank but also universities around the world. The Human Development Network is a project of the UNDP involving 144 representatives from national governments, NGOs, and research institutions.[109] The Human Development Network is designed to link those interested in a "concept of sustainable human development as an . . . approach [that] regards people's well-being as the goal of development."[110] Expansion of educational opportunities is considered an important part of sustainable human development.

The written introduction to the conference supported public-private partnerships because of the inability of some governments to finance the expansion of educational opportunities. Encompassed under the conference's concept of public-private partnerships were "a wide range of providers, including for-profit schools (that operate as enterprises), religious schools, non-profit schools run by NGOs, public funded schools operated by private boards, and community owned schools."[111] The inclusion of for-profit schools links the network to global learning corporations, which will be discussed later in the book.

An example of International Finance Corporation's investment in for-profit education is the SABIS International School in Lebanon. It was the first education investment by the International Finance Corporation in the Middle East and North. The investment was US$8 million with the intention of making it the international headquarters and the flagship of the SABIS Group of Schools. Lars Thunell, the International Finance Corporation's executive vice president and CEO, claimed, "Education is vital to ensuring sustainable economic growth, particularly with a rapidly growing and relatively young population across the MENA [Middle Eastern and North Africa] region. By providing high-quality services, the SABIS school is a model for further private investment in education throughout the region."[112] In a World Bank publication, *Mobilizing the Private Sector for Public Education: A View from the Trenches*, SABIS president Carl Bistany describes that "since the mid-1950s SABIS has viewed 'education' as an industry and has subjected it to the rules that govern successful industries and businesses: efficiency, accountability, and optimization of resources."[113] The company started with a school built in a small village in Lebanon in 1886 and is today a "network of 31 K–12 schools in 11 countries, with a total enrollment of 28,000 students from more than 120 nations. Seven of the 31 are charter schools in the United States, and the remaining are private schools." Bistany describes the for-profit attitude of the company regarding education:

> In a country where profit-based economics has played a major role in development and advancement, it comes as no surprise that the United States is leading the way to find appropriate public-private partnerships. It seems natural for the United States to turn to the private sector to seek assistance to enhance public education by subjecting the private sector to the rules inherent in business and industry, that of accountability, efficiency, cost reduction, added value, and results–oriented incentive schemes. SABIS shares the same views and has been successful in implementing the approach to the SABIS network of schools for a long time.[114]

Criticisms of the Economization of Education

One criticism of the economic view of education is the preparation of students for the needs of the knowledge economy when there are not enough jobs. Also, so-called knowledge work has been routinized allowing for the hiring of less skilled workers. "It is, therefore," Phillip Brown and Hugh Lauder conclude, "not just a matter of the oversupply of skills that threatens the equation between high skills and high income, where knowledge is 'routinized' it can be substituted with less-skilled and cheaper workers at home or further afield."[115]

Brown and Lauder argue that multinational corporations are able to keep salaries low by encouraging nations to invest in schools that prepare for the knowledge economy. For instance, there was an increased demand for higher education in India where computer programmers earn annually between US$2,200 and US$2,900 (1997 U.S. dollars) as compared to programmers in the United States who earn between US$35,500 and US$39,000 (1997 U.S. dollars).[116] The result was a migration of computer programmers from India to the United States resulting in putting a lid on wage increases in the United States, while depleting the human capital resources of India.

Another effect is so-called brain waste where well-educated school graduates are unable to find jobs commensurate with their skills. This results in dampening income growth for college graduates in industrial countries and forcing many into occupations not requiring a high level of education. Brain waste can occur in high-income countries when there are only a limited number of jobs requiring high levels of education. Brown and Lauder write, "Britain, along with America, is not a high-skilled, high-waged economy but one in which this accurately reflects only a minority of workers, who stand alongside an increasingly large proportion of well-qualified but low-waged workers, who in turn stand beside the low-skilled and low-waged."[117]

As a result of pressure to expand educational opportunities to meet the demand of the global knowledge economy, Brown and Lauder conclude that "vast numbers of highly-skilled are available in developing economies, the global expansion of tertiary education has outstripped the demand for high-skilled workers, creating downward pressure on the incomes of skilled workers in developed countries along with some upward pressure on those in emerging economies."[118]

The consequence for developing countries has been disastrous with governments being forced to pay back educational loans to the World Bank while experiencing little economic growth from investment in schooling. In addition, educated workers from developing nations have become part of the so-called "brain migration" moving from their countries to wealthier nations where salaries are higher. Thus, a developing nation invests in education but does not receive the expected rewards from improving its knowledge economy. Some countries have experienced extraordinary depletion of their skilled and educated workforce. According to statistics provided by the OECD, 89 percent of skilled workers have emigrated from Guyana, 85.1 percent from Jamaica, 63.3 percent from Gambia, 62.2 from Fiji, 46.9 from Ghana, and 38.4 percent from Kenya.[119]

A good percentage of these immigrants are unable to obtain in their host countries employment commensurate with their education. For example, statistics released by the U.S. Census Bureau show that many immigrants with bachelor's degrees are unable to obtain skilled jobs in the United States. The most successful group of immigrants with college degrees who were able to gain skilled employment were from Ireland (69%), the United Kingdom (65%), Australia (67%), and Canada (64%). Even these percentages suggest some level of brain waste.[120]

The oversupply of educated workers, it could be argued, depresses wages to the advantage of employers. Therefore, arguments for the knowledge economy may have a disrupting effect on human lives and may cause national educational expenditures to favor higher education. In seeking high-paying jobs, citizens may pressure governments to provide more opportunities for higher education or stimulate the development of private higher education institutions. This demand might redirect government money away from support of needed social programs such as those for health, nutrition, and shelter. The result might be frustrated college graduates who face the prospect of "brain waste" and seek global employment through "brain migration."

Also, the World Bank's advocacy of a knowledge economy can have a negative effect on local cultural practices. For instance, the World Bank advocates replacing traditional farming methods with scientific agricultural methods and corporate farming. The World Bank warns, "Lagging countries will miss out on opportunities to improve their economies through, for example, more efficient agricultural production and distribution systems which would increase yields and lower the proportion of food wasted due to poor distribution."[121] In other words, it claims, knowledge applied to agriculture will increase productivity.

However, the World Bank recommends the use of genetically modified crops that would increase yields, enhance nutritional values, and create plants resistant "to drought, pests, salinity, and *herbicides* [my emphasis]."[122] In other words, traditional plants and cultivation should be replaced by products of biotechnology and chemical eradication of unwanted plants that interfere with crop growth. The result is corporate farming with the little family plot replaced with large-scale scientific farming.

The World Bank recognizes the dangers from genetically modified plants and chemical crop sprays to human health and the environment. Its answer to these problems is improving the knowledge base of a country. In other words, knowledge, in this case biotechnology and chemistry, might change agricultural production to the detriment of the local population, which can be corrected, the Bank claims, by further growth of the knowledge economy. Referring to biosafety and risk management, the World Bank asserts: "To make informed decisions on how to address these challenges, countries need to call on highly qualified specialists—who will not be available unless investment in advanced human capital are made."[123] This convoluted logic results in calls for further expansion of the educational system to correct problems caused by the original application of knowledge.

Postcolonial critics of the Bank's agricultural programs argue they are seriously flawed by a lack of understanding of local agricultural conditions and land ownership. The result has been making the rich richer and the poor poorer. Richard Peet writes regarding the World Bank's policies when applied in Africa, "It turned out little was known about rain-fed tropical agriculture in Africa . . . that attitudes and local conditions were more difficult to change than technology . . . land tenure reforms were a prerequisite of any agricultural development aimed at the poor."[124] The result was that the loans went mainly to rich farmers, according to Peet, which caused "increasing income inequalities."[125]

Robin Shields argues that World Bank policy "embeds a belief that the spread of global capitalism is both inevitable and egalitarian, that competition creates better lives for everyone, and that economic growth is always desirable." He claims that the economization of knowledge favors technology and science and that "critical thinking and democratic citizenship are implicitly unvalued by the little attention they receive in official documents."[126]

In summary, criticisms of World Bank policies are that they serve the interests of corporations by keeping down wages for skilled workers, cause global brain migration to the detriment of developing economies, undermine local cultures, and ensure corporate domination by not preparing school graduates who think critically and are democratically oriented.

KEY POINTS: CRITICISMS OF EDUCATION FOR THE KNOWLEDGE ECONOMY

1. Not enough jobs in the knowledge economy to absorb school graduates
2. Oversupply of educated workers keeps salaries low, which benefits multi-national corporations
3. Brain migration of educated workers from developing to developed countries
4. Brain waste resulting from oversupply of educated workers
5. Overinvestment in higher education to the detriment of other social services
6. Destruction of local cultures
7. Does not prepare school graduates who think critically and are democratically oriented

Conclusion

In summary, the World Bank is able to advance its educational agenda through an extensive global network that includes IGOs and NGOs, national governments, local officials, and multinational corporations. Global discourses on education for the knowledge economy and lifelong learning are strongly influenced by the World Bank's agenda. However, as I mentioned at the beginning of this chapter, the World Bank's views on the knowledge economy and lifelong learning are not shared by all global education players. In the next chapter, I will explore the global agendas and discourses of some other major global institutions, including the United Nations and OECD.

KEY POINTS: SUMMARY OF THE WORLD BANK'S GLOBAL EDUCATION AGENDA

1. Support of public-private partnerships and networks in education, particularly between national education systems, private school groups, and education corporations
2. Financial support of for-profit global learning corporations through loans from the World Bank Group's International Finance Corporation
3. Advocacy of education for a knowledge economy as the key to economic growth
4. Advocacy of education for self-autonomy, in contrast to a collectivist personality, for the worker in the global economy

5. Advocacy of education for working in multicultural workplaces, including the possibility of learners being part of the world's brain migration
6. Support of a global school curriculum that would focus on literacy, math and science, foreign languages for the global economy (mainly English), and education for civic responsibilities
7. Support of learner-centered instruction and learning by doing so that global workers will be able to utilize new knowledge in their jobs and lives
8. Support of lifelong learning so that global workers will be able to adapt to new technological advances, job changes, and possible global migration

The World Bank plays a major role in disseminating the economic model of education through its global networks. Through these networks, it emphasizes the economization of education by turning educational research over to economists and making educational growth the primary objective of school policies. The World Bank supports the idea of the audit state by calling for performance measurements of school systems, such as PISA and TIMSS. I will discuss in the next chapter that these tests come from another global organization, the OECD.

Notes

1 Steven J. Klees, "World Bank and Education: Ideological Premises and Ideological Conclusions," in *The World Bank and Education: Critiques and Alternatives*, edited by Steven J. Klees, Joel Samoff, and Nelly P. Stromquist (Boston: Sense Publishers, 2012), p. 49.
2 World Bank, "Education: Overview—Context." Retrieved from http://web.worldbank.org/WBSITE/EXTERNAL/TOPICS/EXTEDUCATION/0,,contentMDK:20575742~menuPK:282393~pagePK:210058~piPK:210062~theSitePK:282386,00.html on October 7, 2013.
3 Joel Spring, *Education and the Rise of the Global Economy* (Mahwah, NJ: Lawrence Erlbaum, 1998), pp. 159–189.
4 Gita Steiner-Khamsi, "For All by All? The World Bank's Global Framework for Education," in *The World Bank and Education: Critiques and Alternatives*, p. 11.
5 World Bank, "Economics of Education." Retrieved from http://web.worldbank.org/WBSITE/EXTERNAL/TOPICS/EXTEDUCATION/0,,contentMDK:20264769~menuPK:613701~pagePK:148956~piPK:216618~theSitePK:282386,00.html on October, 11, 2013.
6 Ibid.
7 Ibid.
8 World Bank, "SABER: Systems Approach for Better Education Results; Strengthening Education Systems to Achieve Learning for All." Retrieved from http://siteresources.worldbank.org/EDUCATION/Resources/278200-1221666119663/saber.html on October 11, 2013.
9. Ibid.

10 See Collete Chabbott, "Development INGOS," in *Constructing World Culture: International Nongovernment Organizations Since 1875*, edited by John Boli and George Thomas (Palo Alto: Stanford University Press, 1999), pp. 222–248; and Leslie Sklair, "Sociology of the Global System," in *The Globalization Reader*, edited by Frank Lechner and John Boli (Malden, MA: Blackwell Publishing, 2004), pp. 70–76.

11 For example, Michael Goldman, *Imperial Nature: The World Bank and Struggles for Social Justice* (New Haven, CT: Yale University Press, 2005); and Richard Peet, *Unholy Trinity: The IMF, World Bank and WTO* (London: Zed Books, 2003).

12 See Manuel Castells, *The Rise of the Network Society* (Oxford: Blackwell, 2000), pp. 77–147, 216–247.

13 Bjorn H. Nordtveit, "World Bank Poetry: How the Education Strategy 2020 Imagines the World," in *The World Bank and Education: Critiques and Alternatives*, p. 29.

14 International Bank for Reconstruction and Development/World Bank, *Learning for All: Investing in People's Knowledge and Skills to Promote Development-World Bank Group Education Strategy 2020* (Washington, DC: International Bank for Reconstruction and Development/World Bank, 2011), p. 5.

15 Gita Steiner-Khamsi, "For All by All?" p. 5.

16 Ibid.

17 International Bank for Reconstruction and Development/World Bank, *Learning for All*, p. 7.

18 Ibid., p. 6.

19 Ibid.

20 World Bank, "Education: Overview." Retrieved from http://web.worldbank.org/WBSITE/EXTERNAL/TOPICS/EXTEDUCATION/0,,contentMDK:20575742˜menuPK:282393˜pagePK:210058˜piPK:210062˜theSitePK:282386,00.html on October 8, 2013.

21 The three other members of the World Bank Group are the International Finance Corporation, the Multilateral Investment Guarantee Agency, and the International Centre for Settlement of Investment Disputes.

22 Goldman, *Imperial Nature*, p. 69.

23 World Bank, "Education Overview." Retrieved from www.worldbank.org/en/topic/education/overview on April 21, 2014.

24 World Bank, *Annual Report 2013*, p. 7. Retrieved from http://web.worldbank.org/WBSITE/EXTERNAL/EXTABOUTUS/EXTANNREP/EXTANNREP2013/0,,menuPK:9304895˜pagePK:64168427˜piPK:64168435˜theSitePK:9304888,00.html on October 7, 2013.

25 Ibid.

26 World Bank, *A Guide to the World Bank: Second Edition* (Washington, DC: World Bank, 2007), pp. 11–12.

27 Ibid., p. 43.

28 United Nations, *We Can End Poverty: Millennium Development Goals and Beyond 2015: Education*. Retrieved from www.un.org/millenniumgoals/education.shtml on October 8, 2013.

29 United Nations, *We Can End Poverty: Millennium Development Goals and Beyond 2015: Gender*. Retrieved from www.un.org/millenniumgoals/gender.shtml on October 10, 2013.

30 UNESCO, "Education for All (EFA) International Coordination: The Six EFA Goals and MDGs." Retrieved from http://portal.unesco.org/education/en/ev.php-URL_ID=53844URL_DO=DO_TOPIC&URL_SECTION=201.html on October 5, 2007.

31 UNESCO, "Education for All (EFA) International Coordination: The EFA Move-ment." Retrieved from http://portal.unesco.org/education/en/ev.php-URL_ID=54370&URL_DO=DO_TOPIC&URL_SECTION=201.html on October 5, 2007.

32 UNESCO, "Education for All (EFA) International Coordination: Mechanisms Involv-ing International Organizations." Retrieved from http://portal.unesco.org/education/en/ev.php-URL_ID=47539&URL_DO=DO_TOPIC&URL_SECTION=201.html on October 5, 2007.

33 UNESCO, "Education for All (EFA) International Coordination: Collective Consulta-tion of NGOs." Retrieved from http://portal.unesco.org/education/en/ev.php-URL_ID=47477&URL_DO=DO_TOPIC&URL_SECTION=201&reload=114567740 on October 5, 2007.

34 International Bank for Reconstruction and Development/World Bank, *Learning for All*, p. v.

35 Ibid.

36 Ibid., p. 3.

37 Ibid.

38 Ibid., p. 5.

39 Ibid., p. 9.

40 Ibid., p. 13.

41 Ibid.

42 Ibid., p. 33.

43 Ibid.

44 Ibid.

45 Ibid., p. 31.

46 Ibid., p. 33.

47 Robin Shields, Globalization and International Education (London: Bloomsbury Aca-demic, 2013), p. 89.

48 World Bank, *Constructing Knowledge Societies: New Challenges for Tertiary Education* (Washington, DC: The World Bank, 2002), p. 7.

49 Ibid.

50 The World Bank Education, "Education for the Knowledge Economy." Retrieved from http://web.worldbank.org/wBSTIE/EXTERNAL/TOPICS/EXTEDUCATION/0,,contentMDX:20161496~menuPK:540092~pagePK:148956~piPK:216618~theSitePK:282386,00.html on October 10, 2007.

51 Ibid.

52 See Brian Keeley, *Human Capital: How What You Know Shapes Your Life* (Paris: OECD, 2007), pp. 28–35; and Phillip Brown and Hugh Lauder, "Globalization, Knowledge and the Myth of the Magnet Economy," in *Education, Globalization & Social Change*, edited by Hugh Lauder, Phillip Brown, Jo-Anne Dillabough, and A.H. Halsey (Oxford: Oxford University Press, 2006), pp. 317–340.

53 As quoted in Keeley, *Human Capital*, p. 29.

54 Gary Becker, *Human Capital* (New York: Columbia University Press, 1964).

55 Gary Becker, "The Age of Human Capital," in *Education, Globalization & Social Change*, edited by Hugh Lauder, Phillip Brown, Jo-Anne Dillabough, and A.H. Halsey (Oxford: Oxford University Press, 2006), p. 292.

56 Ibid.

57 Daniel Bell, *The Coming of the Post-Industrial Society* (New York: Basic Books, 1973).

58 Peter Drucker, *Post-Capitalist Society* (London: Butterworth/Heinemann, 1993).

59 Robert Reich, *The Work of Nations: A Blueprint for the Future* (New York: Vintage, 1991).
60 Castells, *The Rise of the Network Society*, p. 77.
61 Ibid.
62 Ibid.
63 World Bank, *Constructing Knowledge Societies*, p. 9.
64 Ibid., p. 10.
65 World Bank, *Lifelong Learning in the Global Knowledge Economy: Challenges for Developing Countries* (Washington, DC: World Bank, 2003).
66 William Rideout, Jr., "Globalization and Decentralization in Sub-Saharan Africa: Focus Lesotho," in *Globalization and Education: Integration and Contestation across Cultures*, edited by Nelly Stromquist and Karen Monkman (Lanham, MD: Rowman & Littlefield, 2000), pp. 255–274.
67 World Bank, "Public-Private Partnerships in Education." Retrieved from http://web.worldbank.org/WBSITE/EXTERNAL/TOPICS/EXTEDUCATION/0,,content MDK:20756247~menuPK:2448342~pagePK:210058~piPK:210062~theSitePK:282386 ~isCURL:Y~isCURL:Y,00.html on April 21, 2014.
68 Directorate-General for Education and Culture, *Education and Training in Europe: Diverse Systems, Shared Goals for 2010* (Luxembourg: Office for Official Publications of the European Communities, 2002), p. 7.
69 Commission of the European Communities, "Communication from the Commission, Mobilizing the Brainpower of Europe: Enabling Universities to Make Their Full Contribution to the Lisbon Strategy" (Brussels: The European Commission, April 4, 2005).
70 Directorate-General for Education and Culture, *Education and Training in Europe*, p. 12.
71 World Bank, *Lifelong Learning in the Global Knowledge Economy*, p. 21.
72 Quoted by Stephen Stoer and António Magalhaes in "Education, Knowledge and the Network Society," *Globalisation, Societies and Education* 2(3), 2004 p. 325.
73 For a summary of character traits in individualist and collectivist societies, see Harry C. Triandis, "Individualism and Collectivism: Past, Present, and Future," in *The Handbook of Culture and Psychology*, edited by David Matsumoto (New York: Oxford University Press, 2001), pp. 35–50.
74 Shigehiro Oishi, "Goals as Cornerstones of Subjective Well-Being: Linking Individuals and Cultures," in *Culture and Subjective Well-Being*, edited by Ed Diener and Eunkook M. Suh (Cambridge, MA: Massachusetts Institute of Technology Press, 2000), p. 100. Puerto Rico is actually listed as the sixth most individualist society. However, Puerto Rico is not a country but a possession of the United States, and it has been influenced by U.S. culture since the early twentieth century.
75 Ibid.
76 World Bank, *Lifelong Learning in the Global Knowledge Economy*, p. 22.
77 Ibid.
78 Ibid., pp. 3–4.
79 Hassan M. Fattah, "Saudis Rethink Taboo on Women Behind the Wheel," *New York Times* (September 28, 2007). Retrieved from www.nytimes.com/2007/09/28/world/middleeast/28drive.html?_r=0 on September 28, 2007.
80 World Bank, *Lifelong Learning in the Global Knowledge Economy*, p. 22.
81 Organization for Economic Cooperation and Development, "Adult Literacy." Retrieved from http: www.oecde.org/dataoecd/27/24/2345257.pdf on October 16, 2007.
82 Ibid.
83 World Bank, *Lifelong Learning in the Global Knowledge Economy*, p. 23.

84 Ibid., p. 25.

85 Ibid.

86 Ibid.

87 Ibid., p. 27.

88 Ibid., p. 32.

89 Ibid.

90 Ibid., p. 33.

91 Ibid.

92 Ibid., p. 36.

93 Ibid., p. 43.

94 Michael Trucano, Mobile Learning and Textbooks of the Future, E-reading and Edtech Policies: Trends in Technology Use in Education in Developing Countries, Excerpts from the World Bank's EduTech Blog, Volume IV (Washington, DC: The World Bank, 2013).

95 See Carmel Borg and Peter Mayo, "The EU Memorandum on Lifelong Learning. Old Wine in New Bottles?" *Globalisation, Societies and Education* 3(2005), pp. 203–225; and Spring, *Education and the Rise of the Global Economy*.

96 World Bank, *Lifelong Learning in the Global Knowledge Economy*, p. xix.

97 CEC, *Commission Staff Working Paper. A Memorandum on Lifelong Learning* (Brussels: The European Commission, 2005), p. 3.

98 Kai Ming Cheng and Hak Kwong Yip, *Facing the Knowledge Society: Reforming Secondary Education in Hong Kong and Shanghai* (Washington, DC: World Bank, 2006), p. 34.

99 Cedefop and Eurydice, *National Actions to Implement Lifelong Learning in Europe* (Brussels: Eurydice, 2001), p. 31.

100 UNESCO, "Education for All (EFA) International Coordination: Public–Private Partnerships." Retrieved from http://portal.unesco.org/education/en/ev.php-URL_ID=47544&URL_DO=DO_TOPIC&URL_SECTION=201.html on October 5, 2007.

101 Gita Steiner-Khamsi, "For All by All?" p. 6.

102 Tiphaine Bertsch, Rebecca Bouchet, Joanna Godrecka, Kiira Karkkainen, and Tyra Malzy, *A Study for UNESCO: Corporate Sector Involvement in Education for All: Partnerships with Corporate Involvement for the Improvement of Basic Education, Gender Equality, and Adult Literacy in Developing Countries* (Paris: Fondation Naionale Des Sciences Politiques/Institut D'Etudes Politiques De Paris, 2005).

103 Ibid., p. 12.

104 Ibid.

105 Ibid.

106 Ibid., p. 4.

107 International Finance Corporation World Bank Group, "EdInvest." Retrieved from www.ifc.org/wps/wcm/connect/Topics_Ext_Content/IFC_External_Corporate_Site/EdInvest_Home/ on October 11, 2013.

108 International Finance Corporation World Bank Group, "Education." Retrieved from http//www.ifc.org/ifcext/che.nsf/Content/Education on October 9, 2007.

109 Human Development Network, "About HDN." Retrieved from www.hdn.org.ph/abouthdn.html on October 9, 2007.

110 Human Development Network, "What Is Sustainable Development?" Retrieved from www.hdn.org.ph/whatis.html on October 9, 2007.

111 World Bank, "Public-Private Partnerships in Education: Overview." Retrieved from http://web.worldbank.org/WBSITE/EXTERNAL/TOPICS/EXTEDUCATION/ 0,,contentMDK:21317057~menuPK:282391~pagePK:64020865~piPK:51164185~ theSitePK:282386,00.html on October 9, 2007.

112 International Finance Corporation World Bank Group, "SABIS School, Lebanon: Flagship of IFC Education Activities in MENA." Retrieved from http//www.ifc.org/ ifcext/che.nsf/Content/AttachmentsBy Title/Factsheet_SabisSchoolLebanon/$File/ Sabis+School+Lebanon-Fact+Sheet.pdf on October 9, 2007.

113 Carl Bistany, "True Partners in Public-Private Partnerships," in *Mobilizing the Private Sector for Public Education: A View from the Trenches*, edited by Harry Patrinos and Shobhana Sosale (Washington, DC: World Bank, 2007), p. 31.

114 Ibid., p. 33.

115 Brown and Lauder, "Globalization, Knowledge and the Myth of the Magnet Economy," p. 320.

116 Ibid., p. 323.

117 Ibid., p. 324.

118 Ibid., p. 329.

119 Frédéric Docquier and Abdeslam Marfouk, "International Migration by Education Attainment, 1990–2000," in *International Migration, Remittances & the Brain Drain*, edited by Çaglar Özden and Maurice Schiff (New York: Palgrave Macmillan, 2006), pp. 175–185.

120 Çaglar Özden, "Educated Migrants: Is There Brain Waste?" in *International Migration, Remittances & the Brain Drain*, p. 238.

121 World Bank, *Constructing Knowledge Societies*, p. 11.

122 Ibid.

123 Ibid.

124 Peet, *Unholy Trinity*, p. 120.

125 Ibid.

126 Robin Shields, Globalization and International Education, p. 88.

3

THE WORLD MINISTRY OF EDUCATION AND HUMAN RIGHTS EDUCATION

OECD and the United Nations

The World Ministry of Education is what Heinz Meyer calls the Organization for Economic Cooperation and Development (OECD).[1] OECD is linked to the United Nations and the World Bank. OECD, like the World Bank, supports the economic model of education, while the United Nations is concerned with human rights and peace education. Both organizations contribute to a world education culture while emphasizing differing educational perspectives.

OECD

The OECD has the same global reach as the World Bank. The OECD's 1961 founding document states that its goal is "to achieve the highest sustainable economic growth and employment and a rising standard of living in Member countries, while maintaining financial stability, and thus to contribute to the development of the world economy."[2] From its original membership of 20 nations it has expanded to 34 of the richest nations of the world. In addition, OECD provides expertise and exchanges ideas with more than 100 other countries including the least developed countries in Africa. In 2013, OECD offered this description of its activities:

> The OECD provides a forum in which governments can work together to share experiences and seek solutions to common problems. We work with governments to understand what drives economic, social and environmental change. We measure productivity and global flows of trade and investment. We analyze and compare data to predict future trends. We set international standards on a wide range of things, from agriculture and tax to the safety of chemicals.[3]

OECD describes its educational work as follows: "We compare how different countries' school systems are readying their young people for modern life."[4]

OECD assumes an activist role in trying to influence national policies: "Drawing on facts and real-life experience, we recommend policies designed to make the lives of ordinary people better."[5] Like the World Bank, OECD promotes education for economic growth and development. Along with economic growth, OECD leaders also hope that national populations share the same values to ensure against social disintegration and crime. Regarding the value of education, the OECD states: "Both individuals and countries benefit from education. For individuals, the potential benefits lie in general quality of life and in the economic returns of sustained, satisfying employment. For countries, the potential benefits lie in economic growth and the development of shared values that underpin social cohesion."[6]

To help achieve education benefits for member nations and cooperating nations, OECD:

- Develops and reviews policies to enhance the efficiency and the effectiveness of education provisions and the equity with which their benefits are shared;
- Collects detailed statistical information on education systems, including measures of the competence levels of individuals;
- Reviews and analyzes policies related to aid provided by OECD members for expansion of education and training in developing nations.[7]

OECD operates four important education programs: Centre for Educational Research and Innovation (CERI), the Programme on Institutional Management in Higher Education (IMHE), the Programme on Educational Building (PEB), and the Programme for International Student Assessment (PISA). OECD supports educational privatization in the context of free markets. Fazal Rizvi and Bob Lingard state, "OECD . . . has largely constituted globalization in a performative way . . . [including for education] marketization and privatization on the one hand and strong systems of accountability on the other."[8]

OECD plays a major role in global standardization of education through its assessment program PISA and, as I describe in the next section, in promoting an economic model of education.[9] By becoming an international standard, PISA influences local education policies. The organization also gathers and offers education data and country comparisons through what it calls Education GPS: "Education GPS is the source for internationally comparable data on education policies and practices, opportunities and outcomes. Accessible any time, in real time, the Education GPS provides you with the latest information on how countries are working to develop high-quality and equitable education systems."[10] Education GPS allows the user to find data for each country, compare education systems, and review education policies.

KEY POINTS: LABOR MARKET AND EDUCATIONAL CONCERNS OF OECD COUNTRIES

1. Development of human capital for competition in the knowledge economy
    a. Same policies advocated by the World Bank as discussed in Chapter 2
2. Labor shortage because of declining birth rates and aging of population
    a. Need for immigrants and contract foreign workers for labor shortage
        i. Problem: Tensions between local populations and immigrants and contract foreign workers
        ii. Solution: Education to improve social capital
    b. Bring more women into the workforce
        i.   Problem: Ensuring a sustained and high birth rate
        ii. Solution: Preschool education as preparation for further schooling to free mothers to work
        iii. Problem: Lack of equal educational opportunity for women
        iv. Solution: Policies that ensure educational equity for women and support women's educational efforts
    c. Increase retirement age and keep people working longer
        i. Problem: Increasing portion of retirees in relation to workforce
        ii. Solution: Lifelong learning and policies that prepare older workers to continue working

---

Economization of Education: *Better Skills, Better Jobs, Better Lives*

Similar to the World Bank, OECD links school policies to skills needed in the job market. OECD's 2012 report *Better Skills, Better Jobs, Better Lives: A Strategic Approach to Skills Policies* declares that "skills have become the global currency of 21st-century economies."[11] Furthermore, the report claims that "skills are also key to tackling inequality and promoting social mobility."[12]

What does OECD mean when it uses the word *skills*"? One way of answering this is to consider the content of OECD's International Assessment of Adult Competencies. OECD released the first result of this international survey in 2013 and, at the time, provided this description: "The Survey of Adult Skills is an international survey conducted in 33 countries as part of the Programme for the International Assessment of Adult Competencies (PIAAC). It measures the key cognitive and workplace skills needed for individuals to participate in society and for economies to prosper."[13] Relating the assessment to education, OECD stated, "The evidence from this Survey will help countries better understand how education and training systems can nurture these skills. Educators, policy makers and labour economists will use this information to develop economic, education and social policies that will continue to enhance the skills of adults."[14] The PIAAC "assesses key skills (literacy, numeracy, problem solving in technology-rich environments) and the use of skills in the workplace, and collects information on the antecedents, outcomes and context of skills development and use."[15]

In its economization of the school curriculum, OECD makes a distinction between skills, knowledge and character (soft skills). The word *knowledge* is most often associated with new technology. The 2007 OECD book *Human Capital* asserts: "In *developed* economies, the value of knowledge and information in all their forms is becoming ever more apparent, a trend that is being facilitated by the rapid spread of high-speed information technology [author's emphasis]."[16] OECD claims that the knowledge learned in school should be a reflection of labor market needs. OECD asserts that "fundamental changes in employment imply a rise in the demand for non-routine cognitive and interpersonal skills and a decline in the demand for routine cognitive and craft skills, physical labour and repetitive physical tasks."[17]

A proposal to redesign the twenty-first century curricula is based on the labor market needs. Regarding the category of "knowledge," the redesign plan recommends that school subjects be relevant to real-world situations. Using this criteria, the redesign raises questions about changing school curricula to make it more relevant to the world of work. For instance, "Should engineering become a standard part of the curriculum?" This subject would fulfill an employment need.

One question about the redesign suggests dropping a subject and replacing it with one more suited for workplace: "Should trigonometry be replaced by more statistics?"[18] Also, personal economic issues are suggested: "Should personal finance be taught to everyone—and starting in which grade?"[19] Reflecting the economic influences on the proposed redesign is the following question: "Should entrepreneurship be mandatory?"[20] In other words, should school prepare students to start their own businesses?

The economization of the curriculum results in questioning the relevancy of certain subjects, such as the following question: "What is significant and relevant in history?"[21] OECD raises the questions regarding relevancy of other topics: "Should ethics be re-valued? What is the role of the arts—and can they be used to foster creativity in all disciplines?"[22]

In teaching skills, the redesign plan relates them to work performance: "Higher-order skills ('21st-Century Skills'), such as the '4 C's' of Creativity, Critical thinking, Communication, Collaboration, and others are essential for absorbing knowledge as well as for *work performance* [author's emphasis]."[23] The redesign plan argues that the curriculum is overburdened with content and suggests trimming the knowledge base in favor of increasing skill instruction by going into more depth in fewer subjects: "There is a reasonable global consensus on what the skills are, and how teaching methods via projects can affect skills acquisition, but there is little time available during the school year, given the overwhelming amount of content to be covered."[24] OECD plans to monitor changes in job skill requirements of the employment market through a system of occupational forecasting. The focus is on management and professional skills and not on skills needed by the service industry or in routine factory jobs.

Is OECD's real goal to flood the labor market with highly trained workers to keep wages down and decrease the ability of workers to demand better employment conditions? This is suggested in the organization's report *Better Skills, Better Jobs, Better Lives: A Strategic Approach to Skills Policies*, which warns: "Skills shortages can affect growth through their adverse effects on labour productivity. Shortages *increase the hiring cost per skilled worker*, leading firms to employ less-productive unskilled workers instead. Shortages may also put workers in a *stronger bargaining position to demand an easier pace of work* [author's emphasis]."[25]

OECD and the Economization of Personality

Similar to the World Bank, OECD emphasizes character traits needed by the global economy without any consideration of cultural differences. Under the category "Character (behaviors, attitudes, values)" in the previously mentioned proposal for redesigning the curriculum for the twenty-first century, the following was asserted: "As complexities increase, humankind is rediscovering the importance of teaching character traits, such as performance-related traits (adaptability, persistence, resilience) and moral-related traits (integrity, justice, empathy, ethics)."[26]

An example of educating for particular character traits is the story told in the opening pages of the OECD's book *Human Capital*.[27] The story is about Linda who lives in a Paris suburb with other immigrants from North Africa. The suburb was the scene of youth riots resulting in the burning of thousands of cars. Linda is described as being raised in a "traditionally minded North African family."[28] At a local community center, men sit listening to rap music, while Linda and three other unemployed women from differing ethnic backgrounds meet with an employment counselor. All the women complain that getting a job is difficult because of transportation problems and prejudice and discrimination.

Linda regrets that her schooling was cut short even though she was a model student. Her father believed that women shouldn't work and that they should stay home until marriage. Consequently, her father withdrew her from school before she could graduate. Married as a teenager and then separated, she faces a potential life of unemployment. Faced with this situation, the author comments, "To get on, to get a better job and to improve their incomes, the women know they need to have an education."[29]

However, in this story education is not just about getting a job. It is also about reducing the potential for more riots in French immigrant communities. Human capital is tied to both job skills and reducing community tensions by teaching shared values in schools. "Indeed," the author writes, "even the relationships and shared values in societies can be seen as a *form of capital* that makes it easier for people to work together and achieve economic success."[30] This form of capital is often called "social capita."

A concern among OECD nations is cultural tensions resulting from the growth of immigrant populations. OECD members want education to increase social cohesion to reduce conflicts between immigrant communities and populations in host countries.

Consequently, OECD policymakers give special emphasis to the social capital aspects of human capital. Using the language of networks, OECD defines social capital as "networks together with shared norms, values and understandings that facilitate co-operation within and among groups."[31] The organization divides social capital into three main categories. The first category is the *bonds* linking people to a shared identity through family, close friends, and culture. The second category is the *bridges* that link people to those who do not share a common identity. The last category is the *linkages* that connect people to those up and down the social scale or, in other words, between social classes.

A problem with the first category is that *bonds* created through a shared identity might be so strong that they hinder making *bridges* to others. This, the OECD claims, is a problem with some immigrant communities in member nations. Consequently, schools need to ensure an education that builds these bridges to others and linkages that reduce conflict between social classes. OECD warns that "companies and organizations can also suffer if they have the wrong sort of social capital—relationships between colleagues that are too inward-looking and fail to take account of what's going on in the wider world."[32]

Economization of Family Life

OECD nations are turning to foreign workers to compensate for declining birth rates. OECD asserts that women must have 2.1 children each to maintain a nation's population. Since the 1970s, the birth rate in OECD countries fell below that rate. For example, in Austria, Germany, Italy, and Korea, the birth rate declined to an average of 1.3 children per woman. With the decline in birth rate, OECD nations filled labor shortages using immigration policies. The result, as exemplified previously, is increasing tensions between immigrant families and local populations.

Adding to the problem of declining birth rates is increasing life expectancy. As people live longer in OECD nations, there is greater dependence of retirees on a shrinking labor force. According to the OECD, "Part of the answer is getting women working."[33] OECD's policymakers hail the fact that more and more women are working in OECD countries and are helping to expand the workforce. The OECD's *Employment Outlook 2006* celebrated the fact that "increased female participation has been a major component in labor supply growth during past decades."[34]

How do you balance the need for women to work and to have more babies? One answer is more preschools to free mothers to enter the workforce. What should these preschools look like? OECD studies show a range of approaches to preschool in member nations ranging from French- and English-speaking countries where the emphasis is getting children ready for school, to schools in Nordic countries where children spend many hours learning in outdoor settings. In Finland, children attend day-care centers before entering school at the age of seven. There is only a minimum of academic training in these day-care centers.

Using a human capital perspective, OECD policies support preschools that prepare students for elementary school. Calling for more coordination of school policies in OECD nations, the organization calls for "giving thought to both children's care and learning needs and ensuring that there's *continuity between their preschool and school years* [author's emphasis]."[35]

On the other end of the age scale, OECD wants people to delay retirement and work more years to ensure an adequate labor supply. In OECD countries, there is a general fear about the ability of government pension and other retirement plans to support retirees when there is an increased proportion of retired individuals in relationship to the number of people in the workforce. "Not surprisingly," OECD states, "governments in developed countries are encouraging people to work for longer."[36]

Lifelong learning is one answer to keeping people working longer. This adds another dimension to the lifelong learning policies discussed in Chapter 2 regarding the World Bank. The reader will recall that lifelong learning was promoted as an antidote to technological change and changes in occupational requirements. The worker in the knowledge economy, according to this reasoning, must be prepared to update and learn new skills. In the scenario for advanced economic countries of OECD, lifelong learning serves the dual purpose of preparing workers for changing job requirements and ensuring that older workers can remain active in the labor force.

Cynics might argue that it is exploitive of workers to use lifelong learning as a means of increasing the retirement age to solve labor shortages and reduce the costs of supporting a retired generation. In the past, early retirement was considered a benefit. Now, OECD claims that early retirement shortens one's life. The organization cites a study by Shell Oil that workers who retire at 55 were twice as likely to die in ten years then those who retire at 60 or 65. Within the framework of this reasoning, OECD concludes: "If we need to go on working for longer, we'll also have to go on upgrading our skills, education and abilities—our human capital—throughout our lives."[37]

In summary, the concerns of the developed nations in OECD are somewhat different from those of the World Bank. Both institutions share the same beliefs about the role of human capital education in the knowledge economy. As a result of labor shortages, OECD countries, while still emphasizing education for the knowledge economy, are concerned with multicultural education as a result of their foreign and immigrant workforces. In addition, preschool education is championed to free women to enter the workforce along with lifelong education to keep people working for more years.

International Testing and the World Culture of Education

OECD contributes to the creation of a world education culture through the development and implementation of the PISA and Trends in International Mathematics and Science Study (TIMSS). The possibility of international testing and comparisons was proved by the International Association for the Evaluation of Educational Achievement (IEA). Founded in 1967 with origins dating back to a UNESCO gathering in 1958, the IEA attempted to identify through testing effective educational methods that could be shared between nations. According to the organization's official history, the original group of psychometricians, educational psychologists, and sociologists thought of education as global enterprise to be evaluated by national comparisons of test scores. They "viewed the world as a natural educational laboratory, where different school systems experiment in different ways to obtain optimal results in the education of their youth."[38] They assumed that educational goals were similar between nations but that the methods of achieving those goals were different. International testing, it was believed, would reveal to the world community the best educational practices. The organization tried to prove that large-scale cross-cultural testing was possible between 1959 and 1962 when they tested 13-year-olds in 12 countries in mathematics, reading comprehension, geography, science, and nonverbal ability. The results of this project showed, according to an IEA statement, that "it is possible to construct common tests and questionnaires that 'work' cross-culturally. Furthermore, the study revealed that the effects of language differences can be minimized through the careful translation of instruments."[39]

Besides demonstrating the possibility of global testing programs, IEA claimed to have an effect on the curriculum of participating nations. After a 1970 seminar on curriculum development and evaluation involving 23 countries, IEA officials claimed that "this seminar had a major influence on curriculum development in at least two-thirds of the countries that attended."[40] Through the years, IEA has conducted a number international testing programs and studies, including First International Mathematics Study (FIMS), Second International Mathematics Study (SIMS), International Science Study (ISS), Preprimary Education (PPP), Computers in Education Study (COMPED), Information Technology in Education (ITE), Civic Education Study (CIVED), and Languages in Education Study (LES).

In 1995, IEA worked with OECD to collect data for the Third International Mathematics and Science Study. IEA officials called the 1995 Third International Mathematics and Science Study "the largest and most ambitious study of comparative education undertaken."[41] They claimed that "it was made possible by virtue of IEA experience and expertise, developed through the years of consecutive studies, which saw research vision combining with practical needs as defined by educational policy-makers."[42]

Today, IEA remains a possible source for creating uniform worldwide educational practices. The organization's stated goal is to create global educational benchmarks by which educational systems can be judged. In fact, the mission statement given subsequently includes the creation of a global network of educational evaluators.

IEA Mission Statement

Through its comparative research and assessment projects, IEA aims to accomplish the following:

1. Provide international benchmarks that may assist policy-makers in identifying the comparative strength and weaknesses of their educational systems;
2. Provide high-quality data that will increase policy-makers' understanding of key school- and non-school-based factors that influence teaching and learning;
3. Provide high-quality data which will serve as a resource for identifying areas of concern and action, and for preparing and evaluating educational reforms;
4. Develop and improve educational systems' capacity to engage in national strategies for educational monitoring and improvement;
5. Contribute to development of the world-wide community of researchers in educational evaluation.[43]

PISA: Global Testing and a World Education Culture

PISA testing has created a global academic Olympiad with nations vying for top scores. An issue with PISA, as stated by Heinz-Dieter Meyer and Aaron Benavot, is "the presumption that the quality of a nation's school system can be evaluated through an assessment exercise claiming to be a politically and ideologically neutral undertaking—an act of technocratic rationality—which produces disinterested data to galvanize education reforms around the world."[44]

OECD states that PISA is in response to "member countries' demands for regular and reliable data on the knowledge and skills of their students and the performance of their education systems."[45] The testing program began in 1997, and OECD claims: "PISA benefits from its worldwide scope and its regularity. More than 70 countries and economies have taken part in PISA so far and the surveys, which are given every three years, allow them to track their progress in meeting key learning goals."[46] PISA is creating global standards for the knowledge required to function in what OECD defines as the everyday life of a global economy. By shifting the emphasis from national curricula to global needs, PISA is defining educational standards for a global economy.

What is the global influence of international assessment? Wanting to impress their national leaders, school officials hope their students do well on these tests in comparison to other countries. The consequence is a trend to uniformity national curricula as school leaders attempt to prepare their students to do well on the test. Writing about the effect of PISA and TIMSS on world education culture, David Baker and Gerald LeTendre assert, "After the first set of TIMSS results became public, the United States went into a kind of soul searching . . . The release of the more recent international study on OECD nations called PISA led Germany into a national education crisis. Around the world, countries are using the results of international tests as a kind of Academic Olympiad, serving as a referendum on their school system's performance."[47]

The potential global influence of PISA is vast since the participating member nations and partners represent, according to OECD, 90 percent of the world economy.[48] The assessments are on a three-year cycle beginning in 2000 with each assessment year devoted to a particular topic. OECD promotes PISA as providing data that will influence national policies: "*Public policy issues*: Governments, principals, teachers and parents all want answers to questions such as 'Are our schools adequately preparing young people for the challenges of adult life?', 'Are some kinds of teaching and schools more effective than others?' and 'Can schools contribute to improving the futures of students from immigrant or disadvantaged backgrounds?'"[49]

However, educational achievement is influenced by many factors outside of school, such as family life, and cultural and economic conditions. Can one nation actually take school practices that work in one country and transplant them to their own? For instance, the 2009 PISA results ranked as the top three in reading and math Shanghai, China; Korea; and Finland. The schools in these places are nested in a particular cultural, political, and economic system. In addition, as compared to a country like the United States, these places have a relatively small population and are located in small geographical area. Shanghai, China, is one city in a large country with the world's largest population with its schools operating under the control of the Chinese Communist Party. Korea and Finland are small countries with relatively homogenous population. The schools in these three places operate in different ways and are nested in different cultures and economic systems. Some scholars doubt that practices in Finnish schools can actually be transplanted to other nations.[50]

The potential for creating global educational uniformity is in PISA's definition of literacy: "The assessment focuses on young people's ability to use their knowledge and skills to meet real-life challenges, rather than merely on the extent to which they have mastered a specific school curriculum. This approach is called 'literacy'."[51] This definition makes a distinction between literacy mastered in school and literacy needed for "real-life challenges."

As an example of a shared network of global influences, the World Bank, as discussed in Chapter 2, bases its definition of literacy on the International Adult Literacy Survey created by OECD in partnership with other organizations. Consequently, there are close parallels between PISA's definition of reading literacy and that used by the World Bank. For the World Bank, the literacy standard includes the ability to cope with the demands of everyday life and work in a complex, advanced society with a skill level required for successful secondary school completion and college entry. Similar to the World Bank, the definition of literacy used by PISA is focused on work and living in modern society without any suggestion that literacy should include critical literacy for understanding controversial political and social ideas. In other words, both institutions stress functional literacy.

It is important to emphasize that OECD's definition of literacy ignores national curricula in favor of what it conceives as the literacy skills needed for living in the global economy. In a similar fashion, PISA's math assessment is directed to problems of everyday life and not as an assessment of national curricula:

> The mathematics questions in PISA aim at assessing the capacity of students to draw upon their mathematical competencies to meet the challenges of their current and future daily lives. Citizens have to use mathematics in many daily situations, such as when consulting media presenting information on a wide range of subjects in the form of tables, charts and graphs, when reading timetables, when carrying out money transactions and when determining the best buy at the market.[52]

OECD/PISA's science assessment contains a similar emphasis on knowledge to be used in everyday life: "Science questions in PISA aim at evaluating how well students apply scientific ways of thinking to situations they could encounter in their everyday lives."[53]

OECD and the World Bank

Both OECD and the World Bank reinforce the idea in global networks that the core global curricula needed for the knowledge economy should consist of literacy, math, science, and the skills needed for lifelong learning and the tools to use information and data. Both organizations propagate the message that some form of multicultural education is needed for adjustment to global migration. OECD does not emphasize the teaching of foreign languages or civic education to teach the rule of law. Despite these minor differences, OECD and the World Bank are disseminating similar ideas.

A major difference between the two organizations is the World Bank's stress on individualism (acting autonomously) versus OECD's concern with social bonds. These are conflicting messages being sent over global networks. This could be a result of differences in focus. The World Bank is interested instilling in developing nations a competitive spirit of individualism associated with market economies, while advanced OECD countries are concerned with conflicts between immigrant and resident populations, as well as crime.

OECD and World Education

In summary, OECD/PISA contributes to world education culture by using common assessments for OECD countries and partners representing 90 percent of the world economy. These assessments ignore specific national curricula and focus on what test designers consider as the basic skills needed to function in a global knowledge economy. Of course, national school leaders might take the comparative scores resulting from PISA as a judgment about the quality of their schools. Consequently, they might be inclined to adjust their curricula to prepare students to do well on the assessments. This could result in a growing similarity in the skills taught in global school systems or, in other words, a global education culture. Also, PISA contributes to the formulation of the ideal person needed for a global knowledge economy. Regarding the global impact of PISA, sociologist David Kamens states: "Test scores become symbols of a nation's viability in the modern world, and thus impact national self-perceptions . . . The result is that testing produces cycles of reform within countries and across groups of countries whose school children have not done well on particular kinds of international tests. Furthermore, perceived 'failure' is much more visible than 'success'."[54] Table 3.1 summarizes both the World Bank and OECD/PISA's conceptions of the ideal educated person for the knowledge economy.

TABLE 3.1 The Ideal Person for the Knowledge Economy according to the World Bank and OECD/PISA

World Bank Social Capital	OECD/PISA Social Capital	World Bank Educational Capital	OECD/PISA Educational Capital
Acts autonomously	Establishes *bonds* linking them to a shared identity through family, close friends, and culture	Literacy to manipulate information	Literacy to function in modern global society
Uses tools interactively	Has knowledge and skills needed to function in a knowledge economy *for future life*	Science and math with an emphasis on all students becoming scientifically literate to function in global economy	Science and math literacy to function in modern global society
Can function in socially heterogeneous groups (multicultural workforce and community)	Builds bridges and linkages to those who do not share a common identity or social class (multicultural workforce and community)	Foreign language instruction, particularly in English	
		Lifelong learning Civic education to achieve rule by law and a good government able to achieve economic development	Lifelong learning

UNESCO and Lifelong Learning: A Different Vision

UNESCO, which shares global education networks with both OECD and the World Bank, offers an alternative global discourse and an alternative view of the ideal global person and curriculum. The World Bank and OECD are *not* monolithic forces shaping global education discourses and practices.

UNESCO has contributed to the global discourse on lifelong learning with a more humanistic vision as compared to the economic arguments of the World Bank and OECD. This difference represents competing ideas within global education discourses. In reviewing UNESCO's ideas on lifelong learning, Madhu Singh of the UNESCO Institute of Education describes the ideas of organizations like the World Bank, OECD, and some national government leaders: "The official discourse is narrowly economic and instrumental and often means little more than short-term retraining and adaptation. Most governments are concerned more with national competitiveness and economic growth than individual development."[55]

UNESCO's discourse focuses on the full development of the individual. UNESCO's first major report on lifelong learning appeared in 1972 with the sponsorship of the International Commission on the Development of Education. The report was titled *Learning to Be: The World of Education Today and Tomorrow*.[56] The report's lead author, Edgar Faure, chair of the International Commission on the Development of Education and former prime minister of France, gave four assumptions underlying the arguments in *Learning to Be*. The first was that the world is progressing to a common unity of cultures and political organizations. This common global culture embodied principles of human rights. In other words, the report supported the ideas of world culture theorists but placed emphasis on human rights as part of the learning society and a component of lifelong learning.

The second assumption was the universal value of democracy. The Commission defined democracy "as implying each man's right to realize his own potential and to share in the building of his own future. The keystone of democracy ... is education."[57] However, the Commission did not believe that any form of education would promote democracy. After all, education can be used to support despotic governments. Therefore, they wanted a learning society to teach about and support democracy.

The third assumption of the report focused on the development of the individual in contrast to economic development. This concept of development goes far beyond the concerns of the World Bank and OECD. The report states that

> the aim of development is the complete fulfilment of man, in all the richness of his personality, the complexity of his forms of expression and his various commitments—as individual, member of a family and of a community, citizen and producer, inventor of techniques and creative dreamer.[58]

The fourth assumption was that lifelong learning is a cure for individual and social problems caused by modern society, namely alienation from others and a loss of a sense of community. "Lifelong learning," the report dramatically claims, "can produce the kind of complete man the need for whom is increasing with the continually more stringent constraints tearing the individual asunder."[59] The "complete man" will be educated for political action. Education for political action, the report suggests, is an important part of education for the new age of information. For instance, the report contends that one result of the new information and media age is the obsolescence of representative democracy. Representative democracy, according to the report, "is not capable of providing him [the individual] with an adequate share of the benefits of expansion or with the possibility of influencing his own fate in a world of flux and change; nor does it allow him to develop his own potential to best advantage."[60] In the information and media age, individuals must exert their own control in contrast to turning it over to an elected government representative. The exercise of this individual democratic power requires, according to the report, changes in education. "The new man," the report declares, "must be capable of understanding the global consequences of individual behavior, of conceiving of priorities and shouldering his share of the joint responsibility involved in the destiny of the human race."[61]

What type of education will produce this "new man?" The Commission proposed an education based on scientific humanism focused on the use of technological and scientific advances to enhance the welfare of humans and democracy. The Commission's explanation of education for scientific humanism emphasizes individual control and power.

> For these reasons the commission considered that it was essential for science and technology to become fundamental, ever-present elements in any educational enterprises for them to become part of all educational activities designed for children, young people and adults, *so as to help the individual to control not only natural and productive forces, but social forces too, and in so doing to acquire mastery over himself, his choices and actions; and, finally, for them to help man to develop a scientific frame of mind in order to promote the sciences without becoming enslaved by them* [author's emphasis].[62]

Achieving scientific humanism, the report argued, requires changes in motivation and teaching methods. In a fascinating assertion, considering the World Bank and OECD's emphasis on lifelong learning for economic growth, the Commission states: "Modern democratic education requires a revival of man's natural drive towards knowledge."[63] The Commission specifically rejected a reliance on future employment as a motivation for learning. Education for employment quickly reduced, according to the Commission, schooling to a joyless and boring activity. Contributing to damping of the spark of joy in learning was an excessive emphasis on theory and memory. Instead, the Commission argued, the emphasis should be on learning to learn. Educational systems should not be concerned with achieving a match between schooling and the needs of the labor market. The emphasis should be on the joy of learning, learning to learn, and development of the whole person. In this regard, the Commission states, "The aim of education is to enable man to be himself . . . and the aim of education in relation to employment and economic progress should be not so much to prepare . . . for a specific, lifetime vocation, as to 'optimise' mobility among the professions and afford permanent stimulus to the desire to learn and to train oneself.[64]

From the Commission's perspective, the love of learning creates a desire for lifelong learning and maintenance of a learning society. In this context, the goal of lifelong learning is to give people the power to exercise democratic control over economic, scientific, and technological development. Lifelong learning provides the tools to ensure that scientific and technological progress result in benefitting all. The learning society is one in which people continually develop the skills and knowledge needed to enhance their well-being and ensure a democratic society.

In the 1990s, UNESCO's humanistic approach to lifelong learning was swept up in the rhetoric of the knowledge economy and human capital development. UNESCO reports did not mention the economic arguments for lifelong learning. This continuing humanistic concern is evident in UNESCO's 1996 report on lifelong learning called *Learning: The Treasure Within*. The report was a product of the work the International Commission on Education for the Twenty-First Century, chaired by Jacques Delors, the former President of the European Commission (1985–95) and former French Minister of Economy and Finance.[65]

The extensive worldwide network involved in completing the report highlights the global network articulating a different discourse on lifelong learning than that being propagated by the OECD and the World Bank. The International Commission on Education included representatives from 14 different countries, many of whom were or had been government officials. Three members did not, and to the best of my knowledge, have not held government positions.[66] Eight members of the Commission were current or past ministers of Departments of Education, Social Development and Family Affairs.[67] One member had been a prime minister, another was a member of Parliament, and another was a member of an international governing organization.[68]

The differences in global discourses between the Commission, the World Bank, and OECD were captured in the opening lines of the report's introduction, aptly titled "Education: the Necessary Utopia." Written by Jacques Delors, it declares that education is "an indispensable asset in its attempt to attain the ideals of peace, freedom and social justice."[69] Delors expresses a desire to foster "a deeper and more harmonious form of human development and thereby to reduce poverty, exclusion, ignorance, oppression and war."[70]

The Commission suggested that lifelong learning would solve multiple educational ills and be a "process of forming whole human beings—their knowledge and aptitudes, as well as the critical faculty and the ability to act."[71] For the Commission, education for a knowledge economy required the teaching of how to acquire, renew, and use knowledge in the context of an information society. Preparation for the information society, according to the Commission and similar to the World Bank and OECD, required learning to select, arrange, manage, and use data. Consequently, lifelong learning requires, the Commission asserted, a basic education that includes the following:

- Learning to know
- Learning to do
- Learning to be[72]

According to the Commission, these intellectual skills provide the tools for lifelong learning and a learning society. "Learning to know" and "learning to do" are similar to the human capital definitions of the World Bank and OECD. "Learning to know," according to the Commission's definition, involves a broad general education based on an in-depth study of a selected number of subjects. This would, the Commission contended, provide the foundation for the ability and the desire to continue learning. "Learning to do" involves work skills and the acquisition of "competence that enables people to deal with a variety of situations often unforeseeable ... by becoming involved in work experience schemes or social work while they are still in education."[73]

"Learning to be" reflects the more humanistic thrust of UNESCO. "Learning to be" was to resolve the potential tension between personal independence and common goals. The Commission was concerned that competitive markets might destroy a sense of unity. The Commission hoped to wed the individual to common goals by developing the untapped "buried treasure in every person."[74] The unleashing of this buried treasure, the Commission asserted, would create a desire to work for common goals. The Commission located the source of social unity in the inherent psychological makeup of the individual. Education releases the inherent drive for cultural unity. What are these inherent psychological characteristics? The Commission's list includes "memory, reasoning power, imagination, physical ability, aesthetic sense, the aptitude to communicate with others and the natural charisma of the group leader."[75]

Creating a world culture was an important part of the Commission's discussion of social unity. The Commission asserted that the world is in "erratic progress towards a certain unity."[76] Commission members believed that education should play a major role in this supposed inevitable progress to world unity. How? Their answer was an "emphasis on the moral and cultural dimensions of education," which would enable each person to grasp the individuality of other people and to understand the world's progression toward cultural unity.[77] An emphasis on the moral and cultural dimensions of education should begin, according to the Commission, with "self-understanding through an inner voyage whose milestones are knowledge, mediation and the practice of self-criticism."[78]

Sustainable Development and World Culture

Another example of creating a world culture of education is the request by the United Nations General Assembly for UNESCO to lead the United Nations Decade of Education for Sustainable Development from 2005 to 2014. UNESCO was asked to tap its global network to develop an International Implementation Scheme for the Decade. UNESCO's plan for education for sustainable development takes place "within a perspective of lifelong learning, engaging all possible spaces of learning, formal, non-formal and informal, from early childhood to adult life."[79]

A world culture of shared environmental beliefs may result from UNESCO's efforts. Its plan declares, "Networks and alliances will be the crucial element, forging a *common agenda* in relevant forums [author's emphasis]."[80] In another document, UNESCO announces its leadership role would be used to "catalyze new partnerships with the private sector, with youth, and with media groups."[81] Through these consciously created global networks, UNESCO supports an education agenda that encompasses some of the organization's earlier pronouncements on lifelong learning along with environmental education. Present are earlier concerns with education for democratic power and social cohesion.

In contrast to the World Bank and OECD, the focus is on the environment and not economic growth. The elements of education for sustainable development are given as follows:

- Society: an understanding of social institutions and their role in change and development, as well as the democratic and participatory systems which give opportunity for the expression of opinion, the selection of governments, the forging of consensus and the resolution of differences;
- Environment: an awareness of the resources and fragility of the physical environment and the effects on it of human activity and decisions, with a commitment to factoring environmental concerns into social and economic policy development;
- Economy: a sensitivity to the limits and potential of economic growth and their impact on society and on the environment, with a commitment to assess personal and societal levels of consumption out of concern for the environment and for social justice.[82]

As stated previously, UNESCO's global educational discourse includes preparing citizens to actively wield political power and to understand environmental problems.

Global education for sustainable development is to create an awareness of the potential negative impact of economic growth on the environment and a concern for social justice. Through its global networks UNESCO provides an alternative educational discourse to that of the World Bank and OECD. This is most evident when UNESCO lists the characteristics of what it considers high-quality instruction. According to UNESCO's plan, education for sustainable development encompasses the following characteristics:

- Interdisciplinary and holistic: learning for sustainable development embedded in the whole curriculum, not as a separate subject;
- Values-driven: sharing the values and principles underpinning sustainable development;
- Critical thinking and problem solving: leading to confidence in addressing the dilemmas and challenges of sustainable development;
- Multi-method: word, art, drama, debate, experience, . . . different pedagogies which model the processes;
- Participatory decision-making: learners participate in decisions on how they are to learn;
- Locally relevant: addressing local as well as global issues, and using the language(s) which learners most commonly use.[83]

Table 3.2 reflects the competing global discourses on education between UNESCO's education for sustainable development and the World Bank's education for the knowledge economy.

TABLE 3.2 Competing Global Discourses on Instruction: World Bank and UNESCO

World Bank	*UNESCO*
Learner centered: instruction is related to what students already know	Participatory decision making: learners participate in decisions on how they are to learn
Knowledge-rich learning: involves teaching a few subjects in depth as contrasted with superficial treatment of many subjects	Interdisciplinary and holistic: learning for sustainable development embedded in the whole curriculum, not as a separate subject
Learning by doing: students apply newly gained knowledge to real or simulated problems	Critical thinking and problem solving: leading to confidence in addressing the dilemmas and challenges of sustainable development
Assessment-driven instruction	Multimethod: word, art, drama, debate, experience, etc.
Group work: preparation for working with others in sharing and manipulation of information with real-life problems	Values driven: sharing the values and principles underpinning sustainable development
Information and communication technology (ICT): allows the adaptation of globally available information to local learning situations	Locally relevant: addressing local as well as global issues, and using the language(s) that learners most commonly use

An examination of Table 3.2 shows dramatic differences between the world education culture disseminated by the World Bank and UNESCO. First is the difference in the extent of student control over instructional methods with the World Bank advocating learner-centered instruction using the student's existing knowledge and that learning should involve work on real-world problems. In contrast, UNESCO calls for student participation in deciding instructional methods and a focus on critical thinking and problem solving. One might construe the World Bank's focus on solving real-world problems as being similar to critical thinking and problem solving. However, there is a major difference between saying that instruction will be based on a learner's prior knowledge and giving students an active part in deciding the method of instruction. The approach to curricula is quite different between the two organizations with the World Bank calling for a focus on a few subjects, while UNESCO calls for an interdisciplinary and holistic approach with all subjects combined and interrelated with sustainable development issues. While the World Bank wants group work so that students can share manipulation of information and real-life problems, UNESCO wants students to share the values of sustainable development. In adjusting learning to local cultures and conditions, the World Bank advocates doing it with information and communication technology, while UNESCO wants instruction to consider local problems and use the common language of the students.

Is there a concise way of describing these differences? One might say that the World Bank's instructional methods are designed to educate a worker for the global knowledge economy who is able to use the global flow of information to solve real-world problems. In contrast, UNESCO's instructional approach might be described as preparing students to exercise political power and think critically to solve problems that threaten the well-being of the planet and human life. These differences are highlighted by the United Nations' Cyberschoolbus website.

A Global Human Rights Curriculum: Cyberschoolbus

Will human rights be part of a world culture? The United Nation's Cyberschoolbus would like it to be. Its stated goals are as follows:

- To create an on-line global education community;
- To create educational action projects to show students that they have a role in finding solutions to global problems;
- To give students a voice in global issues;
- To provide high-quality teaching resources to a wide range of educators in a cost-effective manner.[84]

The global reach of the Cyberschoolbus is demonstrated by the following testimonials:

THIS IS A BEST SITE I HAVE EVER SEEN!!!!!
Good Job

Enes Kazazic
Bosnia and Herzegovina

Wow! I must say that you are making me look like a candidate for teacher of the year. Thanks to your program for teachers, I am able to prepare excellent courses while I learn and keep abreast of certain world issues. My students really appreciate the work and so do I. You really make us feel that we can make a difference.

Paul Bougie
Trois-Rivieres, Quebec, Canada

This program has become an essential part of our Social Studies Curriculum which is centered around World Citizenship and a Global Ethic.

Robert Siegel, Headmaster
St. Joseph School, Temuco, Chile

Thanks for all the mail. We have a thriving Peace program in our college and the information has been invaluable in running it.

Richard Laryea
SOS-Hermann Gmeiner International College, Ghana[85]

The Cyberschoolbus lists the following as its major projects:

- Our interactive database, InfoNation, is accessed by thousands of users monthly who pull up accurate official and up-to-date information and statistics regarding the countries of the world.
- Our Schools Demining Schools project brought schools together around the issue of landmines. After learning about the topic, schools ran their own fundraising drives to raise money to clear school grounds of mines. Students could follow the results of their actions through email exchanges with the demining teams in Afghanistan and Mozambique.
- The Model UN Discussion Area attracts thousands of students who gather to discuss international issues, request information and exchange ideas.
- For the Health module, classes from around the world connected with each other on a discussion board to discuss, then define health, before getting together on-line to question experts from the Pan American Health Organization and the World Health Organization about their concerns.

• Cities of Today, Cities of Tomorrow includes a comprehensive 6-unit teaching module on urban issues that covers everything from the history of urban development to profiles of today's important cities to issues facing the cities of tomorrow.[86]

The Cyberschoolbus website was created in 1996 as the online education component of the United Nations Global Teaching and Learning Project. This project provides teaching materials for educational use (at primary, intermediate, and secondary school levels) and for training teachers. It offers curricula and lesson plans for Peace Education, Poverty, Schools Demining Schools, Human Rights, Cities of the World, World Hunger, Indigenous People, Rights at Work, Ethnic Discrimination, and Racial Discrimination.[87] An important part of the Cyberschoolbus's curriculum is human rights. A goal of its ABC Human Rights curriculum is embed human rights in global culture.[88]

Sesame Street: Global Preschool for Social Justice and World Education Culture

The creators of *Sesame Street* envisioned a preschool education that would create a world culture of peace, tolerance, and social harmony. The program spans the globe carrying a similar message to the world's children. The original *Sesame Street* was broadcast in 1969 as part of the so-called American war on poverty. The idea of creating an educational program for educating preschool children from low-income families was proposed by Lloyd Morrisett who at the time worked as a supervisor of grants for the Carnegie Corporation. Morrisett worried that preschool education, which he considered important for the cognitive development of children, "would slowly, if at all, reach many of the children who needed them, particularly underprivileged children for whom preschool facilities might not be available." The answer to this problem, he felt, was in using television to reach large numbers of children.[89]

Gerald Lesser, professor of education and developmental psychology at Harvard, was chosen as chief advisor for the program. He believed that television had certain elements that made it superior to schools. Schools, he maintained, depended on control of the student by others, public humiliation, and the continuous threat of failure. Television learning contained none of these elements. In front of the television, Lesser argued, the child learns without fear of a teacher. Consequently, he believed that television was an ideal educator. It was nonpunitive, and it provided a shelter from the emotional stresses of society. "We may regret the conditions in our society that make sanctuaries necessary and must guard against a child's permanent retreat into them," Lesser wrote, "but sanctuaries are needed, and television is one of the few shelters children have."[90]

Later *Sesame Street* producers would consider television learning a welcome sanctuary for the world's poor children, particularly those forced to work at a young age. For instance, in the production of the program for Bangladesh, one of the world's poorest nations, it was estimated that while a majority of young children were not in school, almost 80 percent watched television.[91] Under these conditions, educational television was considered the best hope for any form of education to reach poor children.

Another vision carried around the world was that *Sesame Street* characters could serve as models for children's future actions. Originally, Lesser believed that a great deal of learning took place through modeling. According to Lesser, children do not need to interact to learn; they can model themselves after television characters. In fact, modeling fit Lesser's concept of a nonpunitive form of education. "The child," Lesser wrote, "imitates the model without being induced or compelled to do so. . . . By watching televised models, children learn both socially desirable and undesirable behaviors."[92] Through preschool education on television with the use of appropriate models, Lesser asserted that "surely it can . . . help them [children] toward a more humane vision of life."[93]

A founder of *Sesame Street*, Jane Cooney, emphasized the attempt to create a world culture by invoking the image of missionaries: "Our producers are like old-fashioned missionaries . . . it's not religion that they're spreading, but it is learning and tolerance and love and mutual respect, and in a way, you have to say it must be the most wonderful job in the world."[94]

Sesame Workshop is engaged in a global effort to adapt a particular television framework on local cultures. By hiring local experts, the program hopes to escape the charge of cultural imperialism. A basic element of the program is the use of Muppets. For instance, coproducers for the South African program introduced the Muppet Kami who is HIV positive. The South African producers were concerned about the large numbers of South African children who are HIV positive. The goal was to create toleration of HIV-positive children and disseminate information about the disease.[95] In the Bangladesh program, a production goal was promoting equality between social classes, genders, castes, and religions.[96]

In summary, *Sesame Street* is another effort to create a world culture of peace and harmony similar to that of the Cyberschoolbus. It might prove very effective by reaching global households with young children.

United Nations and Millennial Goals: A Network of World Education Culture

The linkages in developing global education policies are highlighted by the United Nations Millennium Goals endorsed by 189 countries at the 2000 United Nations Millennium Assembly.[97] As discussed in Chapter 2, the World Bank is a supporter of these goals. So is OECD.[98]

The overall Millennium Goal of eradicating world poverty fits both the economic goals of the World Bank and OECD, as well as the United Nations' concern about human rights education. As stated in Chapter 2, the Millennium Goals for education are as follows:

- Target 2.A: Ensure that, by 2015, children everywhere, boys and girls alike, will be able to complete a full course of primary schooling;[99]
- Target 3.A: Eliminate gender disparity in primary and secondary education, preferably by 2005, and in all levels of education no later than 2015.[100]

These two education goals are part of eight goals described as:

> The eight Millennium Development Goals (MDGs)—which range from halving extreme poverty to halting the spread of HIV/AIDS and providing universal primary education, all by the target date of 2015—form a blueprint agreed to by all the world's countries and all the world's leading development institutions. They have galvanized unprecedented efforts to meet the needs of the world's poorest.[101]

The other six Millennium Goals, except for Goal 8, are human welfare goals:

> Target 1.A: Halve, between 1990 and 2015, the proportion of people whose income is less than $1.25 a day;
> Target 4.A: Reduce by two thirds, between 1990 and 2015, the under-five mortality rate;
> Target 5.A: Reduce by three quarters the maternal mortality ratio;
> Target 6.A: Have halted by 2015 and begun to reverse the spread of HIV/AIDS;
> Target 7.A: Integrate the principles of sustainable development into country policies and programmes and reverse the loss of environmental resources;
> Target 8.A: Develop further an open, rule-based, predictable, non-discriminatory trading and financial system.[102]

Goal 8 reflects a belief that global free markets will benefit all nations and contribute to increasing global wealth.

OECD supports the Millennium Goals and describes its role in collecting data for the effort:

> Since 2000, the OECD has played a key role in work to track progress on the MDGs [Millennium Development Goals]. It was a founding member of the Inter-Agency Expert Group that tested and refined the MDG indicators, and has contributed to the UN's annual MDG progress reports and the MDG "gap" reports devoted to Goal 8, which tracks global partnership efforts in support of the MDGs. A vital part of this work has been to supply statistics and commentary on aid flows.[103]

Contributing to a world education culture, the global network supporting Millennium Development links together representatives from 160 nations ranging from Afghanistan to Zambia. In addition, there are more than 50 different global development organizations ranging from Abu Dhabi Fund for Development to the World Business Council for Sustainable Development.[104] These nations and aid organizations signed the Busan Partnership for Effective Development Co-operation in Busan, Korea, in 2011.

Global networking is highlighted in the Busan's opening declaration supporting Millennium Goals: "We, Heads of State, Ministers and representatives of developing and developed countries, heads of multilateral and bilateral institutions, representatives of different types of public, civil society, private, parliamentary, local and regional organizations."[105] The Busan declaration also emphasizes values shared by others, such as those represented by the Cyberschoolbus: "Moreover, the Declaration identifies that promoting human rights, democracy and good governance are an integral part of our development efforts."[106]

Thus, the United Nations Millennium Goals create or add on more links to existing global networks. Members of this network are not always in agreement about school policies, particularly with the United Nations stressing education for human rights, environmental protection, and peace, and the World Bank and OECD focusing on economic growth. It could be argued that there is an inherent conflict between the economization of education and environmental protection. The economization of education focuses on educating productive workers for a consumerist culture. However, a throwaway consumer culture may be part of the environmental problem.

Conclusion: Spreading a World Education Culture—Economization and Human Rights

Global networks linking the World Bank, OECD, and the United Nations contribute a world culture of education but with differing emphases. These differences are summarized in Table 3.3.

Table 3.3 highlights various approaches to world education culture between the World Bank, OECD, UNESCO, the Cyberschoolbus, and *Sesame Street*. Exemplifying these differing approaches is the common goal of gender equity, which is supported by these organizations for differing reasons. The World Bank advocates gender equality, particularly in education, as a key to ensuring the health of children and expanding global labor markets. Also, OECD advocates gender equality to expand the labor supply in developed nations, in other words, to free women to work. UNESCO, the United Nations Cyberschoolbus, and the Sesame Street Workshop International support gender equality in the context of human rights. Whatever the reasons, these organizations create a world education culture that values gender equality but with varying responses from local cultures. Gender

TABLE 3.3 World Education Culture: Educating the Global Citizen

	World Bank	OECD	UNESCO: Sustainable Development	United Nations: Cyberschoolbus	Sesame Street Workshop International
Goals	Educating workers for the knowledge economy; ability to function in a multicultural society and workforce; gender equality; social cohesion	Educating workers for the knowledge economy; ability to function in a multicultural society and workforce; gender equality; social cohesion	Educating global citizens committed to sustainable development; sustain and protect cultures and languages; gender equality; activist citizen	Social justice: peace, human rights, antipoverty; human rights; gender equality; antiracism; multicultural cooperation; activist citizen	To give young children models for promoting social justice and ability to live in a multicultural world and gender equality; provide poor children the basic tools for further education
Instruction	Standardized curriculum; assessment driven; ICT; learner centered; knowledge rich; group work	Standardized curriculum; assessment driven; ICT; learner centered; knowledge rich; group work	Participatory decision making; interdisciplinary and holistic; critical thinking; locally relevant; values–driven sustainable development	Internet learning; games, information, and curricular materials made available on peace education, human rights, and other social justice issues	Television as sanctuary from emotional stress of living; instruction in basic educational concepts; nonpunitive; behavioral models

equity might be rejected or modified by local cultures because of its impact on traditional family structures and gender roles.

Consider some of the differences in Table 3.3—the goals of the World Bank and OECD being the education of workers for the knowledge economy and UNESCO's concern being with education for sustainable development, protection of cultures and languages, and activist citizens. Then there is the Cyberschoolbus's curriculum of social justice, peace, human rights, antipoverty, antiracism, multicultural cooperation, and active citizenship, and the Sesame Street Workshop International's goal of providing poor children with basic education tools and teaching social justice and harmony in a multicultural world. There is a world culture of education, but there are important tensions and differences within that education culture. Also, local cultures will vary in their acceptance of this world education culture.

Notes

1 David H. Kamens, "Globalization and the Emergence of an Audit Culture: PISA and the Search for 'Best Practices' and Magic Bullets," in *PISA, Power, and Policy: The Emergence of Global Educational Governments*, edited by Heinz-Dieter Meyer and Aaron Benavot (Oxford: Symposium Books, 2013), p. 123.

2 OECD, *Internationalization of Higher Education* (Paris: OECD, 1996), p. 2.

3 OECD, "Our Mission." Retrieved from www.oecd.org/about/ on October 14, 2013.

4 Ibid.

5 Ibid.

6 OECD, "Education: About." Retrieved from www.oecd.org/about/0,3347 ,en_2649_37455_1_1_1_1_374,00.html on November 7, 2007.

7 Ibid.

8 Fazal Rizi and Bob Lingard, "Globalization and the Changing Nature of the OECD's Educational Work," in *Education, Globalization & Social Change*, edited by H. Lauder, P. Brown, J. Dillabough, and H. Halsey (Oxford: Oxford University Press, 2006), p. 259.

9 Ibid., p. 248.

10 OECD, "Education GPS." Retrieved from http://gpseducation.oecd.org/ on October 14, 2013.

11 OECD, *Better Skills, Better Jobs, Better Lives: A Strategic Approach to Skills Policies* (Paris: OECD, 2012), p. 10. Retrieved from http://dx.doi.org/10.1787/9789264177338-en on October 14, 2013.

12 Ibid., p. 11.

13 OECD, "About the Survey of Adult Skills (PIAAC)." Retrieved from www.oecd.org/ site/piaac/surveyofadultskills.htm on October 14, 2013.

14 Ibid.

15 OECD, *Better Skills, Better Jobs, Better Lives*, p. 12.

16 Brian Keeley, *Human Capital: How What You Know Shapes Your Life* (Paris: OECD, 2007), p. 14.

17 OECD, *Better Skills, Better Jobs, Better Lives*, p. 21.

18 Ibid., p. 27.

19 Ibid.

20 Ibid.
21 Ibid.
22 Ibid.
23 Ibid.
24 Ibid.
25 Ibid., pp. 21–22.
26 Ibid., p. 27.
27 Keeley, *Human Capital*, pp. 10–11.
28 Ibid., p. 10.
29 Ibid., p. 11.
30 Ibid.
31 Ibid., p. 103.
32 Ibid., p. 104
33 Ibid., p. 45.
34 As quoted in Ibid., p. 46.
35 Ibid., p. 56.
36 Ibid., p. 82.
37 Ibid., p. 81.
38 International Association for the Evaluation of Educational Achievement, "Brief History of IEA." Retrieved from www.iea.nl/brief_history_iea.html on January 28, 2008.
39 Ibid.
40 Ibid.
41 Ibid.
42 Ibid.
43 International Association for the Evaluation of Educational Achievement, "Mission Statement." Retrieved from www.ies.nl/mission_statement.html on January 28, 2008.
44 Heinz-Dieter Meyer and Aaron Benavot, "Introduction," in *PISA, Power, and Policy: The Emergence of Global Educational Governments*, p. 11.
45 PISA, "Background and Basics." Retrieved from www.oecd.org/pisa/pisaproducts/Take%20the%20test%20e%20book.pdf on October 17, 2013.
46 Ibid.
47 David Baker and Gerald LeTendre, *National Differences, Global Similarities: World Culture and the Future of Schooling* (Palo Alto, CA: Stanford University Press, 2005), p. 150.
48 OECD, *PISA—The OECD Programme for International Student Assessment* (Paris: OECD, 2007), p. 4.
49 PISA, "Background and Basics."
50 See Jane Varjo, Hannu Simola, and Risto Rinne, "Finland's PISA Results: An Analysis of Dynamics in Education Politics" pp. 51–76; and Tilna Silander and Jouni Valijari, "The Theory and Practice of Building Pedagogical Skill in Finnish Teacher Education," pp. 77–99 in *PISA, Power, and Policy: The Emergence of Global Educational Governments*.
51 PISA, *Take the Test: Sample Questions from the OECD's PISA Assessments* (Paris: OECD, 2009), p. 13. Retrieved from http://unesdoc.unesco.org/images/0014/001486/148654e.pdf on October 18, 2013.
52 Ibid., p. 98
53 Ibid., p. 188.
54 Kamens, p. 135.
55 Madhu Singh, "The Global and International Discourse of Lifelong Learning from the Perspective of UNESCO," in *Lifelong Learning: One Focus, Different Systems*, edited by Klaus Harney, Anja Heikkinen, Sylvia Rahn, and Michael Shemmann (Frankfurt am Main: Peter Lang, 2002), p. 18.

56 Edgar Faure, Felipe Herrera, Abdul-Razzak Kaddoura, Henri Lopes, Arthur V. Petro-vsky, Majid Rahnema, and Frederick Champion Ward, *Learning to Be: The World of Education Today and Tomorrow* (Paris: UNESCO, 1972).

57 Ibid., p. vi.

58 Ibid.

59 Ibid.

60 Ibid., p. xxv.

61 Ibid.

62 Ibid., p. xxvi–xxvii.

63 Ibid., p. xxix.

64 Ibid., pp. xxxi–xxxii.

65 Jacques Delors, *Learning: The Treasure Within: Report to UNESCO of the International Commission on Education for the Twenty-First Century* (Paris: UNESCO, 1996).

66 William Gorham (United States), President of the Urban Institute in Washington, DC; Aleksandra Kornhauser (Solvenia), Director, International Centre for Chemical Studies; and Rodolfo Stavenhagen (Mexico), Professor at the Centre of Sociological Studies, El Colegio de Mexico.

67 In'am Al Mufti (Jordan), former Minister of Social Development; Isao Amagi (Japan), Adviser to the Minister of Education; Roberto Carneiro (Portugal), former Minister of Education and Minister of State; Fay Chung (Zimbabwe), former Minister of Education; Marisela Quero (Venezuela), former Minister of the Family; Karan Singh (India), several times Minister for Education and Health; Myong Won Suhr (Republic of Korea); former Minister of Education; and Zhou Nanzhao (China), Vice-President, China National Institute for Educational Research.

68 Other members, in addition to Jacques Delors, are Bronislaw Geremek (Poland), Member of Parliament; Michael Manley (Jamaica), Prime Minister (1872–80); and Marie-Angelique Savane (Senegal), member of the Commission on Global Governance and Director, Africa Division, UNFPA.

69 Delors, *Learning*, p. 11.

70 Ibid.

71 Ibid., p. 19.

72 Ibid., pp. 86–97.

73 Ibid., p. 21.

74 Ibid.

75 Ibid.

76 Ibid., p. 17.

77 Ibid.

78 Ibid.

79 UNESCO, "International Implementation Scheme (IIS)." Retrieved from http://portal.unesco.org/education/en/ev.php-URL_ID = 23280&URL_DO = DO_TOPIC&URL_SECTION = 201.html on November 17, 2013.

80 Ibid.

81 UNESCO, *Education for Sustainable Development United Nations Decade 2005–2014: Highlights on ESD Progress to Date April 2007* (Paris: UNESCO, 2007), p. 2.

82 UNESCO, "International Implementation Scheme (IIS)."

83 Ibid.

84 United Nations Cyberschoolbus, "Mission Statement." Retrieved from www.un.org/Pubs/CyberSchoolBus/miss.html on October 21, 2013.

85 United Nations Cyberschoolbus, "About Us." Retrieved from www.un.org/cyberschoolbus/aboutus.html on October 21, 2013.

86 United Nations Cyberschoolbus, "About Us: Project Highlights." Retrieved from www.un.org/cyberschoolbus/aboutus.html#project on October 21, 2013.

87 United Nations Cyberschoolbus, "Curriculum." Retrieved from www.un.org/cyber schoolbus/index.shtml on October 21, 2013.

88 United Nations Cyberschoolbus, "ABC Human Rights." Retrieved from www. un.org/cyberschoolbus/index.shtml on October 21, 2013.

89 Lloyd Morrisett, "Introduction," in Gerald S. Lesser, *Children and Television: Lessons from "Sesame Street"* (New York: Vintage, 1975), p. xxi.

90 Lesser, *Children and Television*, p. 23.

91 Information provided in *The World According to Sesame Street: A Global Documentary of Local Proportions*, DVD, produced and directed Linda Goldstein Knowlton and Linda Hawkins Costigan (New York: Participant Productions, 2006).

92 Lesser, *Children and Television*, pp. 24–25.

93 Ibid., pp. 254–255.

94 PBS, "The World According to Sesame Street." Retrieved from www.pbs.org/inde pendentlens/worldaccordingtosesamestreet/film.html on October 21, 2013.

95 For a documentary on the South African production, see "The World According to Sesame Street."

96 For a documentary on the Bangladesh production, see "The World According to Sesame Street."

97 United Nations, "We Can End Poverty: Millennium Development Goals and Beyond 2015." Retrieved from www.un.org/millenniumgoals/ on October 22, 2013.

98 OECD, "The OECD and the Millennium Development Goals." Retrieved from www.oecd.org/dac/theoecdandthemillenniumdevelopmentgoals.htm#DAC_role on October 22, 2013.

99 United Nations, "We Can End Poverty: Millennium Development Goals and Beyond 2015: Education." Retrieved from www.un.org/millenniumgoals/education.shtml on October 8, 2013.

100 United Nations, "We Can End Poverty: Millennium Development Goals and Beyond 2015: Home." Retrieved from www.un.org/millenniumgoals on October 10, 2013.

101 United Nations, "We Can End Poverty: Millennium Development Goals and Beyond 2015: Background." Retrieved from www.un.org/millenniumgoals/bkgd.shtml on October 22, 2013.

102 United Nations, "We Can End Poverty: Millennium Development Goals and Beyond 2015: Home."

103 OECD, "The OECD and the Millennium Development Goals." Retrieved from www.oecd.org/dac/theoecdandthemillenniumdevelopmentgoals.htm#DAC_role on October 22, 2013.

104 OECD, "Countries, Territories and Organizations Adhering to the Busan Partnership for Effective Development Co-operation." Retrieved from www.oecd.org/dac/effec tiveness/busanadherents.htm on October 22, 2013.

105 OECD, "The Busan Partnership for Effective Development Co-operation." Retrieved from www.oecd.org/dac/effectiveness/49650173.pdf on October 22, 2013.

106 Ibid.

4

THE WORLD TRADE ORGANIZATION AND THE GLOBAL CULTURE OF HIGHER EDUCATION

In 2013, the *Washington Post* reported that "the global education market is now worth $4.4 trillion—that's TRILLION—and is set to grow a lot over the next five years."[1] Exemplifying the growing global education market was the creation of a free trade zone for educational services in Dubai. The free trade zone was called Knowledge Village.[2] Dubai's actions exemplify the worldwide marketing of higher education and the activities of multinational learning corporations. These enterprises add another dimension to the global superstructure of educational practices and policies and the evolution of a world education culture. Many of these global corporations support the economic model of education. Emblazoned on the Knowledge Village website are the words "Empowering Human Capital." Its description states, "Dubai Knowledge Village (DKV) is the world's only Free Zone area dedicated to Human Resource Management and . . . aims to develop the region's talent pool and establish the UAE as a knowledge-based economy."[3]

Global trade in educational products is sanctioned by the World Trade Organization's (WTO) General Agreement on Trade in Services (GATS) and Agreement on Trade-Related Intellectual Property Rights (TRIPS). The WTO, GATS, and TRIPS by sanctioning the sale of education products contribute to the growth of a global education culture. However, as I indicated in Chapter 3, this global education culture is not uniform and contains contradictory ideas and emphasis. Also, as I suggested in Chapter 1, there are global religious education models outside this more general trend to a world education culture.

Trade in educational services did exist prior to being sanctioned by the WTO. In previous times, missionaries and colonialists transported education to other countries, students and scholars traveled between nations, and some national schools opened branches in other countries. This early story should not be thought of as just another example of Western cultural imperialism. Certainly, the West played a major role in providing international educational services, but many countries outside of the West also traded in educational services, such as Chinese scholars studying in Japan in the nineteenth century and the centuries of international movement of Islamic scholars and students. The past history of international education is important, but my focus is on the present globalized trade in educational services.[4]

GATS and TRIPS

The 1995 creation of the WTO opened the door to free trade in educational materials and services, as well as the marketing of higher education. The WTO was an outgrowth of the 1948 General Agreement on Tariffs and Trade, which was called the "third institution" after the World Bank and the International Monetary Fund. The general goal was to reduce national tariffs and promote free trade in goods. The Uruguay Round of trade talks from 1986 to 1994 resulted in GATS and TRIPS. GATS expanded free trade to include a free trade in services. TRIPS provides protection for the global sale of so-called knowledge-related products.

TRIPS protects intellectual property sold by individuals, universities, corporations, and other institutions. TRIPS also covers software, compilation of data, recorded media, digital online media, and patents on industrial, health, and agricultural technologies. Also included are integrated circuit designs, utility models, industrial designs, trademarks, trade names, and geographical names.[5]

How many countries are involved in GATS and TRIPS? As of 2013, the WTO had 159 member countries and 25 observer countries.[6] The WTO is controlled by member nations with all major decisions requiring agreement by all members. GATS and TRIPS are governed by the three fundamental obligations of WTO members. The first obligation is equal and consistent treatment of all trading partners. For instance, if a foreign university is allowed to establish a branch in another country, then that country must allow other foreign universities to establish branches. The same is true of other educational services. The second obligation is that all foreign providers of educational services receive equal treatment within the host country. The third is that each country determines the extent of market access to foreign providers. In other words, if a country decides to allow one branch campus of a foreign university, then it must allow other foreign universities to do the same. The same obligations cover the protection of intellectual property under TRIPS.[7]

GATS and TRIPS can transform higher education into business enterprises that sell services and knowledge.[8] As Helen Raduntz explains:

> Universities as idea-generating powerhouses are prime targets for investment, by those knowledge-based industries involved in telecommunications, computers, electronics, and biotechnology. As lucrative sites of investment, their potential has been enhanced by the protection of ideas, as intellectual property generated by research, under copyright and patent laws and global trade agreements.[9]

Global free trade contributes to creating a world education culture. Trade can result in the exchange of cultural artifacts and knowledge. Free trade might have a major impact on local cultures and contribute to the making of world culture. Legal scholar Christopher Arup wrote about the global impact of GATS: "Services, particularly those with intellectual content, carry far deeper messages than goods."[10] Arup worries that "not only do services comprise a growing proportion of international trade overall, but the ways in which services are supplied provide potential to undermine the economic sufficiency, political sovereignty and cultural identity of the locality."[11]

KEY POINTS: WTO, GATS, AND TRIPS

WTO

1. Origins and Structure
    a. Outgrowth of 1948 General Agreement on Tariffs and Trade
    b. The Uruguay Round of Trade Talks 1986–1994 resulted in the creation of the WTO, GATS, and TRIPS
    c. WTO membership in 2007: 151 member nations and 31 observer nations
    d. Rules enforced by members
2. General Trade Obligations
    a. Equal and consistent treatment of all trading partners
    b. All foreign traders and companies will receive equal treatment in host country
    c. Each country determines the extent of market access to foreign companies and traders

GATS

1. Trade in services governed by the general trade obligations of the WTO
2. Agreement includes the production, distribution, marketing, sale, and delivery of a service
3. Classification of educational services under GATS
    a. Cross-border supply such as distance learning, e-learning, and virtual universities
    b. Consumption abroad involves students who go to another country to study
    c. Commercial presence of facilities in another country such as branch campuses and franchising arrangements in another country
    d. Presence of natural persons includes the travel of scholars, researchers, and teachers to another country to work

> **TRIPS**
>
> 1. Protects intellectual property sold by individuals, corporations, and universities
> 2. Intellectual property includes copyrighted printed material; software; compilation of data; recorded media; digital online media; patents on industrial, health, and agricultural technologies; integrated circuit designs; utility models; industrial designs; trademarks; trade names; and geographical names

GATS and the Globalization of Higher Education

GATS provisions affect the global marketing of higher education. Jane Knight writes in Trade in Higher Education; The Implications of GATS, "The GATS defines four ways in which a service can be traded, known as 'modes of supply'. These four modes of trade apply to all service sectors in GATS."[12] Table 4.1 represents these four modes of trade identified by Knight. She uses the term "borderless education" for these four modes of trade in higher education.

TABLE 4.1 GATS and Trade in High Education

Mode of Supply according to GATS	Description	Higher Education Examples	Potential Market
Cross-Border Supply	Service crosses borders	Distance education; e-learning; virtual universities	Great potential for continued growth
Consumption Abroad	Movement of consumer to the country of the supplier	Students who study in another country	Major share of global market in educational services
Commercial Presence	Service provider establishes commercial presence in another country	Establish local branch of university located in another country; partnerships with institution in another country; franchising arrangements with local institutions	Major area of growth
Presence of Natural Persons	Persons travelling to another country to provide temporary service	Professors, teachers, and researchers working abroad	Strong market with an emphasis on professional mobility

Source: Adapted from "Chart One: Mode of Supply," in Jane Knight, *Trade in Higher Education; The Implications of GATS* (London: The Observatory on Borderless Higher Education, 2002), p. 5.

Cross-Border Supply: E-Learning and World Education Culture

Global higher education online courses are contributing to a world culture of higher education. In "Cross-Border Supply" in Table 4.1, e-learning and virtual universities are protected under GATS and represent an important area of global growth. One area is Massive Open Online Courses (MOOCs). For instance in 2011, 160,000 students in 190 countries enrolled in Stanford's Artificial Intelligence course. The course required translations into 44 languages, Facebook groups, and online discussions.[13] Stanford backed the course, and in a statement by Stanford's provost John Etchemendy, he referred to education as a global business: "Our business is education, and I'm all in favor of supporting anything that can help educate more people around the world."[14]

Without leaving their countries, students in Stanford's MOOC shared a common knowledge about artificial intelligence and opinions on the topic through global online discussions. The course was launched through Udacity, a for-profit created to distribute the course, with the stated purpose: "Our mission is to bring accessible, affordable, engaging, and highly effective higher education to the world. We believe that higher education is a basic human right, and we seek to empower our students to advance their education and careers."[15]

For-profits like Udacity are playing major roles in marketing MOOCs and contribute to a global higher education culture. Since its birth with the launch of the Stanford Artificial Intelligence course and protected by GATS, Udacity has expanded its MOOC offerings. The company claims, "Higher education is broken with increasingly higher costs for both students and our society at large. Education is no longer a one-time event but a lifelong experience. Education should be less passive listening (no long lectures) and more active doing. Education should empower students to succeed not just in school but in life."[16]

Using the language of the economization of education, Udacity states its mission as follows: "We are reinventing education for the 21st century by bridging the gap between real-world skills, relevant education, and employment. Our students will be fluent in new technology, modern mathematics, science, and critical thinking. They will marry skills with creativity and humanity to learn, think, and do. Udacians are curious and engaged world citizens."[17] In 2013, Udacity offered 29 courses that supposedly reflected skills needed by the global knowledge economy. Some were basic introduction courses in physics, algebra, statistics, and psychology. The majority of the courses were related computer software, such as Web Development, Algorithms: Crunching Social Networks, HTML5 Game Development, Mobile Web Development, Software Testing, Software Debugging, Design of Computer Programs, and Artificial Intelligence for Robotics.[18]

Udacity is only one of many other global Internet education programs operated by private companies and universities. Some are operated by for-profit enterprises, such as University of Phoenix and the American Public University. The University of Phoenix markets itself as a global online program: "A global classroom for a global world. . . . international students have the option of earning a college degree online. Our mission is to make quality higher education highly accessible to working adults like you who have other lifestyle commitments."[19] American Public University states as a goal, "Relevance in a global society . . . we educate and support more than 100,000 distance learners studying in 50 states and more than 100 countries."[20]

As a major step in creating a world higher education culture, the U.S. State Department signed an agreement with Coursera to create "learning hubs" around the world where students can get Internet access to free online courses with discussions led by local teachers. At the time of the 2013 agreement, Coursera had enrolled five million students in free online courses.[21] The learning hubs are to provide Internet access for those lacking it.

Adaptation of global courses to local cultures is aided by hiring local teachers or other facilitators at each learning hub. "Our mission is education for everyone," said Lila Ibrahim, the president of Coursera, "and we've seen that when we can bring a community of learners together with a facilitator or teacher who can engage the students, it enhances the learning experience and increases the completion rate." The actual nature of these local facilitators, according Ibrahim, "will vary with the location and the organization we're working with, but we want to bring in some teacher or facilitator who can be the glue for the class."[22]

There is an element of cultural imperialism embedded in the U.S. State Department's efforts to support global online courses. Along with Coursera and other online providers, the State Department has piloted global "online courses in priority fields, including science and technology subjects, Americana and entrepreneurship."[23] The "Americana" aspect of these courses is designed to spread positive feelings about American culture. The science, technology, and entrepreneurship courses, of course, reflect an emphasis on building skills for the global economy.

The U.S. State Department calls this endeavor MOOC Camp and houses it in the State Department's Bureau of Educational and Cultural Affairs. In 2013, MOOC Camp was described as "a new initiative of the Department of State to host facilitated discussions around massive open online courses (MOOCs) at U.S. Embassies, Consulates, American Spaces, and other public spaces around the world."[24] U.S. Embassies and Consulates in 40 countries were participating. An official description of MOOC Camp states, "Course content is drawn from major MOOC providers, including Coursera and edX, as well as from multiple Open CourseWare providers."[25] The goal of the effort fits the economic model of education to "help meet the aspirations of young people around the world, and offer skills and knowledge that they can use to succeed in life."[26]

Another goal of MOOC Camp is to attract foreign students to American colleges and universities. This effort falls under the "Consumption Aboard" category of Table 4.1, which will be discussed in more detail in the next section.

Regarding MOOC Camp's attempt to attract foreign students, it is stated: "all the while offering students a chance to test-drive a U.S. higher education experience. Program participants will also be able to learn more about opportunities to study in the United States through EducationUSA, a network of hundreds of student advising centers around the world that the State Department supports."[27]

Teaming up with MOOC Camp reflects Coursera's goal of "connecting people to a great education so that anyone around the world can learn without limits."[28] Coursera describes itself as "an education company that partners with the top universities and organizations in the world to offer courses online for anyone to take, for free. Our technology enables our partners to teach millions of students rather than hundreds."[29] Coursera lists more than 90 global partner universities and educational institutions.

While Coursera exemplifies the role of online education in creating a global higher education culture, edX, one of the other partners in the MOOC Camp, has created a global consortium of universities to offer online courses. EdX claims, "The colleges and universities that comprise the edX consortium are among the best in the world. They are dedicated to quality education both on campus and online. EdX is honored they have chosen to become part of the initiative by opening their virtual doors to the world."[30]

Companies like Coursera and edX are operated for-profit while providing free online courses. According to the *Financial Times*, one source of income for Coursera is selling "certificates of achievement" to students for US$30 to $100. It also shares revenues and profits with universities: "This collaborative model sees 15 per cent of revenues associated with a given class directed to the respective university, plus 20 per cent of its gross profits."[31] Coursera's goal is to sell certificates for a majority of its courses. EdX follows a similar model with students paying the course provider to verify their identity as a kind of certification of achievement. In addition, edX is selling software for its MOOC platform.[32]

In summary, global online learning will continue to expand, particularly with the aid of for-profit companies like Coursera, Udacity, and edX. Supported by the U.S. State Department, these American-based online providers act as a form of cultural imperialism. GATS protects this trade in services, listed in Table 4.1 as "Cross-Border Supply," which in this case means online learning. This "Cross-Border Supply" contributes to a world higher education culture.

Consumption Abroad: Foreign Students and Globalization of Higher Education

Students traveling abroad for higher education provide a sharing of cultures between two countries and accelerate the development of a world higher education culture. International students also provide income to host institutions and countries. However, there are certain countries that host the largest number of students. These countries may have greater impact on shaping world education cultures than countries that host few foreign students. Students return to their own nations with ideas about higher education and culture from their host countries.

In 2011, according to Organization for Economic Cooperation and Development (OECD), the United States had the largest number of foreign students with 709,565, followed by Great Britain 419,946; Australia 262,597; Germany 176,682; Japan 138,563; and Canada 106,284.[33] Other countries had only limited numbers of foreign students.

English, it is important to note, is the national language of the previously mentioned countries except for Germany and Japan. This fact helps to make English a world language. Students traveling to these countries must know English before leaving their homelands.

Global Rankings, English, and World Higher Education Culture

Standardization of global higher education is strongly influenced by the world rankings of the *Times Higher Education* Supplement. These rankings favor English-speaking countries. Similar to Programme for International Student Assessment (PISA), the rankings are now part of a higher education Olympiad to see who is best. The rankings started in 2004 and now influence university administrators and political officials who want their schools to be at the top of the list. The ranking criteria influence educational decisions by university officials and politicians. In other words, higher education policies are implemented that help higher education institutions meet the criteria of the rating system. These rankings are also used to define the meaning of world-class universities. The *Times Higher Education* World University Rankings website states:

> The *Times Higher Education* World University Rankings 2013–2014, powered by Thomson Reuters, are the only global university performance tables to judge world-class universities across all of their core missions—teaching, research, knowledge transfer and international outlook. The top universities rankings employ 13 carefully calibrated performance indicators to provide the most comprehensive and balanced comparisons available, which are trusted by students, academics, university leaders, industry and governments.[34]

In his study of the impact of these world rankings on Osaka University, Mayumi Ishikawa writes, "The Global rankings demonstrate the existing reality of a global hierarchy in higher education in a plain, explicit, and blatant manner. They portray the powerful image of the world's top-class universities in a way that overshadows the most competitive domestic counterparts."[35]

The World University Rankings are based on 13 performance indicators. These indicators influence policy decisions by those wanting to increase the prestige of their schools. Also, they contribute to a growing uniformity of global higher education institutions. The 13 performance indicators are grouped into five areas:

1. Teaching: the learning environment (worth 30 per cent of the overall ranking score)
    a. The dominant indicator here uses the results of the world's largest invitation-only academic reputation survey.
2. Research: volume, income and reputation (worth 30 per cent)
    a. This category is made up of three indicators. The most prominent, given a weighting of 18 per cent, looks at a university's reputation for research excellence among its peers, based on the 16,000-plus responses to our annual academic reputation survey.
3. Citations: research influence (worth 30 per cent)
    a. Our research influence indicator is the flagship. Weighted at 30 per cent of the overall score, it is the single most influential of the 13 indicators, and looks at the role of universities in spreading new knowledge and ideas.
    b. We exclude from the rankings any institution that publishes fewer than 200 papers a year to ensure that we have enough data to make statistically valid comparisons.
4. Industry income: innovation (worth 2.5 per cent)
    a. A university's ability to help industry with innovations, inventions and consultancy has become a core mission of the contemporary global academy.
5. International outlook: staff, students and research (worth 7.5 per cent).
    a. This category looks at diversity on campus and to what degree academics collaborate with international colleagues on research projects—both signs of how global an institution is in its outlook. The ability of a university to attract undergraduates and postgraduates from all over the planet is key to its success on the world stage.[36]

The reputational survey methods used in the criteria may simply affirm past ideas about a particular higher education institution. For instance, the "Teaching: the learning environment" criterion is based on a reputational survey. In other words, people are asked what they think of the quality of teaching at a particular school in what is described as the "world's largest invitation-only academic reputation survey." The actual teaching at a school is not evaluated by classroom observation or student evaluation of courses. The teaching criterion is determined by the reputation of the school. For instance, in the subsequent list, the California Institute of Technology is listed as the number one school in the 2012–13 rankings. While the institution might have a good reputation, the actual teaching might be poor. A reputational method is also used as part of the "Research" criterion—that is, the "university's reputation for research excellence among its peers, based on the 16,000-plus responses to our annual academic reputation survey." Being ranked at the top almost guarantees a continued positive reputation in these categories and might ensure the continued high ratings of the institution.

Globalization of higher education is embedded in the criterion "International outlook," which is based on the diversity of the student body and international research cooperation. To achieve a high score in this criterion, schools must seek foreign students so that the institution will be a "success on the world stage." This internationalizes schools seeking a high rank.

What were the world-class universities according to these criteria in 2012–13? The top ten are in these rankings are considered "world-class."[37] The following are the schools in this category:[38]

1. California Institute of Technology	United States	95.5
2. University of Oxford	United Kingdom	93.7
2. Stanford University	United States	93.7
4. Harvard University	United States	93.6
5. Massachusetts Institute of Technology	United States	93.1
6. Princeton University	United States	92.7
7. University of Cambridge	United Kingdom	92.6
8. Imperial College London	United Kingdom	90.6
9. University of California, Berkeley	United States	90.5
10. University of Chicago	United States	90.4

It is not difficult to suggest that there is a level of cultural imperialism in these rankings with the top ten being in the United States and the United Kingdom. An important issue is that all of these are English-speaking institutions, which accelerates the growth of English as the dominant global language. It also results in other institutions in this higher education Olympiad trying to raise their rankings by improving on those areas judged by the criteria. Obviously, these rankings influence choices made by foreign students whom institutions want to attract to ensure their rankings. Since the "world-class" schools are English-speaking, this reinforces the academic use of English by students and the global dominance of English in higher education.

Reinforcing the Global Role of English

English as a world language is strength by higher education rankings, the international movement of students and academics, and the reliance on English in academic publications. The importance of English is illustrated by demonstrations broke out in France in the spring of 2013 when it was proposed that French universities offer courses in English as a means of attracting more foreign students. As reported by Maïa De La Baume, the law requiring English courses "is intended simply to increase the number of students from abroad, in particular from emerging countries like India, Brazil and China, who often prefer to go to universities in English-speaking countries."[39] The French parliament declared that the lack of English was a major cause of France's decline in the world economy. Geneviève Fioraso, France's minister of higher education, stated that France was losing its attractiveness for foreign students because "Germany went past us by developing courses in English."[40]

The importance of English in academic publications was noted by Philip Altbach, director of Boston College's Center for International Higher Education, in an article in the center's publication *International Higher Education* titled "Globalization and Forces for Change in Higher Education." In the article, Altbach suggests that massification of higher education (mass access to higher education) reflects global inequalities with developing nations being at a disadvantage. Altbach argues, "Academic systems and institutions that at one time could grow within national boundaries now find themselves competing internationally. National languages compete with English even within national borders. Domestic academic journals, for example, often compete with international publications within national academic systems, and scholars are pressured to publish internationally."[41] The Center for International Higher Education's African network in part is designed to overcome these inequalities. Altbach recognizes that global networks in higher education are having a profound effect on the global usage of English:

> The growth of information technology (IT) has created a virtual global community of scholarship and science. *The increasing dominance of English as the key language of communicating academic knowledge is enhanced by IT* [author's emphasis]. Global science provides everyone immediate access to the latest knowledge.[42]

Consumption Abroad: Global Marketing of Higher Education

As noted previously, speaking English is important for students wanting to study abroad. As noted in the previous example of France wanting higher education courses taught in English, spending on tuition and living expenses by foreign students provides an important source of national income. Higher education systems and countries work hard to attract students, including, as discussed subsequently, engaging in advertising and public relations campaigns. Ravinder Sidhu's *Universities and Globalization: To Market, To Market* captures the commodification of higher education by examining marketing strategies.[43] Branding is an important aspect of this marketing. The concept of branding dates back to the early twentieth century when manufacturers used advertising to create brand loyalty and confidence among consumers that they could trust a particular brand.[44] University administrators attempt to accomplish the same thing by creating symbols and slogans to attract students. Sidhu investigates this branding and marketing phenomenon in universities in the three major English-speaking countries engaged in global marketing—the United States, the United Kingdom, and Australia.

Sidhu's first examples are Stanford University and Stony Brook State University of New York. Stanford's approach to marketing is low-key, reflecting, according to Sidhu, the elite status of the school. It is already an established brand name among global universities. The marketing emphasis at Stanford is on interdisciplinary inquiry and a culture of innovation as captured in its motto "the wind of freedom blows" and website examples like "Stanford ideas that changed the world."[45] Stony Brook issued a generic promotional brochure filled with images highlighting a diverse faculty and student body. Designed to attract foreign students, the pamphlet presents the university as a showcase, according to Sidhu, for "multidisciplinary and multicultural talents." [46]

In the 1990s, the United Kingdom developed a new image for global markets. This was the goal of the 1998 Brand Report of the British Council's Education Counseling Services, which involved the hiring of companies involved in market research, public relations, and advertising. The British education brand stresses terms, such as elite, investment, ambition, ownership, and movers and shakers. Foreign students are presented as "ambitious . . . movers and shakers when they return to their countries . . . They know that an education in an English-speaking country is a passport to intellectual citizenship in the world."[47] Using a combination of historical images, UK institutions promise economic success and that foreign student will have, "A chance to be the best."[48] One British Council ad that Sidhu includes in her book shows a generic dark-skinned male staring supposedly with an overlay of the words "Postgraduate courses" intersected at 90 degrees with the words "Be the best you can be." Inside the commonly used *o* is the "UK" logo.[49] Another ad shows a Japanese student with the logo "UK" superimposed on her statement, "I was a bit nervous to begin with, but I'm settling in now and making friends from so many different countries."[50]

Australian universities have tried to use their advantages in being close to Asian nations and being English-speaking. Jan Currie, the vice chancellor of Murdoch University, issued his vision of higher education in a 1996 report titled *Preparing the University for the Twenty-First Century*. Based on this vision, the university developed what it called its "Four Pillars," which could be used by any corporation:

1. Develop market attractiveness;
2. Diversify income streams;
3. Build on management efficiency and effectiveness;
4. Create an entrepreneurial culture.[51]

Developing "market attractiveness" and diversifying "income streams," reflected efforts by Australian schools to attract foreign students and establish branches in other countries. This led to major advertising efforts. For instance one ad for

QUT, an amalgamation of the Queensland Institute of Technology and Kelvin Grove College of Advanced Education, shows a runner wearing a tee shirt emblazoned with the name Accenture, which is described as one of the world's leading consultants on management and technology. Across the picture are splashed the words: "QUT business graduate," "Real global giant," and "Runner."[52] QUT positioned itself as a global university to attract foreign students with the ad, "Our campuses are cosmopolitan . . . a significant proportion of our students speak at least one other language than English."[53]

Commercial Presence: Branch Campuses

As noted in Table 4.1, GATS provides for the commercial presence of branch campuses. Dubai's Knowledge Village exemplifies the trade in higher education services. The Knowledge Village claims to be "the world's only Free Zone totally focused on professional training and learning support services."[54] Dubai, one of seven emirates in the federation of United Arab Emirates, founded Dubai Knowledge Village, according to its official website, "as part of a long-term economic strategy to develop the region's talent pool and accelerate its move into a knowledge-based economy."[55] Inviting educational services from other nations to participate, the government promised protection of their income: "Benefits for Dubai Knowledge Village partners include 100% foreign ownership, 100% freedom from taxes, 100% repatriation of assets and profits and effortless visa issuance procedures."[56] Knowledge Village consists of branches of universities located in India, Russia, Pakistan, Iran, England, and Australia. One member of the Knowledge Village is SAE Institute, which is the largest global provider of training in educational media services with branches throughout Asia, Europe, North America, and the Middle East. SAE's mission statement expresses its goals:

> As the world's largest network of media Institutes, SAE Institute will continue to set the pace for a new level of Higher Education & Vocational Technology training on its existing individual, corporate and government platform by an ongoing process of updating its worldwide campuses. . . . SAE will also maintain its focus capitalizing on its existing internationally recognized quality profile & accreditation.[57]

Nearby, another member of United Arab Emirates, Abu Dhabi, contracted with Singapore's National Institute of Education (NIE) to help establish the Emirates College for Advanced Education (ECEA), which has the stated mission "to become the premier center for teacher education and develop the UAE and the Gulf."[58] Reflecting the commercial nature of selling educational services in an international market, Singapore's NIE reported its contract with Abu Dhabi under "Corporate Developments" in its quarterly publication *News*. The publication explained the financial relationship: "NIE was pivotal in the founding of ECEA after signing a contract with Abu Dhabi Education Council in October 2006 on the provision of related services culminating in the setup of the college."[59]

There are several important things to note about Singapore's sale of educational services to Abu Dhabi and its contribution to the growth of a world education culture. Singapore's NIE relies on global educational research and its own research to guide educational practices and services. For instance, in the same issue of *News* announcing the contract with Abu Dhabi there was an article announcing the founding of a worldwide alliance of deans of education at the NIE in August 2007. The institute hosted deans from Denmark's University of Aarhus, Beijing Normal University, University of London, University of Melbourne, Seoul National University, Ontario Institute for Studies in Education, and the University of Wisconsin-Madison. The goal of this new international network is described as follows: "The alliance acts as a think tank to influence the sector globally, drawing together existing expertise and research ... In doing so, it aims to influence governments, international agencies, funding bodies and the public at large to enhance the profile and quality of education internationally."[60]

Abu Dhabi has also recruited New York University (NYU) to open a branch campus, which will be called "NYU Abu Dhabi." A 2007 NYU press release proudly carried the following subtitles: "Important Step in Transforming NYU into a 'Global Network University'" and "First Comprehensive Liberal Arts Campus Abroad Developed by a Major U.S. Research University."[61] The Abu Dhabi government agreed to provide the land, funding, construction, equipment, and maintenance of the branch campus. The President of NYU, John Sexton, used the term "idea capitals" when referring to research universities. One can imagine a world map dotted with indicators of the "idea capitals." Regarding the global spread of research universities, Sexton stated that "the evolving global dynamic will bring about the emergence of a set of world centers of intellectual, cultural, and educational strength; and a recognition that research universities will be key to these 'idea capitals'."[62]

In summary, higher education is rushing to market its products by engaging in public relations campaigns, branding, recruiting foreign students, and establishing branch campuses. Both government-operated and for-profit schools are tending to operate along the lines of corporations with entrepreneurial faculty and administrators. Will the new global map, as President Sexton of NYU suggests, indicate the location of the new corporate-like idea capitals?

Global Concepts of Higher Education

Western models of higher education were globalized before the advent of GATS. Nothing better symbolizes the assumption that higher education is globally similar in its structure and educational practices than the 1998 issuance by United Nations Educational, Scientific, and Cultural Organization (UNESCO) of the World Declaration on Higher Education for the Twenty-First Century.[63] Similar to other United Nations educational documents that assume that all national school systems are divided into primary and secondary schools, this declaration was issued without any members raising the question about whether or not something called higher education existed worldwide and that it had a similar organization across nations.

There are critics of this trend. Daniel Schugurensky has provided a useful summary of these criticisms against the background of the history of Western higher education.[64] He has identified three historical periods in the history of higher education. First is the early liberal tradition that saw the role of the university as protecting the moral and cultural values. The second is the human capital role of the university as a service station attending to the needs of corporations and public institutions through research and education. A third is the role of the university in promoting social justice and social transformation. This role fits the progressive education model discussed in Chapter 1. Recently, the human capital model combined with the concept of the service university to create institutions interested in expanding markets and making money with academics becoming entrepreneurs and knowledge treated as a commodity. Critics bemoan the loss of the liberal and social justice traditions in higher education.[65]

Global policy statements on higher education have captured some of the historical elements discussed by Schugurensky. There are variations in these statements. For instance, UNESCO's 1998 World Declaration on Higher Education for the Twenty-First Century provides more emphasis on social justice issues than the pronouncements of OECD. However, as I will discuss later in this section, it appears that higher education systems in the twenty-first century are primarily serving corporate enterprises while operating like business enterprises.

The 1998 UNESCO World Conference on Education in the Twenty-First Century was certainly a global affair with representatives from more than 180 countries in attendance along with teachers and students. UNESCO convened the World Conference to establish the principles for reforming higher education in the twenty-first century. Reflecting an acceptance of a globalized form of higher education and the participation of all nations in higher education, UNESCO referred in its World Conference goals to a generalized "mankind" when declaring as its intention to forge and confirm "the values and principles laid down in the constitution of UNESCO for the intellectual and moral solidarity of mankind."[66]

What does "intellectual and moral solidarity" mean in the World Declaration on Higher Education for the Twenty-First Century? Let us consider Article 1 of the declaration, titled "Mission to Educate, to Train and to undertake Research."

1. We affirm that the core missions and values of higher education, in particular the mission to contribute to the sustainable development and improvement of society as a whole, should be preserved, reinforced and further expanded, namely, to:

   a. educate highly qualified graduates and responsible citizens able to meet the needs of all sectors of human activity, by offering relevant qualifications, including professional training, which combine high-level knowledge and skills, using courses and content continually tailored to the present and future needs of society;

   b. provide opportunities for higher learning and for learning throughout life, giving to learners an optimal range of choice and a flexibility of entry and exit points within the system, as well as an opportunity for individual development and social mobility in order to educate for citizenship and for active participation in society, with a worldwide vision, for endogenous capacity-building, and for the consolidation of human rights, sustainable development, democracy and peace, in a context of justice;

   c. advance, create and disseminate knowledge through research and provide, as part of its service to the community, relevant expertise to assist societies in cultural, social and economic development, promoting and developing scientific and technological research as well as research in the social sciences, the humanities and the creative arts;

   d. help understand, interpret, preserve, enhance, promote and disseminate national and regional, international and historic cultures, in a context of cultural pluralism and diversity;

   e. help protect and enhance societal values by training young people in the values which form the basis of democratic citizenship and by providing critical and detached perspectives to assist in the discussion of strategic options and the reinforcement of humanistic perspectives;

   f. contribute to the development and improvement of education at all levels, including through the training of teachers.[67]

First, I would like to reiterate that the missions and goals of the declaration are addressed to all systems of higher education with the assumption that globally they are similar in structure and practices. The first three goals of the declaration place higher education in the categories that Schugurensky called the human capital and service functions of the university. Goals "a" and "b" of Article 1 identify the main goals of higher education to be human capital and lifelong learning, which places higher education in role of preparing students for the knowledge economy. However, goal "b" contains values of social justice when it includes in lifelong learning a goal of "consolidation of human rights, sustainable development, democracy and peace, in a context of justice." Goal "c" identifies the role of higher education as a knowledge-creator in which research serves "cultural, social and economic development."

Goals "d" and "e" can be linked to OECD's concerns with social cohesion discussed in Chapter 3. These include fears of strife between cultures as a result of global migration and the breakdown of a sense of national solidarity alongside concerns with preserving historic cultures in the context of "cultural pluralism and diversity." Goal "e" could be considered as trying to maintain civic order by teaching what Schugurensky's referred to as the liberal and social transformative traditions in higher education. Finally, goal "f" seems to suggest that higher education should train students to be dedicated to the improvement of the current globalized form of primary and secondary education including the training of teachers.

In general, UNESCO's World Declaration on Higher Education for the Twenty-First Century is hardly a revolutionary document. The answer to the previously posed question about the meaning of "intellectual and moral solidarity" is that globalized forms of higher education will teach similar values to all students. For instance, in goal "e" higher education is given the job of protecting "societal values."

Neglecting the progressive qualities of the UNESCO declaration, OECD links the goals of higher education to a knowledge economy. These goals are clearly expressed in Higher Education and Regions: Globally Competitive, Locally Engaged.[68] The opening statement of the Executive Summary of this 2007 book presents a clear statement of the role of higher education in a global knowledge economy:

> In order to be competitive in the globalizing knowledge economy, the OECD countries need to invest in their innovation systems at the national and regional levels. As countries are turning their production towards value-added segments and knowledge-intensive products and services, there is greater dependency on access to new technologies, knowledge and skills . . . HEIs [higher education institutions] must do more than simply educate and research—they must engage with others in their regions, provide opportunities for lifelong learning and contribute to the development of knowledge-intensive jobs.[69]

Regarding human capital, OECD asserts: "Higher education can contribute to human capital development . . . through educating a wider range of individuals in the local area, ensuring that they are employable when they leave education, helping local employers by responding to new skills requirements, ensuring that employees go on learning by supporting continuous professional development, and helping attract talent from outside."[70]

OECD contends that there has been a neglect of social service by higher education: "Regional development is not only about helping business thrive: wider forms of development both serve economic goals and are ends in themselves. HEIs have long seen service to the community as part of their role, yet this function is often underdeveloped."[71] This statement should not be interpreted as

OECD supporting the role of higher education in social transformation. From the examples of how some university systems can render social service, their goals are very limited. They provide four examples. The first is mandatory social service for Mexican university students. The second is the engagement of higher education in public health issues. The third is the role of European universities in creating a sense of unity to the European Union and supporting diversity and multiculturalism. Finally, without mentioning any specific university or higher education system, they suggest that higher education can play an important role in environmentalism.[72] While public health, multiculturalism, and environmentalist are important, there is little emphasis on the liberal tradition that promised a level of humaneness to society or the transformative tradition that hoped that graduates would work for social justice including the elimination of poverty and closing the gap between the rich and poor. Both OECD and UNESCO members assume that national higher education systems are similar in structure and curricula. This global uniformity is highlighted by the ability of universities to globally market their products.

Global Marketing of For-Profit Higher Education

For-profit higher education represents another element in the creation of a world culture of higher education. In 2013, the World Bank's International Finance Corporation (IFC) announced a $150 million investment in the for-profit Laureate Education Inc., which owns 31 institutions in Latin America and 3 in the Middle East and North Africa. Reporter Elizabeth Redden claims that this "investment is the largest-ever in education on the part of the IFC, an arm of the World Bank that focuses exclusively on the private sector in developing countries."[73]

A loan from the IFC helps to promote global for-profit colleges. Redden quoted Douglas L. Becker, Laureate's chairman and CEO:

> It's not a large investment relative to the capital base we have in the company, but the significance for us is relative to the strategic partnership we have with the IFC. It's very important for us in terms of credibility. A lot of people understand that the IFC and the World Bank have incredibly high standards for the environmental and social impacts of the companies that they invest in, and a company would have to be perceived as very highly credible in order to be fortunate enough to have them as an investor.[74]

There is a burgeoning global market for corporate-controlled for-profit higher education. In 2006, the *Chronicle of Higher Education* reported that for-profit colleges were the fastest-growing sector in higher education with the eight largest corporations having a combined market value of about $26 billion.[75] Some economists criticize for-profit higher education institutions for spending more

money on recruitment than other nonprofit and private schools. Stanford economist Samuel Wood, according a report in the *Chronicle of Higher Education*, suggests
that "for-profits have a lot more in common with a chain of Bally's health clubs
than they do with, say, Arizona State or Emory Universities."[76] According to his
calculations, nonprofits spend from 1 to 2 percent of their revenue on recruiting
students, while for-profits spend 23 percent. However, as Wood suggests, this may
change as nonprofit colleges spend more money on advertising and public relations to attract foreign students and to establish branch campuses in other countries; I discuss these aspects of marketing of higher education in a later section.

The corporate structure of Educate Inc. reflects the complex structure of modern for-profit schools and knowledge industries. After the 2007 purchase of Sylvan Learning Centers from Laureate Education Inc., Educate Inc. could boast
about its ownership of Hooked on Phonics, Catapult Learning, Educate Online,
and Progressus Therapy. Educate Inc. markets its products in Europe under the
Schülerhilfe brand.[77] Involved in complex financial connections, Educate Inc. is
owned by Edge Acquisition LLC with Citigroup Capital Partners and Sterling
Capital Partners as investors.[78] The chairman of Edge Acquisition LLC, R. Christopher Hoehn-Saric, is also a trustee of Johns Hopkins University.[79] The interplay of politics and education is evident on the Board of Directors of Educate
Inc. One director, Raul Yzaguirre, is a professor at Arizona State University, the
director of the Mexican American advocacy group LaRaza, and former cochair
of the 2008 Hillary Rodham Clinton presidential campaign.[80] Another director,
Douglas Becker, is chairman and CEO of Laureate Education Inc. along with
being director of Baltimore Gas and Electric Company and director of For Inspiration and Recognition of Science and Technology.[81] Director Cheryl Gordon
Krongard is a regent of the University System of Maryland and director of U.S.
Airways Group Inc.[82] Other directors of Educate Inc. have similar ties to industry,
investment companies, and higher education.

In September of 2007, Laureate made a dramatic move to capture the Asian
market when Douglas L. Becker, its chairman and CEO, announced that he and
his family were moving to Hong Kong to ensure the expansion of the company
and to establish Asian headquarters. In an example of the international financing
of for-profit education, Becker and an investor group engineered a $3.8 billion
private-equity buyout of the company in June 2007. The international investor
group included Harvard University, Citigroup, Microsoft cofounder Paul Allen,
global philanthropist George Soros, Kohlberg Kravis Roberts & Co. (KKR),
S.A.C. Capital Management LLC, SPG Partners, Bregal Investments, Caisse de
depot et placement du Quebec, Sterling Capital, Makena Capital, Torreal S.A.,
and Brenthurst Funds. In reporting the move, a *Chronicle of Higher Education* article
commented, "Mr. Becker devised the transformation of Laureate into an internationally focused higher-education company from its roots as a tutoring business
called Sylvan Learning Systems."[83]

The Apollo Group and the University of Phoenix: A New Model for a Global University?

Are the University of Phoenix and Phoenix University Online the new models for consumer-oriented universities selling prepackaged knowledge? Both for-profit university systems are part of a conglomerate owned by the Apollo Group, which also owns the Institute for Professional Development, the College for Financial Planning, Western International University, and Insight Schools, which is based in Portland, Oregon, and offers K–12 online education.[84] The University of Phoenix operates campus locations for face-to-face instruction in 26 states and Puerto Rico in the United States, and in Canada and the Netherlands. Phoenix University Online enrolls students from 40 different countries.[85]

The University of Phoenix is based on a consumer model of adult education. Founded in 1973 before the advent of online learning, its founder John Sperling believed that "lifelong employment with a single employer would be replaced by lifelong learning and employment with a variety of employers. Lifelong learning requires an institution dedicated solely to the education of working adults."[86] At the time, Sperling found that a gradual shift was occurring in higher education demographics from a student population dominated by youth to one in which approximately half the students were adults, of whom 80 percent worked. According to Sperling, working adult students were invisible on the traditional campus and were treated as second-class citizens.[87]

In the end, Sperling turned higher education into a consumer-oriented enterprise and significantly changed faculty work. Like a factory, the University of Phoenix and Phoenix University Online sell prepackaged courses. The focus on working adults, the company claims, "informs the University's teaching and learning model, approach to designing and providing student services, and academic and administrative structure. It also guides the institution as it plans and prepares to meet the needs of working adult students."[88]

Craig Swenson, provost and senior vice president for academic affairs at the University of Phoenix, describes what it means to provide consumers with a standardized educational experience. Like shopping malls, "campuses and learning centers are located at strategic locations near major freeways and thoroughfares that permit convenient access."[89] Classes are scheduled after the usual working hours and on weekends. This model was significantly changed with the introduction of online courses, which allows students to select learning at their own convenience. According to Swenson, students expect the same level of service as any all-night store, which means "24 x 7 access to student services" including the online purchase of textbooks and class materials, as well as access to learning programs.

How does the University of Phoenix standardize its courses? The most important step is changing the role of faculty members. Swenson refers to this as the unbundling and disaggregation of the traditional faculty model. What this means in practice is taking traditional faculty roles and turning them over to specialists—the factory model. For instance, traditionally individual faculty members make decisions about the reading, class assignments, topics, and assessments in a particular course. The only requirement is that the content of the course is related to its description in the college catalogue.

At the University of Phoenix, a contracted faculty team, meaning they receive compensation for these activities, works under the supervision of a "curriculum development manager" and an "instructional designer" to create syllabi and instructional modules for each course. The contracted team is composed of core full-time faculty and part-time "practitioner" faculty; the university prefers *not* to use the word adjuncts for these part-timers. The curriculum development manager oversees the document process in course planning, while the instructional designer ensures that the syllabi and instructional module fit program objectives and the university's learning goals.[90]

The content of instruction is tightly controlled through a combination of the design process for the syllabi and modules and an assessment system. The university has instituted assessment systems, which it claims to "have brought significant public recognition to University of Phoenix."[91] These assessment systems are reminiscent of those advocated by human capital educators for public school systems. There are two systems: the Academic Quality Management System, which evaluates the performance of faculty, curriculum, and student services; and the Adult Learning Outcomes Assessment, which measures student learning.

Higher Education Networks

For-profit higher education, like Laureate and Phoenix, are part of a vast global network of university administrators, government education officials, research associations, and international scholarly organizations. The list of international scholarly organizations is too vast to discuss in this book, but they range across academic disciplines including, but not limited to, history, literature, languages, science, mathematics, economics, education, sociology, philosophy, political science, geography, and anthropology. Each of these disciplines have subdisciplines that hold international meetings. The existence of these global scholarly organizations and meetings is made possible by the common academic use of English and modern transportation systems.

What is the effect of the increasing international network of academic scholars? It would be interesting to investigate each discipline to determine the consequences of these global academic contacts, a project that would take specialists from each discipline. However, it can be easily imagined what might be the results. First, there is the possibility of worldwide scholarly interactions resulting in common intellectual paradigms within each discipline. Second, there could result a common global academic culture. Third, as part of the process of global academic sharing, there can be mutual influences that fundamentally change the thinking of an academic culture. This has certainly happened in the field of cross-cultural psychology where researchers consistently note cultural differences in thought.[92] Since it is impossible in this book to explore all the academic networks, I will focus on university networks, which seem to creating a global university organization and culture.

One organization that has as a specific goal the globalization of higher education culture and structures is the International Association of Universities (IAU), which was founded in 1950 as a UNESCO-based organization. The membership is drawn from 150 countries and collaborates with other international, regional, and national organizations. The organization's mission statement encourages the globalization of practices in higher education. "By encouraging members to work together," the organization's mission statement asserts, the IAU:

1. Facilitates the exchange of experience and learning and fosters cooperation;
2. Restates and defends the academic values and principles that underlie and determine the proper functioning of universities and other higher education institutions;
3. Upholds and contributes to the development of a long-term vision of universities' role and responsibilities in society;
4. Voices the concerns for higher education with regard to policies of international bodies such as UNESCO, the World Bank and others;
5. Contributes to a better understanding of current trends and policy developments through analysis, research and debate;
6. Provides comprehensive and authoritative information on higher education systems, institutions and qualifications worldwide.[93]

The mission statement promotes common global academic values, such as the goal of defending "the academic values and principles that underlie and determine the proper functioning of universities and other higher education institutions." The assumption in this statement is that there is general standard among the 180 member nations as to the "proper functioning of universities and other higher education institutions." Also, the organization promotes global cooperation in higher education and the sharing of policy developments and information.

The Center for International Higher Education, located at Boston College, has as its stated mission "advancing knowledge about the complex realities of higher education in the contemporary world. The colleagues at the Center believe an international and comparative perspective is central to understanding global realities and national circumstances."[94] As part of this endeavor, the center publishes a quarterly *International Higher Education* and operates an International Higher

Education Clearinghouse. The clearinghouse provides another network linked to other higher education networks, or in the words of the center: "The Clearinghouse create[d] a website that will provide researchers and practitioners with the perfect starting point for searching available resources-web-based 'one-stop shopping'."[95] Often neglected in educational research is the plight of Africa. The center corrects this problem by offering an extensive International Network for Higher Education in Africa.[96]

Altbach believes that inequalities between nations and academic systems work against the creation of "a worldwide academic community based on cooperation and a shared vision of academic development."[97] From his perspective, as long as these inequalities exist there will be no globalized system of higher education.

A Global University through Higher Education Networks?

What is the global university? This was the question addressed at the 2007 London conference on Realizing the Global University.[98] Participants in the conference were members of the global network in higher education. One sponsor of the meeting had the slogan: "The Observatory: Crossing tomorrow's higher education borders today." This is the motto for the Observatory on Borderless Higher Education. The kind of global pressures on higher education administrators and their use of global networks are captured in the following testimonial the by vice chancellor of Britain's Open University Brenda Gourley that it "provides a really important service to the busy and increasingly pressurized leaders in higher education. It targets the kind of information necessary to decision-making about the strategies fundamental to survival in a complex and fast changing HE landscape. Highly recommended."[99] The Observatory on Borderless Higher Education provides information to higher education administrators in 50 countries and is partnered with a vast network of other international organizations including the Association of Commonwealth Universities, Universities UK, UNESCO, the World Bank, the Commonwealth of Learning, the U.S. Distance Learning Association, the European Distance Educational Network, and the Western Co-operative for Educational Telecommunication.

Other sponsors of the Realizing the Global University conference include the Worldwide Universities Network, Universities UK, IAU, and the Association of Commonwealth Universities. Speakers, mostly higher education officials, were from the United Kingdom, the World Bank, the United States, China, Australia, Mexico, and Italy.[100] Searching for a definition of a global university, the conference's announcement declared: "Universities are universal and increasingly international, but they are not yet 'global'. In a world that is globalizing rapidly, in which the central role of universities in the knowledge economy and in civil society is articulated more strongly and more widely than ever, we do not have a clear sense of what it takes or what it means to be a global university."[101] In order to be global, a university must, according to the announcement, do more that attract international students and establish branch campuses overseas; it "requires 'international' to pervade everything a university does and for it to be embedded in a strategic and operational framework."[102]

What does it mean to internationalize a university beyond having foreign students and branch campuses? Being part of international networks was one answer given Graham Spanier, president of Pennsylvania State University: "The call to internationalize the university has gained traction in recent years. Organizations like the Worldwide Universities Network [Spanier was a founder of this organization] provide transcontinental opportunities and bring together leaders in education to focus attention on international education."[103] In addition, he argued, the curriculum should be "internationalized," and students should be taught a global perspective. Also, part of being a global university, Spanier contends, is for the university to participate in cooperative global research.

"Global brand penetration," is another feature of a global university suggested at the conference by Eric Thomas, vice chancellor of the University of Bristol and former chair of Worldwide Universities Network.[104] Most of the world's peoples, he laments, have never heard of his own university or even the location of Bristol, England. In contrast, most people have heard of England's most famous brand schools—Cambridge and Oxford. Of course, he argues, this doesn't mean that every ordinary person recognizes your school as a global brand, but, he states, "I would argue that if you wish to be considered to be a global university it is almost a *sine qua non* that your peers and national policy makers should see you as that."[105] Another qualification, which Thomas asserts in agreement with Spanier, is "the pursuit of innovative global research is the absolutely prime characteristic and without it, a university cannot claim to be global."[106]

Will the global university be a virtual university? In articulating their views on the nature of a global university, Thomas and Spanier were reflecting their efforts working with Worldwide Universities Network. The network is devoted to integrating its members into a "global university" using modern information and communications technology to promote, among other things, e-learning, distance learning, cooperative research efforts, and global virtual seminars. Sixteen universities compose the membership of the Network. These schools are located in the United States, Great Britain, Australia, Canada, China, Norway, and the Netherlands. The network's mission statement emphasizes its global goals:

> The WUN [Worldwide Universities Network] alliance exists to make significant advances in knowledge and understanding in areas of current global concern. By fostering and encouraging collaboration between members, WUN brings together the experience, equipment and expertise necessary to tackle the big issues currently facing societies, governments, corporations and education.[107]

The Worldwide Universities Network is attempting to achieve this mission by creating global research communities through its networks of contacts and using communication devices such as websites, video conferencing, and access grid technology. Also, faculty and students are encouraged to spend time at institutions within the network. There is also an attempt to internationalize the curricula through the "development of elearning theory, practice and programs."[108] Finally, the network organizes online seminars between member institutions. Examples of these online seminars are those held through the networks' Contemporary China Center for the 2007–2008 academic years. These "Virtual Seminars" covered topics involving governance and society, media and security, and environment and sustainability. Advertisements indicated start times for seminar at different locations around the globe.[109]

Competing with the Worldwide Universities Network is Universitas 21: The International Network of Higher Education. This is a network of 21 universities in 13 countries including Australia, Canada, China, Hong Kong, India, Ireland, Japan, Mexico, New Zealand, Singapore, South Korea, Sweden, the United Kingdom, and the United States.[110] This organization claims to be the "leading global network of research universities."[111] As part of the globalization plan, the organization issued in 2003 the "Shanghai Declaration on Universitas 21 Student Mobility," which called for more global student mobility in undergraduate and graduate programs.[112] In its strategic plan, it discusses four methods to guarantee that it is "the leading international higher education network." These methods include ensuring that the organization is recognized as the leading higher education network by national higher education commentators; maintaining links to "decision-makers and opinion-formers of global national or regional significance"; and debating issues of "global significance to higher education."[113]

What is the significance of these global higher education networks for the concept of the global university? Based on the work of higher education networks, something called a global university would probably consist of an organization of universities from around the world that share students and faculties, engage in cooperative research, internationalize and share curricula, use e-learning, and hold virtual seminars. Most importantly, and this hasn't to my knowledge occurred, a diploma would be granted from the network organization rather than from a member university. One can imagine that in this global university local schools would retain their identities while surrendering their degree-granting powers to the global organization. Students at all the national localities would be studying common curricula while utilizing faculty from throughout the network either through e-learning and virtual classes and seminars or by moving from campus to campus. A global university might result from the work of organizations like the Observatory on Borderless Higher Education, the Worldwide Universities Network, the IAU, and Universitas 21.

Conclusion: Name Brands and a Global University

The world system theorists discussed in Chapter 1 might interpret current trends in higher education as helping the richest nations legitimize their power by imposing their educational values on other nations. From this perspective, globalization of higher education might be considered part of an effort to impose particular economic and political agendas that benefit wealthy and rich nations at the expense of the world's poor.

The world system theorists would agree that the WTO and GATS's free trade rules applied to high education have ensured the global dominance of schools in English-speaking countries and the global use of English. Helped by GATS and TRIPS and world rankings, the world trade in education and knowledge-related products could be contributing to a uniformity of higher education institutions based on models in the richest countries. The global marketing of higher education and the establishment of branch campuses contribute to the influences of the richest countries. The international movement of students has aided this process of educational imperialism.

The global use of English is reinforced by the domination of schools in English-speaking countries. Also, English language imperialism is reflected in course offerings taught in English in non-English-speaking countries, as well as in the use of English in international research publications and on the Internet. The standardization of global English has helped for-profit school corporations sell their products on a global market.

Higher education is a global business both in its internal operations and in its marketing systems and establishment of branch campuses. Are we entering a time when university brand names will have a similar recognition as fast-food chains? All of these activities are occurring across global networks composed of scholars, university administrations, for-profit publishing and knowledge companies, intergovernmental organizations, and higher education organizations. These trends are favoring English-speaking nations and universities, established publishing corporations and testing, and name-brand universities. Trends in global higher education support world system theorists' arguments that rich nations are continuing to dominate the globalization of higher education.

Notes

1 Valerie Strauss, "Global Education Market Reaches $4.4 Trillion—and Is Growing," *Washington Post* (February 9, 2013). Retrieved from www.washingtonpost.com/blogs/answer-sheet/wp/2013/02/09/global-education-market-reaches-4-4-trillion-and-is-growing/ on October 27, 2013.
2 Dubai Knowledge Village, "Home." Retrieved from www.kv.ae/ on October 26, 2013.
3 Ibid.
4 There are many histories of the international trade in educational services. For an introduction to different aspects of the field, see John Willinsky, *Learning to Divide the*

World: Education at Empire's End (Minneapolis: University of Minnesota Press, 1998); Theodore Vestal, *International Education: Its History and Promise for Today* (Westport, CT: 1994); Joel Spring, *Pedagogies of Globalization: The Rise of the Educational Security State* (Mahwah, NJ: Lawrence Erlbaum, 2006); and Joel Spring, *Education and the Rise of the Global Economy* (Mahwah, NJ: Lawrence Erlbaum, 1998).

5 Christopher Arup, *The New World Trade Organization Agreements: Globalizing Law through Services and Intellectual Property* (Cambridge: Cambridge University Press, 2000), pp. 177–213.

6 World Trade Organization, "Members and Observers." Retrieved from www.wto.org/english/thewto_e/whatis_e/tif_e/org6_e.htm on October 28, 2013.

7 Jane Knight, "Higher Education and Trade Agreements: What Are the Policy Implications?" in *Universities and Globalization: Private Linkages, Public Trust*, edited by Gilles Breton and Michel Lambert (Quebec, Canada: UNESCO, 2003), pp. 87–89; and Arup, *The New World Trade Organization Agreements*, pp. 95–214.

8 Gary Rhoads and Sheila Slaughter, "Academic Capitalism and the New Economy: Privatization as Shifting the Target of Public Subsidy in Higher Education," in *The University, State, and Market: The Political Economy of Globalization in the Americas*, edited by Roberts Rhoads and Carlos Torres (Palo Alto, CA: Stanford University Press, 2006), pp. 103–104.

9 Helen Raduntz, "The Marketization of Education within the Global Capitalist Economy," in *Globalizing Education: Policies, Pedagogies, & Politics*, edited by Michael Apple, Jane Kenway, and Michael Singh (New York: Peter Lang, 2005), pp. 231–245.

10 Arup, *The New World Trade Organization Agreements*, p. 97.

11 Ibid.

12 Jane Knight, Trade in Higher Education; The Implications of GATS (London: The Observatory on Borderless Higher Education, 2002), p. 5.

13 Tamar Lewin, "Instruction for Masses Knocks Down Campus Walls," *New York Times* (March 4, 2012). Retrieved from www.nytimes.com/2012/03/05/education/moocs-large-courses-open-to-all-topple-campus-walls.html?_r=3&hpw&pagewanted=print on October 28, 2013.

14 Ibid.

15 Udacity, "Our Mission." Retrieved from https://www.Udacity.com/us on October 28, 2013.

16 Ibid.

17 Ibid.

18 Udacity, "Course Catalog." Retrieved from https://www.Udacity.com/courses on October 28, 2013.

19 University of Phoenix, "International Division." Retrieved from www.phoenix.edu/colleges_divisions/global.html on October 29, 2013.

20 American Public University System, "Who We Are." Retrieved from www.apus.edu/about-us/ on October 29, 2013.

21 Tamar Lewin, "U.S. Teams Up with Operator of Online Courses to Plan a Global Network," *New York Times* (October 31, 2013). Retrieved from www.nytimes.com/2013/11/01/education/us-plans-global-network-of-free-online-courses.html?ref=education&_r=0&pagewanted=print on October 31, 2013.

22 Ibid.

23 Ibid.

24 The U.S. Department of State, Bureau of Educational and Cultural Affairs, "MOOC Camp." Retrieved from http://eca.state.gov/programs-initiatives/mooc-camp on November 4, 2013.

25 Ibid.

26 Ibid.

27 Ibid.

28 Coursera, "About Coursera." Retrieved from https://www.coursera.org/#about on November 4, 2013.

29 Ibid.

30 edX, "Schools." Retrieved from https://www.edx.org/schools on November 4, 2013.

31 Adam Palin, "Mooc Platform Coursera Continues Its Expansion," *Financial Times* (February 21, 2013). Retrieved from www.ft.com/cms/s/2/a59cc418–7b54–11e2–8eed-00144feabdc0.html on November 4, 2013.

32 Robinson Meyer, "Harvard and MIT's Online Education Startup Has a New Way to Make Money: Even Non-Profits Need to Eat," *The Atlantic* (October 21, 2013). Retrieved from www.theatlantic.com/technology/archive/2013/10/harvard-and-mits-online-edu cation-startup-has-a-new-way-to-make-money/280700/ on November 4, 2013.

33 OECD, "Foreign/International Students Enrolled," StatExtracts. Retrieved from http://stats.oecd.org/Index.aspx?DataSetCode = RFOREIGN on November 5, 2013.

34 The World University Rankings, "World University Ratings 2013–2014 top 40." Retrieved from www.timeshighereducation.co.uk/world-university-rankings/ on November 10, 2013.

35 Mayumi Ishikawa, "University Rankings, Global Models, and Emerging Hegemony," in *Universities and the Knowledge Sphere: Knowledge Building in the Era of Globalization*, edited by Brian Pusser, Ken Kempner, Simon Marginson, and Imanol Ordorika (London: Routledge, 2012), p. 88.

36 The World University Rankings, "The Essential Elements in Our World-Leading Formula." Retrieved from www.timeshighereducation.co.uk/world-university-rank ings/2012-13/world-ranking/methodology on November 8, 2013.

37 Ishikawa, "University Rankings, Global Models, and Emerging Hegemony," p. 86.

38 The World University Rankings, "World University Rankings 2012–2013." Retrieved from www.timeshighereducation.co.uk/world-university-rankings/2012–13/world ranking on November 10, 2013.

39 Maïa De La Baume, "Bid in France to Add Courses in English Raises Fear for Language," *New York Times* (May 5, 2013). Retrieved from www.nytimes.com/2013/05/24/world/europe/french-upset-over-more-english-proposal.html?ref=todayspaper&_r=0&pagewanted=print on May 6, 2013.

40 Ibid.

41 Philip G. Altbach, "Globalization and Forces for Change in Higher Education," *International Higher Education* 50 (Winter 2008), p. 1.

42 Ibid.

43 Ravinder Sidhu, *Universities and Globalization: To Market, To Market* (Mahwah, NJ: Lawrence Erlbaum, 2006).

44 For a history of schools, advertising, and brand names, see Joel Spring, *Educating the Consumer-Citizen: A History of the Marriage of Schools, Advertising, and Media* (Mahwah, NJ: Lawrence Erlbaum, 2003).

45 Sidhu, *Universities and Globalization*, p. 91.

46 Ibid., p. 106.

47 Ibid., p. 130.

48 Ibid., pp. 131–132.

49 Ibid., p. 135.

50 Ibid., p. 134.

51 Jan Currie, "Australian Universities as Enterprise Universities: Transformed Players on a Global Stage," in *Universities and Globalization: Private Linkages, Public Trust*, edited by Gilles Breton and Michel Lambert (Quebec, Canada: UNESCO, 2003), pp. 185.

52 Sidhu, *Universities and Globalization*, p. 202.

53 As quoted in Ibid., p. 206.

54 Dubai Knowledge Village, "About Dubai Knowledge Village."

55 Ibid.

56 Ibid.

57 SAE Institute, "Mission Statement." Retrieved from http//www.sea.edu/mission_statement on December 18, 2007.

58 Emirates College for Advanced Education, "Mission and Vision." Retrieved from www.ecae.ac.ae/English/Mission.aspx on December 19, 2007.

59 Ibid.

60 "Corporate Developments: Senior NIE Staff Helms Emirates College for Advanced Education," *News* (October 2007) No. 62, p. 4.

61 Press Release, "NYU to Open Campus in Abu Dhabi, Friday, Oct. 12, 2007." Retrieved from www.nyu.edu/public.affairs/rreleases/detail/1787 on January 8, 2008.

62 Ibid.

63 UNESCO, "World Declaration of on Higher Education for the Twenty-First Century: Vision and Action." Retrieved from www.unesco.org/education/educprog/wche/declaration_eng.htm#world%20declaration on January 10, 2008.

64 Daniel Schugurensky, "The Political Economy of Higher Education in the Time of Global Markets: Whither the Social Responsibility of the University?" in *The University, State, and Market: The Political Economy of Globalization in the Americas*, edited by Roberts Rhoads and Carlos Torres (Palo Alto, CA: Stanford University Press, 2006), pp. 301–320.

65 Ibid.

66 UNESCO, "Higher Education: Milestone-World Conference on Higher Education." Retrieved from http://portal.unesco.org/education/en/ev.php-URL_ID=DO_Topic&URL_SECTION=201.html on January 11, 2007.

67 UNESCO, "World Declaration of on Higher Education for the Twenty-First Century: Vision and Action."

68 OECD, *Higher Education and Regions: Globally Competitive, Locally Engaged* (Paris: OECD, 2007).

69 Ibid., p. 11.

70 Ibid., p. 15.

71 Ibid., p. 16.

72 Ibid.

73 Elizabeth Redden, "Global Development and Profits," Inside Higher Ed (January 24, 2013). Retrieved from www.insidehighered.com/news/2013/01/24/world-bank-affiliate-invests-150-million-profit-college-provider#ixzz2jywCQXi5 on November 7, 2013.

74 Ibid.

75 Stephen Burd, "Promises and Profits: A For-Profit College Is under Investigation for Pumping Up Enrollment While Skimping on Education," *Chronicle of Higher Education*

(January 13, 2006). Retrieved from http://chronicle.com/weekly/v52/i19/19a02101.htm on January 18, 2008.

76 Goldie Blumenstyk, "Why For-Profit Colleges Are Like Health Clubs: They Spend More on Recruiting and Less on Instruction than Their Nonprofit Counterparts Do, a Scholar's Model Shows, *Chronicle of Higher Education* (May 5, 2006). Retrieved from http://chronicle.com/weekly/v52/i35/35a03501.htm on January 18, 2008.

77 Educate Inc. "About Us." Retrieved from www.educateinc.com/aboutus.html on July 15, 2007.

78 Muckety, Listings, Edge Acquisition, LLC. "Edge Acquisition, LLC Full Screen Relationship." Retrieved from www.muckety.com/Edge-Acquisition-LLC/5016495.muckety?full = true on January 3, 2007.

79 Ibid.

80 Ibid.

81 Ibid.

82 Ibid.

83 Goldie Blumenstyk, "The Chronicle Index of For-Profit Higher Education," *Chronicle of Higher Education* (August 17, 2007). Retrieved from http://chronicle.com/weekly/v54/i11/fptest.htm on January 18, 2007.

84 Apollo Group Inc. "About Apollo Group." Retrieved from www.apollogrp.edu/About.aspx on July 15, 2007.

85 Craig Swenson, "New Models for Higher Education: Creating an Adult-Centred Institution," in *Universities and Globalization: Private Linkages, Public Trust* edited by Gilles Breton and Michel Lambert (UNESCO: Paris, 2003), p. 196.

86 Ibid.

87 Ibid.

88 Apollo Group Inc. "History." Retrieved from www.apollogrp.edu/History.aspx on January 6, 2008.

89 Swenson, "New Models for Higher Education" p. 202.

90 Ibid., pp. 204–206.

91 Ibid., p. 208.

92 A good example of the development of bicultural perspectives by cross-cultural psychologists is Richard Nisbett's *The Geography of Thought: How Asian and Westerners Think Differently . . . and Why* (New York: Free Press, 2003).

93 International Association of Universities, "General Information." Retrieved from www.unesco.org/iau/assocation/index.html on January 18, 2008.

94 Center for International Higher Education, "Welcome." Retrieved from https://www.bc.edu/content/bc/research/cihe/about.html on January 22, 2008.

95 Ibid.

96 International Network for Higher Education in Africa, "Welcome." Retrieved from www.bc.educ/bc_org/avp/soe/cihe/inhea/index.htm on January 22, 2008.

97 Ibid.

98 Realizing the Global University, "Conference, 15th November, 2007, Thistle Marble Arch Hotel London." Retrieved from www.wun.ac.uk/theglobaluniversity/conference.html on January 20, 2007.

99 The Observatory on Borderless Higher Education, "About the Observatory." Retrieved from www.obhe.ac.uk/aboutus/ on January 18, 2008.

100 Realizing the Global University, "Conference, 15th November, 2007, Thistle Marble Arch Hotel London."

101 Realizing the Global University, "Home." Retrieved from www.wun.ac.uk/theglo baluniersity/index on January 20, 2008.

102 Ibid.

103 Graham Spanier, "Internationalizing Today's Universities" (Paper delivered at the Conference on Realizing the Global University, London, November 15, 2007). Retrieved from www.wun.ac.uk/theglobaluniversity/conference.html on January 20, 2008.

104 Eric Thomas, "Defining A Global University" (Paper delivered at the Conference on Realizing the Global University, London, November 15, 2007). Retrieved from www.wun.ac.uk/theglobaluniversity/conference.html on January 20, 2008.

105 Ibid.

106 Ibid.

107 Worldwide Universities Network, "About Us." Retrieved from www.wun.ac.uk/aboutus.php on January 21, 2008.

108 Ibid.

109 Worldwide Universities Network, "Contemporary China Center Video Seminars." Retrieved from www.wun.ac.uk/chinacenter/documents/poster_USletter.pdf on January 21, 2008.

110 Universitas 21: The International Network of Higher Education, "About Us." Retrieved from www.universitas21.com/about.html on January 21, 2008.

111 Universitas 21: The International Network of Higher Education, *Universitas 21 Strategic Plan 2007–2012*, p. 5. Retrieved from www.universitas21.com/StrategicPlan.pdf on January 21, 2008.

112 Universitas 21: The International Network of Higher Education, "Shanghai Declaration on Universitas 21 Student Mobility." Retrieved from www.universitas21.com/shanghaideclaration.html on January 21, 2008.

113 Universitas 21: The International Network of Higher Education, *Universitas 21 Strategic Plan 2007–2012*, p. 10.

5

CORPORATIZATION OF GLOBAL EDUCATION

Profit Opportunity and Resistance to Corporatization

Corporatization of global education shifts part of the control from national school systems to international publishing, testing, technology, and software corporations. In addition, some international nongovernmental organizations (INGOs), such as human rights and environmental organizations, have become corporatized in structure.[1] Corporatization involves multinational education businesses selling products to local schools and an emphasis on training corporate workers. Education corporations and INGOs are linked to global philanthropic foundations supporting the corporatization of education. This results, as stated by Stephen J. Ball, in education policies being championed because they provide a profit opportunity.[2]

Some environment INGOs offer a radical alternative to corporatization by rejecting the very foundations of a consumer-industrial society. As I will explain in the last part of this chapter, some environmental groups offer multinational corporations a positive public image by working with them, while others say no to a corporatized world.

The operation of education businesses is sanctioned by the World Trade Organization's General Agreement on Trade in Services (GATS), as discussed in Chapter 4, which allows education businesses to sell products across national borders and for an education service provider to establish a commercial presence in another country. This trade arrangement is premised on the idea that free trade in education services will improve global education. As policies have evolved, it supports for-profit education enterprises with an assumption that competition in the marketplace will improve educational services.

Corporatization of global social programs, including education, involves what Janine Wedel calls a "shadow elite" who move between national governments, global corporations, INGOs, and foundations. The potential impact of this "shadow elite" is expressed in the title of Wedel's book: *Shadow Elite: How the World's New Power Brokers Undermine Democracy, Government, and the Free Market*.[3] A similar interpretation is provided by Stephen J. Ball in *Global Education Inc*. Ball refers to the development of a new global policy network and writes, "I contend that policy networks do constitute a new form of governance, albeit not in a single and coherent form, and bring into play policy process new sources of authority and indeed a 'market of authorities'."[4]

People, institutions, and policymakers linked in these policy networks often share similar values. For example, sellers of education products share economic interests and values.

Shared Economic Interests and Values

a. Support of national education policies that promote for-profit schooling, the sale of online instruction, and the purchase of education products;
b. Global trade policies favoring for-profit schools and education corporations;
c. Support of national education policies that rely on testing by for-profit companies and the sale of curriculum aligned with a national curriculum;
d. National, rather than local, education policies, which create uniform markets for the sale of education products.

As I discuss in the next section on the work of Stephen J. Ball, global education networks include shared economic interests and education values. These education networks of shared interests and values include for-profit companies, foundations and think tanks, INGOs, and national education policymakers.

Stephen J. Ball: Policy as Profit

Sociologist Stephen J. Ball has done the most complete analysis of global networks linking business, foundations, INGOs, and national education policymakers.[5] Ball introduces several important concepts in studying global networks. One concept is "policy as a profit opportunity."[6] This refers to global education businesses supporting policies that will result in increasing their profits. For instance, technology firms push global policies, such as online learning, that will increase their sales of hardware and software. In the United States, the Common Core State Standards, supported by the U.S. Chamber of Commerce and the Business Roundtable, created a whole industry of products for implementation and assessment. Established companies like Pearson, Apple, Samsung, and Microsoft raked in revenue from selling tests, software aligned with the Common Core, and computer tablets loaded with text aligned with the Common Core.[7] Also, new endeavors were started to capture these new sources of revenue with the most notable being Rupert Murdoch's NewsCorp creating a new education division called Amplify and the marketing of an Amplify tablet.[8] Supporting the Common Core were foundations, such as the Bill and Melinda Gates Foundation, the Pearson Foundation, and the Foundation for Excellence.[9]

Stephen Ball argues that global corporate and philanthropic influences on existing policy networks are resulting in the transfer of business methods to education policy planning and the functioning of national school systems.[10] Philanthropic organizations give money to educational institutions and policymakers with the requirement that recipients report back using business methods. What is called venture philanthropy designed to change national policies, Ball asserts, wants "to see clear and measurable impacts an outcomes from their 'investments' of time and money."[11] Often this means providing the philanthropic organization with data in form of numbers, such as test scores, school attendance, and other numerical outcomes.

One of many examples used by Ball to show the interplay between philanthropy, business, and global school involves the Clinton Global Initiative Forum, which in 2008 convinced the Deutsche Bank Americas Foundation, the Kellogg Foundation, and the investment firm Gray Matters Capital to support New Globe Schools in bringing low-cost education to Africa. New Globe Schools created a chain of schools in Kenya and India. It became part of the for-profit Bridge International Academies, which then received what was called a "philanthropic investment" from the founder of eBay Pierre Omidyar. In 2009, the for-profit Bridge International Academies received $4.35 million from investment firms.[12]

Bridge International Academies used the money from private investors and philanthropic organizations to franchise something called "school in a box." Local entrepreneurs buying the "school in the box" were promised extremely low costs that would yield profits. The "school in a box" comes with a *School Manager Manual* with detailed methods for handling financial and instructional services. The local entrepreneur is assured that schools can be established within five months at less than US$2,000 per classroom. In Kenya, parents were charged about US$4 a month with each school expected to enroll about 1,000 students. The "school in a box" was expected to be profitable within a year. According to Ball, "Parents pay fees and school owners pay bills using an electronic M-PESA mobile phone system—no money changes hands at school level."[13]

Ball's story of the evolution of "school in the box" illustrates the tangled network between venture philanthropy, investment banking, for-profit education firms, and local schools. In this case, the ideology of the free market penetrates the effort to expand global schooling by relying on local entrepreneurs to unpack the "school in the box." It also illustrates the triumph of education policy as a profit opportunity. Of course, business methods are implemented as franchise operators follow the *School Manager Manual*.

The selling and exporting of education policy based on profit, according to Ball, illustrates "the role of policy itself as a profit opportunity for global edu-businesses ... the [philanthropic] giving away of policy and education services, and the participation of these [education] businesses in national and international education policy communities."[14]

Global Education Businesses

What are the consequences of the growth of multinational global education corporations and the supporting networks of venture philanthropy, national education policymakers, and the shadow elite? While the actual impact is difficult to measure, there are certain hypotheses that can be made. First, global knowledge industries might be creating a level of uniformity in global education culture as the result of the marketing of for-profit schools, the international use of testing products, global databases, and, most importantly, the publishing of textbooks for global markets. Secondly, global knowledge industries might try to exert corporate control of the ideologies disseminated through schools around the world. While it is always possible that textbooks might reflect differing ideologies, it seems unlikely that global publishers would be distributing textbooks that contained ideas that threatened their control of global markets. Thirdly, globally marketed schools and worldwide information and publishing corporations might transform and displace local cultures. Again, these are only speculative hypothesizes without any concrete proof, but they might be supported by reason and common sense regarding the operation of global markets.

An example of the local impact of for-profit knowledge companies is the fear of some public librarians that GATS will result in a reduction of government support of public libraries in favor of for-profit knowledge companies.[15] The International Federation of Library Associations and Institutions warned in 2001 that GATS "has the potential to open up all aspects of a national economy to foreign competition including public sector services such as libraries."[16]

In *Constraining Public Libraries: The World Trade Organization's General Agreement on Trade in Services*, Samuel Trosow and Kirsti Nilsen detail the library services that can be done by for-profit corporations. One area is the selection of books that is increasingly being handled by private-sector international vendors. An example is the Ingram Content Group, which boasts of being "the world's largest and most trusted distributor of physical and digital content. We provide books, music and media content to over 38,000 retailers, libraries, schools and distribution partners in 195 countries. More than 25,000 publishers use Ingram's fully integrated physical and digital solutions and programs to realize the full business potential of books."[17] Another member of the Ingram Book Group, Coutts Information Services, provides a full array of services:

> Coutts Information Services Ltd. offers academic and professional librarians worldwide the broadest inventory of print and electronic content, leading fill rates, and expertly-managed programs and services. We provide service to more than 5,000 libraries and other professional organizations in over 150 countries, leading the way in service and innovation, and shaping the future of book and electronic content acquisition throughout the world of further and higher education. including supplying books, "collection management and shelf-ready services."[18]

There are other information and publishing services that are supplanting libraries, such as the so-called global knowledge companies. These include publishers who benefit from a global free market, such as Bertelsmann, HCIRN, Holtzbrinck Publishers, Informa, Pearson Education, Reed Elsevier, The McGraw-Hill Companies, and Thomson.[19] All of these companies include publishing and vast information systems.

The global publishing and information conglomerates are vast. With home headquarters in Stuttgart, Germany, Holtzbrinck Publishers describes its company as "active in more than 80 countries and publishes works in both print and electronic media, providing information, disseminating knowledge, and serving the needs of educational, professional, and general readership markets."[20] In the United States alone, the company owns Audio Renaissance; Bedford/St. Martin's; Farrar, Straus & Giroux; Henry Holt and Company; Palgrave Macmillan; Picador; St. Martin's Press; Tor Books; W. H. Freeman; Bedford, Freeman, and Worth Publishing Group; and Worth Publishers.[21] Informa, which advertises itself as a "Specialist Information for Global Markets," owns an array of publications including Taylor & Francis Group composed of Routledge, Garland Science, and Psychology Press.[22]

Pearson, headquartered in England, boasts that it "is the world's leading education company. From pre-school to high school, early learning to professional certification, our curriculum materials, multimedia learning tools and testing programmes help to educate millions of people worldwide—more than any other private enterprise."[23] Pearson provides this description of its global reach: "Though we generate approximately 60% of our sales in North America, we operate in more than 70 countries. We publish across the curriculum under a range of respected imprints including Scott Foresman, Prentice Hall, Addison-Wesley, Allyn and Bacon, Benjamin Cummings and Longman."[24] Stephen J. Ball writes that Pearson in its advertising offers solutions to "national policy of raising standards and achieving educational improvements linked to both individual opportunity and national competitiveness ... [it] is a globalizing actor ... through its publishing, assessment ... [and] English language teaching and administration and management products."[25]

The global reach of McGraw-Hill Education into 44 countries and with publications in 60 languages is proudly announced on its website:

> McGraw-Hill Education partners around the world with students, educators, administrators and other professionals to deliver engaging, adaptive and personalized solutions that improve performance and results. We combine proven, research-based content with the best emerging digital technologies to guide assessment, teaching and learning to achieve the best possible outcome for students, instructors and institutions. McGraw-Hill Education employs more than 6,000 people in 44 countries and publishes in more than 60 languages.[26]

In 2013, McGraw-Hill Education was sold to "to investment funds affiliated with Apollo Global Management, LLC."[27] In the same year, it jumped on the technology bandwagon by offering an adaptive e-book called SmartBook, declaring it "the world's first ever adaptive e-book, which revolutionizes college reading by focusing students on content most critical to their learning."[28]

Many of these global information and publishing corporations target developing countries such as Springer Science+Business Media, which states in its Developing Countries Initiatives: "As a global scientific, technical and medical publisher, we are aware of the role we play in the distribution of scientific information and access to knowledge and research. We make a concerted effort to ensure that the knowledge we manage is also accessible in those parts of the world that are still developing."[29]

Global Testing Services: Standardization of School Subjects and English

Global use of the same tests is one result of the worldwide expansion of publishing and information corporations. What is the cultural effect on students preparing for the same examinations? Does the global marketing of tests and the testing programs of international organizations contribute to a uniformity of world education culture and promotion of English as the global language? Is worldwide testing leading to a global standardization of knowledge in professional fields?

At this time any answer would have to be speculative since there is no concrete evidence about the effect of global testing programs. However, one could argue that if students worldwide are preparing for similar tests, then they are being exposed to a uniform educational and professional culture, which might contribute to creating a world culture.

The worldwide standardization of professional knowledge might be a result of the marketing prowess of Pearson, the global corporation discussed in the last section. Pearson markets its international computer-based tests through its Pearson Virtual University Enterprises (VUE) division. According to the company's official history, in 1994 the VUE was established by three pioneers in the field of electronic tests, including the developer of the first electronic system, E. Clarke Porter. Pearson purchased VUE in 2000. In 2006, Pearson acquired Promissor, a provider of knowledge measurement services that certified professionals in a variety of fields. Focusing on the certification of professionals, Pearson VUE serves 175 countries with 4,500 Pearson VUE Testing Centers. "Today," according to its company description,

> Pearson VUE (www.pearsonvue.com) is the global leader in electronic testing for information technology, academic, government and professional clients, providing a full suite of services from test development to data management. From operational centers in the United States, the United

Kingdom, India, Japan, and China, the business provides a variety of services to the electronic testing market. Currently serving over 175 countries, Pearson VUE partners with more than 4,500 Pearson VUE Authorized Test Centers in its rapidly expanding network. Pearson VUE also owns and operates over 400 Pearson Professional Centers throughout the world, serving professional licensing and certification sponsors.[30]

The range of computer-based tests offered by Pearson is astonishing, and it is beyond the scope of this book to list all the tests. The company lists tests for Academic/Admissions, IT Certification, Financial Services, Government Services, Health and Medicine, and for government regulatory licensing.[31]

As I was writing the first edition of this book, the Technology Training Center of my school, Queens College of the City University of New York, sent an e-mail to faculty announcing that "Queens College is now part of the Pearson VUE Test Center family."[32] The e-mail claimed, "Our Technology Training Center has partnered with Pearson VUE to offer the best service in delivering exams for technology, business, and other professional industry certifications. We also provide advanced, reliable technology access to many exclusive promotions and exam vouchers."[33] It was planned that the Queens College VUE test center would offer testing for admission, licensing, and employment for about 48 organizations and companies.

While Pearson VUE may be aiding the global standardization of professions and government licensing, worldwide language testing is possibly resulting in the standardization of a global English language as contrasted with forms of English associated with particular cultures or nations. As I discuss subsequently, global standardization of English, which in part involves the global reach of the U.S.-based Educational Testing Services (ETS), seems to be in the form of a global business English that allows communication across cultures in the world's workplaces. Focused primarily on work situations, it may result in teaching a limited vocabulary. This form of English may, and again I want to stress the word *may*, limit the ability of workers to express in English their discontent and demands for change regarding economic, political, and social conditions. This framework for global English was reflected on a sign I saw in Shanghai, which read "Learn the English words your boss wants to hear!"

Until 2000, ETS primarily focused on the U.S. testing market. In 2000, businessman Kurt Landgraf became president and CEO turning a nonprofit organization into one that looks like a for-profit with earnings of more than $800 million a year. As part of Landgraf's planning, the company expanded into 180 countries. "Our mission is not just a U.S.-oriented mission but a global mission," Landgraf is quoted, "We can offer educational systems to the world, but to do that, you have to take a *lesson from the commercial world* [author's emphasis]."[34] The official corporate description of this global marketing is that "ETS develops, administers and scores more than 50 million tests annually—including the TOEFL and TOEIC tests, the GRE General and Subject Tests and The Praxis

Series assessments—in more than 180 countries, at more than 9,000 locations worldwide."[35]

Corporatization of Global English

An important function of ETS is standardizing English as a global language. Many of its products are for English language learners. It markets the widely used Test of English as a Foreign Language (TOEFL), Test of English for International Communication (TOEIC), and Test of Spoken English (TSE). TOEFL serves as an assessment tool for determining the English language ability of foreign students seeking admission into English-speaking universities. Regarding its promotion of English, ETS states, "We conduct educational research, analysis and policy studies and develop a variety of customized services and products for teacher certification, English language learning and elementary, secondary and postsecondary education."[36]

Highlighting the growth of global English was the 6th Annual Meeting of English as a Lingua Franca in Rome in September for 2013.[37] English as a lingua franca refers to communication in English between nonnative speakers of English. It is estimated that only one out of four English speakers in the world is a native speaker of English.[38] As Barbara Seidlhofer writes, English as a lingua franca can be "a 'contact language' between persons who share neither a common native tongue nor a common (national) culture, and for whom English is the chosen foreign language of communication."[39]

Standardization of global English is one of the consequences of considering it as a lingua franca. There are a variety of world Englishes including those spoken in Africa, India, Pakistan, the United Kingdom, and the Americas. This complicates global communications by second language learners of English. Therefore, English as a lingua franca in global communications is standardized to ensure intelligibility. Seidlhofer argues that teaching English as a lingua franca should focus on international understanding. She writes, "The features of English which tend to be crucial for international intelligibility and therefore need to be taught . . . are being distinguished from the ('non-native') features that tend not to cause misunderstandings and thus do not need to constitute a focus for . . . those learners who intend to use English mainly in international settings."[40]

The domination of English-speaking institutions in the global trade in educational services contributes to the growth of English as the global language. English also dominates global academic discourses. The director of the Center for International Higher Education, Philip Altbach, describes the dominant role of English in the global trade in educational services in an article with the descriptive title, "The Imperial Tongue: English as the Dominating Academic Language."[41] Besides being the language of global commerce, Altbach states, "English now serves as the main international academic language."[42] The reasons for the dominant role of English in academic circles are clear. The United States spends half of the world's R&D funds, and English-speaking nations (United States, Canada,

Great Britain, and Australia) accommodate more half of the world's international students. In addition, according to Altbach, the editors of the major scientific and scholarly journals primarily work at English-speaking universities, and the journals are published in English. Also, English is the world's most widely studied second language at all levels of the education ladder. The majority of academic websites are in English. Universities throughout the world are offering degree programs in English.[43]

As a result, English-speaking countries are in the forefront of establishing branch campuses in other countries. As Altbach states, "The worldwide branch campus movement for the most part uses English as the medium of instruction. The United States, Australia, and the United Kingdom have been most active in establishing branch campuses, and it is not surprising that English is the medium of instruction."[44] Even branches of universities from non-English-speaking countries often use English as the medium of instruction. In addition, Altbach claims that curricular developments in higher education are reported in English and often come from English-speaking countries.

This aids the development of a global education culture. Altbach predicts the continued domination of English and, as a result, the domination of trade in educational services from English-speaking countries. Altbach concludes, "If globalization determines the direction of the world economy, science, and other factors, then the growth of English as the global language of science and scholarship is inevitable for the foreseeable future."[45] In the context of GATS, Altbach argues that it will force nations to be receptive to foreign educational services. He asserts, "Should GATS be widely implemented, this will inevitably mean the English-language institutions and programs will further entrench themselves worldwide."[46]

In summary, English is the main language in the global trade in educational services resulting in English-speaking nations being in the forefront of the worldwide marketing of educational services. Also, the recognition of English as a lingua franca that is different from world Englishes might contribute to its global standardization. The expansion of international testing might result in global standardization of English. It would be interesting to analyze the content of the all the various tests offered by Pearson on the standardization of professional knowledge. By using online tests, Pearson is able to engage in global marketing. ETS's range of English tests and its online services in English composition have a global impact on how English is spoken and written. Can English as a global language be standardized so that it is not identified with a particular culture or nation? Is global English to be corporatized as the language of international corporations?

INGOs: Part of the Shadow Elite?

There is controversy about the global role of INGOs. World culture theorists consider INGOs important for the evolution of a common global culture. Two world culture theorists, John Boli and George Thomas, highlight the importance of INGOs for world culture theory in their book *Constructing World Culture:*

International Nongovernment Organizations since 1875.[47] They write, "Our analysis depicts INGOs as embodiments of universalism, individualism, rational voluntaristic authority, progress, and world citizenship."[48] World citizenship, according to John Boli, Thomas Loya, and Teresa Loftin, is the result of the growth of INGOs. In their analysis, they found that Western nations do not dominate the membership of INGOs. While in the nineteenth century international INGOs tended to be concentrated in Western countries, by the twenty-first century the researchers found INGO participation "in all geographical regions of the world, across all levels of development, for old and new countries, for countries of every dominant religion."[49] With regard to Western influence, the authors conclude that "world culture is increasingly global, decreasingly the provenance of the Europeans and Anglo-Americans, who dominated it in its early stages."[50]

In contrast to world culture theorists, critics of INGOs brand them as a form of "humanitarian imperialism" serving the interests of "global capitalist governance."[51] In the tradition of world system theorists, INGOs are supporting global capitalism. Human rights organizations, one of the largest groups of INGOs, are criticized for supporting an agenda of "Western liberal internationalism," which is "generally compatible with the maintenance of existing geopolitical structure of authority and wealth in the world."[52] Others argue that the "NGO-led processes of human rights intervention are often inherently imperialist and colonial."[53] Environmental INGOs, the other largest group of INGOs, are criticized for humanizing "capitalist exploitation" and "often serve elite economic and political interests."[54]

The argument that INGOs tend to represent Western and corporate interests is supported by their affiliation with the World Bank. Leaders of INGOs that work with the World Bank might be considered part of the global shadow elite. The World Bank places INGOs in the category of "civil society." The World Bank describes its work with "civil society organizations" as follows:

> The World Bank first began to interact with civil society in the 1970s through dialogue with non-governmental organizations (NGOs) on environmental concerns. Today the World Bank consults and collaborates with thousands of members of Civil Society Organizations (CSOs) throughout the world, such as community-based organizations, NGOs, social movements, labor unions, faith-based groups, and foundations.[55]

The World Bank clearly states that its work with civil society organizations, including INGOs, is for the purpose of advancing their agenda:

> The World Bank has learned through these three decades of interaction that the participation of CSOs in government development projects and programs can enhance their operational performance by contributing local knowledge, providing technical expertise, and leveraging social capital. Further, CSOs can bring innovative ideas and solutions, as well as participatory approaches, to solving local problems.[56]

The World Bank describes their interactions with civil society groups as ranging from policy discussions to active collaboration with the Bank's activities: "There are many examples of active partnerships in the areas of forest conservation, AIDS vaccines, rural poverty, micro-credit, and internet development."[57]

Of course, human rights and environmental organizations agree more with the world culturalist description that they are an embodiment of "universalism" and "world citizenship." They might disagree with the labels of "individualism" and "progress" that are embodied in the phrase "humanitarian imperialism." Certainly, ecotage groups, as I discuss later in this chapter, such as Earth First!, see themselves working against the consumer-industrial model of global corporatization. The educational characteristics of these organizations tend not to follow the human capital education model and rely on progress education methods.

Similar to other worldwide organizations, there are differences between the global rhetoric of INGOs and the actual implementation of policies in local communities. One investigator of this disparity, Dana Burde, agrees with world culture theorists: "Insofar as INGOs' burgeoning presence in the world and increased influence on civil society have allowed, they have been able to promote world-cultural principles."[58] However, in his case study about the introduction of national parent-teachers associations in the former Yugoslavia by an INGO, he found a major difference between the global rhetoric and the results of implementation. The goals of the INGO were to promote high-quality early childhood education through an alliance of parent-teachers associations. Besides training the parents in early childhood development, the associations were to provide support groups for early childhood education programs. The results of his case study supported the idea of a growth of a world culture of education: "INGO model reforms do seem to be converging on an international level—most INGOs . . . share model program interventions and best practices . . . even among the local staff . . . there is a convergence . . . their rhetoric."[59] However, when it came to actual implementation: "Program beneficiaries . . . seem to either participate in old ways that are familiar to them . . . or are left out of the process altogether."[60]

INGOs and a Global Civil Society

INGOs are often thought of as part of a global civil society, as exemplified by the previous discussion about the World Bank, which are attempting to influence the actions of governments or acting as a parallel system of power to national governments. This suggests that leaders of INGOs might actually be a shadow elite working with global organizations and national political structures.

Some writers refer to the combination of INGOS, intergovernmental organizations (IGOs), and multinational corporations as the key elements of a global civil society. In *Global Community: The Role of International Organizations in the Making of the Contemporary World*, Akira Iriye contends that traditional histories of international relations primarily focus on national governments and diplomacy.[61]

What is missing from this historical perspective, he asserts, is the growth of a global civil society composed of a tangled web of interrelationships between IGOs and INGOS. Since the nineteenth century, the network of INGOS forming this global civil society sometimes supplants and competes with the actions of nation-states. In his history of the global community, Iriye divides the organizations of global civil society by their functions, such as humanitarian relief, cultural exchange, peace and disarmament, developmental assistance, religious, human rights, and environmentalism.[62] Intertwined with global civil society are IGOs such as the World Bank. Together, these form the basic structure of Iriye's *global community*. Iriye uses the International Red Cross as an example of the intertwined roles of INGOS and governments. In 1864, the Swiss government convened an international conference of government leaders to write a treaty that would ensure better treatment of those wounded in war. However, prior private efforts had already created the Red Cross headquarters in Geneva. Government representatives attending the conference signed a treaty supporting the Red Cross. The intergovernmental treaty contributed to the Red Cross as an INGO humanitarian organization being caught up in international politics. For instance, Japan insisted that Korea, which it had colonized in the early twentieth century, not be allowed to ratify the original treaty as a separate nation. The International Red Cross acceded to Japan's wishes, and the Korean Red Cross was put under the jurisdiction of the Japanese Red Cross. Iriye concludes, "The line between the state apparatus and a nonstate organization was never clear-cut."[63]

In a global civil society, human rights organizations form the largest group of INGOs. Human rights and other INGOs developed rapidly after World War II. Since 1850, 35,000 not-for-profit INGOs appeared on the world stage. While many of these disappeared overtime, after World War II the rate of dissolutions declined. For instance, in 1969 approximately 134 new INGOs were created while only about 20 dissolved.[64] The number of human rights organizations increased from 33 in 1953 to 168 in 1993, and they represent about 26.6 percent of the total global INGOs. The next largest number of INGOs is environmental with 90 groups in 1993 forming 14.3 percent of the global number. Environmental INGOs have been the fastest growing with only two groups having existed in 1953. Following environmentalist groups are women's rights INGOs whose numbers grew from 10 in 1953 to 61 in 1993. Other INGOs, in descending order of total number of organizations, are concerned with Peace, Esperanto, World Order, Development, Ethnic Unity/Group rights, and International Law.[65]

Human Rights INGOs and Progressive Education

Most instructional programs of human rights and environmental INGOs use progressive education methods that emphasize group work and cooperation, as well as education for social and activism. As I will explain later, the premise of many environmental groups is not the inevitable "progress" of human development but the potential destruction of humanity and the planet as a result of industrial-consumerism.

Human rights INGOs use progressive education methods to try and create a global human rights culture. This requires educators to develop in students a conscious awareness of human rights protections and abuses, as well as a desire to defend the human rights of others. In this context, consciousness or awareness of human rights requires all people to think about and interpret events in the context of human rights. This is supposed to create a global culture that shares an interpretative lens that makes sense of social actions by using a common set of human rights values. In other words, in a human rights culture people are to think about how their behavior and the behavior of others might or might not violate human rights. Education is to alert students to abuses of human rights and how to take action to correct them. Also, education is to prepare students to interpret their own actions according to whether they support or violate human rights.

Human rights education includes welfare issues such as the right to shelter, nutrition, medical care, and employment at a living wage. Many human rights educators argue that if people share a belief in welfare rights, then people's interpretative lenses would be calibrated to include an evaluation of the welfare of others as part of human rights. This would mean seeing the world through a framework that asks whether all people's human rights are protected and if they have adequate shelter, nutrition, medical care, and employment.[66]

The commitment of most human rights education is to promote a form of activism that will lead to the protection of the human rights of others. This represents the social activist part of the progressive education. An example is the Canadian Human Rights Foundation's instructional module for training human rights teachers, called *The Global Human Rights Context*. The objectives of this training module are to introduce human rights teachers to the "impact of globalization on human rights" and "issues related to global governance and their impact on civil society."[67] In the instructional module, globalization is presented as a complex phenomenon with both positive and negative effects. In the module's first unit, small groups of teachers are asked to read newspaper headlines with short quotes from the article. Examples of the headlines are "Amazon Tribe Sues for Survival," "Languages Are in Danger of Extinction," "Information Technology in the 21st Century," "Police Say Toronto a World Hub for Child Porn," and "New Front in Aids War."[68] They are then asked to compose lists of what they feel are the positive and negative influences of globalization and present them to the entire class. Two questions are for discussion: "In what ways can globalization create opportunities to better promote and protect human rights? In what ways do certain dimensions of globalization threaten or pose a danger to human rights?"[69] The second and third activities require human rights teachers to examine the impact of globalization on different world regions. The central question is, "How would you try, in this context, to promote respect for human rights in your community and region?"[70]

As illustrated in these training modules, the Canadian Human Rights Foundation wants students educated to participate in the regulating the effects of globalization on human rights. In Unit 2 of *The Global Human Rights Context*, module teachers are trained to effect specific organizations by creating a "Spheres of Influence" diagram. At the beginning of the module, human rights educators are told, "An understanding of power relations and structures at all levels of society (i.e., international, national and local) is an essential tool for the protection of human rights and social change. The aim of this activity is to identify the key actors and their influence on the globalization process in our societies."[71] The class is asked to consider how they might influence groups in the globalization process. These groups include the following: globalized economic institutions, the World Bank, the International Monetary Fund, regional development banks, multilateral trade organizations (such as the WTO), transnational corporations, national governments, ministries of international trade, ministries of education, ministries of finance, INGOs, and the global communications industry.

Power relations are central to this lesson. After completing the "Spheres of Influence" diagram, the class is given a statement designed to provoke discussion about the role of human rights educators in influencing power relations in a global society. The statement is an excerpt from the International Consultation on the Pedagogical Foundations of Human Rights Education declaration "Towards a Pedagogy of Human Rights Education." It begins, "Human rights education should be approached in a fashion that includes the analysis, understanding and reading of power relations and social forces so as to enable a struggle to change those power relations that impede the full realization of human rights."[72]

Another example of promoting human rights activism is the college textbook *Educating for Human Dignity: Learning about Rights and Responsibilities* written by Betty Reardon, a well-known U.S. leader in human rights and peace education.[73] The book provides instructional guidelines and models of lessons on human rights that can be used in classes ranging from kindergarten to the twelfth grade. An example of activist education is a twelfth-grade lesson titled, "Moral Development—From Awareness to Commitment, the Making of Human Rights Heroes."[74] Accompanying the lesson is a guide to "Phases in the Development of Moral Inclusion." These phases of "moral inclusion" move from "Spectator" to "Solidarity/Victim/Martyr." The guide emphasizes creating a global moral community: "The universal recognition of the full range of human rights for all peoples of the world depends in large part on widening our moral community and extending its boundaries to include all human beings."[75] Supposedly, members of a global human rights community would actively intervene, even to the extent of martyrdom, to protect universal human rights. "Moral inclusion" is defined as "a capacity that can be developed through both experiential and academic learning."[76]

According to Reardon, proper instruction can change the mere spectator into a martyr. In her steps of moral inclusion, the first three stages involve progressively greater involvement in human rights issues from "Spectator," "Observer," to "Witness." At the next stage, "Advocate," moral concerns about human rights cause them "to join advocacy groups, write letters to the editor, speak to schools, church groups, etc. Such people *advocate* the cause of the victims." "Advocate" is followed by "Activist" when people are "moved to the acceptance of personal responsibility and risk [in defending human rights]."[77] Activists assume personal responsibility to try and stop human rights' violations. At the final "Solidarity/Victim/Martyr," the person begins to take on personal risk in defending human rights. Reardon provides the following description of the "Solidarity/Victim/Martyr" stage of moral inclusion:

> Activism is most often pursued within one's own group or country, but some activists actually join in *solidarity* with the struggle and suffering of victims to work for human rights as a member of the victimized group. Such an activist risks being victimized herself even to the point of losing her life and thus becoming a *martyr* in the struggle for human rights. Do you know of such martyrs who are now considered heroes of human rights?[78]

Betty Reardon uses the interests of the child and activity-based instruction to have children develop their concepts of human rights. In the following human rights lesson, human rights are considered human needs. In her model second-grade lesson, "Wishing a World Fit for Children—Understanding Human Needs," Reardon instructs the teacher, "Tell the children that when we make wishes we use our imaginations. When we imagine good things and a better world, we actually begin to make the world better."[79] In the lesson, children write down wishes as gifts for a newborn baby. The gifts are supposed to represent things the baby will actually need, such as a bed, clothes, and food. The wishes are for something that will make the child's life more secure and happy. A class discussion of wishes and needs yields two lists, "Needs of a Child" and "Wishes for a Better World." The lesson concludes with teachers asking the second graders to "look at the list of wishes for a better world and think about what we need to learn to make a better world."[80]

Separating needs from wants is another method for students to construct their own human rights list. The following lesson is part of a larger text called *Human Rights Here & Now: Celebrating the Universal Declaration of Human Rights* issued by the Human Rights Educators' Network and Amnesty International USA.[81] An important feature of the book is linking human rights concepts to developmental stages of children's growth. In the context of developmental psychology, learning to differentiate between needs and wants is an activity for upper primary, ages 8 to 11. During these ages, there is an emphasis on teaching social responsibility and distinguishing wants from needs. The concept of needs, as opposed to wants, is then related to human rights. All the lessons are geared toward educating an activist citizen. In early childhood, which includes preschool and lower primary grades, it is recommended that human rights education begin with teaching respect for self, parents, teachers, and others. For this age group, the key learning concept is responsibility to the community by practicing in group situations self-expression and listening to others. Age-appropriate lessons are introduced on racism, sexism, unfairness, and hurting people. Concepts are introduced related to individual and group rights, freedom, equality, justice, and rule by law. Students learn to value diversity and to distinguish fact from opinion. Also, they perform school and community service. Students between the ages of 12 and 14 are taught about the content of human rights documents. They learn about international law, world peace, world developmental and economic issues, and legal and moral rights. They are taught how to understand another person's point of view, to do research on human rights issues, and to practice sharing information about community activities. In the final years of high school, students integrate human rights into their personal awareness and behaviors by participating in civic organizations and learning the power of civil disobedience.

Environmental INGOs and Progressive Education

Environmental INGOs, the second largest group of global nongovernment organizations, also emphasizes education for social and political activism. Environmental INGOs are important in promoting a sustainable environment. A combination of INGOs and the United Nations (the World Conservation Union, the United Nations Environment Programme, and the World Wide Fund for Nature) were responsible for the landmark 1991 Second World Conservation Report, *Caring for the Earth*, which declared, "We must act globally . . . The environment links all nations."[82] INGOs played a role in the demand for global civil action at both of the two major world environmental summits in the 1992 and 2002. In 1992, the Rio Earth Summit issued a declaration defining the basic elements of civic action from local to national levels. Meeting in Rio de Janeiro, the summit attracted representatives from 172 governments including 108 heads of state along with 2,400 representatives from INGOs. "Environmental issues," states the *Rio Declaration on Environment and Development* or, as it has been called, *Agenda 21*, "are best handled with the participation of all concerned citizens, at the relevant level. At the national level, each individual shall have appropriate access to information concerning the environment that is held by public authorities, including information on hazardous materials and activities in their communities, and the opportunity to participate in decision-making processes."[83] This was a call for direct participation and action by citizens as opposed to a reliance on elected representatives. The Rio Declaration calls on governments to ensure that the public is given information about environmental issues. "States shall facilitate and encourage public awareness," the declaration demands, "by making information widely available."[84] Civil society, including INGOs, is to spearhead environmental efforts.

Ten years after the Rio summit, another earth summit was held in Johannesburg with a similar global participation. Meeting at the Johannesburg summit, the Global People's Forum issued a "Civil Society Declaration." This declaration claims that the Global People's Forum represents those oppressed social groups named in *Agenda 21* of the Rio summit, including "women, youth, labour, indigenous peoples, farmers, NGOs, and others including disabled people, the elderly, faith-based organizations, peoples of African descent, social movements, people under foreign occupation and other under-represented groups."[85] In other words, the dispossessed and disadvantaged who feel their interests are not represented by nation-states. The declaration asserts that "as the key agents of social change and sustainable development, we are determined to take leadership for our future with utmost seriousness."[86]

Holistic education was supported by the Johannesburg declaration. Holistic education is a form of progressive education where the barriers between disciplines are broken down. Both John Dewey and Paulo Freire were holistic educators. Holistic education has two important meanings. In the first meaning, all human issues are interrelated with each other and the environment. The second meaning considers all arenas of human knowledge as a whole rather than separated into specific disciplines such as history, economics, physics, and biology. The Johannesburg declaration emphasizes the holistic nature of human and environmental issues in its description of a global civil society and its role in environmental protection.

> The definition of civil society includes, the major groups defined in Agenda 21, formal and informal community-based organizations, INGOs that work with and represent peoples who are victims of racism. Organizations of civil society have a central role to play in the translation of the Rio Principles and Agenda 21 into concrete programs, projects and implementation strategies for sustainable development . . . We affirm that solidarity and partnerships for sustainable development are those entered into on the basis of clearly defined human needs and related goals, objectives and actions for the elimination of poverty and the enhancement and restoration of the physical, social, and universal spiritual environment.[87]

The social activist aspect of environmental education is embodied in a 1969 definition by William Stapp of the University of Michigan. Stapp later coauthored important texts on environmental education. His 1969 definition is as follows: "Environmental education is aimed at producing a citizenry that is knowledgeable concerning the biophysical environment and its associated problems, aware of how to help solve these problems, and motivation to work toward their solution."[88]

In other words, social activism is supported by the WWF (formerly known as the World Wildlife Fund), which is a major INGO promoting environmental education. It differentiates between a narrow and broad focus in environmental education based on the degree of social activism. The WWF considers narrowly focused instruction as developing a "caring interest in the environment." This type of education does not attempt to engage the student in direct civic action. Activities are usually limited to picking up trash or planting a tree. In contrast, a broad instructional focus examines the relationship between "human behavior and global eco-systems" and develops "concerned awareness and participatory skills [civic action]."[89] These skills prepare students to engage in a range of activities from simply writing letters to political leaders to the direct action methods against perpetrators of environmental destruction.

Cultivating an awareness of environmental problems without teaching civic activism typifies the actual educational programs of the WWF. There is little instruction in social activism, which might explain its ties to the World Bank, UNESCO, governments, and other INGOs that make it a key player in the global civil society. Officially, the organization's mission

> Is to stop the degradation of our planet's natural environment, and build a future in which humans live in harmony with nature.
> In order to achieve this mission, WWF focuses its efforts on two broad areas:

> Biodiversity
> Footprint

> The first, is to ensure that the earth's web of life—biodiversity—stays healthy and vibrant for generations to come. We are strategically focusing on conserving critical places and critical species that are particularly important for the conservation of our earth's rich biodiversity.
> The second is to reduce the negative impacts of human activity—our ecological footprint. We are working to ensure that the natural resources required for life—land, water, air—are managed sustainably and equitably.[90]

Radical Environmentalism and Rejection of Global Corporatization

In contrast to INGOs that work with organizations promoting global corporatism, some environmental INGOS reject the very organization of the current economic system and oppose growing global corporatization. For instance, the EcoJustice education movement focuses on changing cultural values that are supportive of current economic systems. EcoJustice education advocates reject "commodification: or turning everything into a product for sale on the market. Expressed in the idea that 'education is an investment in the future'" for "non-commodified: traditions maintained based on intrinsic value and meaning.

Markets and monetary transactions are a small part of culture."[91] Most importantly, EcoJustice education rejects the concept that humans are the most important species and, consequently, should dominate all other species. Changing the belief that the earth exists primarily to serve the human species is central to the efforts of animal rights groups. Also, the belief in primacy of humans allows for wanton exploitation of natural resources and the extinction of other species. There is also a rejection of "mechanism: sees the world and life processes as being like a machine. Exhibited in such terms as 'information processing' and 'feedback systems'" in favor of "holistic/organic: sees world as interconnected like a living thing. Views humans and the rest of nature in reciprocal relationships of interdependence."[92]

Two examples of this radical rejection of humans as the central and dominant species are Earth First! and People for the Ethical Treatment of Animals (PETA). Earth First! teaches methods of direct action, such as tree sitting and blockading logging trucks to save forests or what it refers to as "monkeywrenching." Officially, Earth First! explains its activism as follows: "We believe in using all of the tools in the toolbox, from grassroots and legal organizing to civil disobedience and monkeywrenching. When the law won't fix the problem, we put our bodies on the line to stop the destruction. Earth First!'s direct-action approach draws attention to the crises facing the natural world, and it saves lives."[93]

"Monkeywrenching" refers to Edward Abbey's book *The Monkeywrench Gang*.[94] Monkeywrenching involves tree spiking, destruction of billboards, removal of surveying stakes, pouring sugar or sand into the fuel tanks of earthmoving machinery, and other forms of sabotage or, as it is called, "ecotage." Monkeywrenching, as described by the organization leaders of Earth First!, is a step beyond civil disobedience. Posted on the Earth First! website are articles supporting monkeywrenching, such as "Taking a Monkey Wrench to Climate Change: Renegade Naturalist Doug Peacock on Saving Ourselves from a Bleak Future." In the article, environmental activist Doug Peacock is portrayed as a "self-described desert rat honed his wilderness affinities under legendary conservationist Edward Abbey, author of Desert Solitaire, and was the inspiration for George Hayduke, the eco-saboteur central to the Monkey Wrench Gang. For anyone who's ever wanted to take a chainsaw to a billboard or watch a dam implode so a river can run free again, Peacock and Abbey have long been totems."[95]

While Earth First! denies any organizational support to monkeywrenching, it does admit that some local groups and individuals participate in this dramatic form of public education. Also, Earth First! distributes Dave Foreman and Bill Haywood's book *ECODEFENSE: A Field Guide to Monkeywrenching*.[96]

Acts of civil disobedience to protect the environment are compared to civil rights movements to end human slavery and discrimination among humans. The new civil rights movement is concerned with the rights of all species of animals and plants. A member of Earth First! proclaimed, "Earth First! shares Dr. King's commitment to individual rights. Today ... we publicly extend his vision to include oppressed members of our planetary society."[97] Bill Duvall describes civil disobedience as an important form of public education. Civil disobedience, he asserts, "is aimed at a larger audience, and the action should always be interpreted by the activists. Smart and creative communication of the message is as important as the action itself."[98]

Ecotage as a form of public education is more controversial because it involves potential harm to other humans and the destruction of property. For instance, the spiking of trees could hurt the logger or lumber mill worker. Similar to the arguments supporting civil disobedience, ecotage is compared to the violence used by abolitionists in their efforts to end human slavery. In addition, the intention of an act like spiking trees is to make the cutting of old growth forests unprofitable rather than harm other humans. The destruction of property, such as the burning of suburban construction sites, is justified according to the property rights of all humans as opposed to property rights of individuals and corporations. Peg Millett, arrested for knocking down an electrical tower in 1989, defines monkeywrenching as "the dismantling of the present industrial system, but I would define it as dismantling the machinery very carefully."[99]

PETA has used a variety of techniques to educate the public about animal rights from throwing acid on fur coats to passing out literature. One of their more interesting projects involves the distribution of packets of 52 cards called *Animal Rights: Weekend Warrior*. Representing each week of the year, the cards carry information and suggestions for civic action. Some of these suggestions are directed at public schools. The card for "Week 4" is titled "Veganize Your Cafeteria" and calls on schools to offer "a healthier, humane lunch program." It is suggested that the card owner meet with school food services and "request that a vegan entrée be offered at every meal, and suggest that cruelty-free alternatives, like vegan margarine, tofu sour cream . . . be made available. Be clear—meat flavorings and vegetables cooked in butter are unacceptable."[100] On another card, "Week 11: Cut Out Dissection," students are urged to write their teacher and principal "to express your feelings about dissection."[101] For "Week 2: Make a Library Display," weekend warriors are told to "educate others in your community about animal rights issues by creating a display for your local library."[102] Other cards suggest that weekend warriors go leather-free, hang banners, leaflet fur stores, and protest animal testing of products.

PETA's activities are having a global effect. For instance, PETA members sued the multinational fast-food franchise KFC to improve its treatment of chickens and to stop making false claims about its humane handling of animals. KFC slaughters more than 700 million chickens a year. In response to criticism from PETA, KFC created an Animal Welfare Advisory Council to establish standards for farms raising chickens for the franchise. In May 2003, PETA agreed to stop its boycott of KFC after the franchise required breeders to expand the cage size for chickens by 30 percent and to install cameras to ensure that the animals were killed in the most painless manner possible. However, in July 2003, PETA filed a legal suit complaining that "the birds raised and killed for the defendants operations suffer great pain and injuries in massive numbers."[103]

What is important about PETA's actions is the resulting establishment of global standards for the ethical treatment of animals. In the case of KFC, the company has officially stated, "As a major purchaser of food products, we have the opportunity, and responsibility, to influence the way animals are treated. We take that responsibility very seriously. We only deal with suppliers who maintain the very highest standards and share our commitment to animal welfare."[104] PETA has also won concessions regarding the treatment of animals from the fast-food franchises McDonald's, Wendy's, and Burger King.

In summary, while some INGOs function as "humanitarian imperialism" with links to corporate advocates like the World Bank, others reject global corporatization, such as Earth First! Most human rights and environmental INGOs use progressive education methods stressing some form of social activism. Consequently, these INGOs have global education models of education that are different from the dominant human capital model. In fact, an INGO like Earth First! rejects the industrial-consumer system on which human capital education is premised. These competing global education models support the contention that there is no single uniform global education culture.

KEY POINTS: GLOBAL CIVIL SOCIETY AND INGOS

1. The global civil society consists of voluntary organizations
   a. Formal and informal community-based organizations
   b. Formal and informal nongovernmental organizations within a nation
   c. INGOs
2. Members of the global civil society issue policies and set standards that influence
   a. Local governments
   b. National governments
   c. Global IGOs such as the World Bank, the United Nations, OECD, etc.
3. The major global INGOs in rank order of numbers of organizations
   a. Human rights
   b. Environmental
   c. Women's rights
   d. Peace
   e. Esperanto
   f. Ethnic unity/group rights
4. INGO's support the following forms of progressive education
   a. Preparation of students for active participation in solving problems of social justice
   b. Preparation of students to actively change the political and economic system
   c. Cultural liberation using Freirian methods

Culturalists: Progressive Education

Rejecting the existence of a single world culture of education, culturalists frequently refer to progressive education models as alternatives in the global discourse. In keeping with the culturalist argument that global practices are adapted to local circumstances, progressive education methods have been adapted to local circumstances.

As presented in Chapter 1, progressive education world models contains the following elements:

Progressive Education World Model

1. Teacher professionalism and autonomy;
2. Learning based on students' interests and participation;
3. Active learning;
4. Protection of local languages;
5. Education for ensuring social justice;
6. Education for active participation in determining social and political change.

These elements take on different meaning depending on the particular locality and educational theorist. For example, the progressivism associated with American educational philosopher John Dewey was borrowed by many Chinese educators after his visit in the early 1920s and by Soviet educators in the 1920s in the form of the Dalton plan.[105] In a different form, Paulo Freire's progressive educational ideas became part of the global educational discourse after the publication of *Pedagogy of the Oppressed* in 1968.[106]

It is not within the scope of this book to review every form of progressive education, but there is one common element in all its forms, namely education for active participation in determining social and political change. This common element is easily contrasted with the human capital model of educating for work within the knowledge economy. The type of participation in social and political method varies with each form of progressive education ranging from working within existing government structures to revolution.

Jürgen Schriewer and Carlos Martinez demonstrated the borrowing of progressive models in their comparative research on the internationalization of educational knowledge.[107] They did a content analysis of education journals in Spain, Russia/Soviet Union, and China from the 1920s to the mid-1990s. They found that all three nations from the 1920s to the early 1930s displayed an intense interest in global education discourses particularly in what Schriewer and Martinez call "the international progressive education movement."[108]

Their findings confirm the early existence of a global progressive education model. In their words, "Based on quantitative data ... our findings have come to confirm the thesis of the internationality of the progressive education reform movement, a thesis supported thus far mainly ... [by] this movement's self interpretations developed by its followers."[109]

This early global movement of progressive education ideas was not revolutionary, but they became associated with revolutionary movements.[110] John Dewey was not a political revolutionary, and his educational ideas were never intended to foment armed rebellion. When Dewey lectured in China, he introduced ideas about basing education on the interest of the child, the social construction of the curriculum, learning by doing, the use of social imagination, and educating students for active participation in the reconstruction of society using the tools of a democratic government. He never told his audiences that they should use his ideas to arm the people to fight against control by wealthy social classes. By the time Dewey left China in 1921, he had given 78 different series of lectures. At the time of his departure, 100,000 copies of his Peking lectures—a 500 page book—were in circulation, and three of his lectures were reprinted as classroom texts.[111] Dewey's visit was sponsored by China's Society for the Promotion of New Education, which used his ideas to justify their reform proposals. In part, this organization was responsible for the Chinese government's School Reform Decree of 1922, which adopted the American school model of six years of elementary school, three years of junior high school, and three years of high school. When Dewey returned from China in 1922, he expressed his doubts on having any meaningful impact on Chinese education:

> The difficulties in the way of a practical extension and regeneration of Chinese education are all but insuperable. Discussion often ends in an impasse: no political reform of China without education; but no development of schools as long as military men and corrupt officials divert funds and oppose schools from motives of self-interest. Here are the materials of a tragedy of the first magnitude.[112]

Mao Zedong was one revolutionary who did become acquainted with Dewey's educational ideas while selling Dewey's lectures from his Cultural Bookstore. Mao opened the bookstore after being trained as a teacher in a Western-style teaching preparation program at the Human Fourth Provincial Normal School. After graduation, Mao experimented with establishing anarchist-communal villages. In 1920, he founded the Self-Study University of Changsha and the Cultural Bookstore. Indicating the interest being taken in John Dewey's Chinese lecture series, more books were sold through the bookstore by anarchist Prince Kropotkin and John Dewey than by Marx. Mao openly rejected Dewey's ideas because they lacked a class analysis despite there being parallels in their educational thought. Dewey and Mao Zedong's pedagogies both stressed linking theory and practice, and having students understand the social origins of knowledge.[113]

Another example of the culturalist's framework of borrowing and lending is the work of Paulo Freire, a truly revolutionary progressive educator. He noted the influence of Mao's progressive educational ideas in *Pedagogy of the Oppressed.* Freire wrote, "This appears to be the fundamental aspect of Mao's Cultural Revolution."[114] Regarding his important proposal for dialogical instruction that helps learners understand how their subjective beliefs shape their interpretation of the objective world, Freire noted,

> Mao-Zedong declared, "You know I've proclaimed for a long time: we must teach the masses clearly what we have received from them confusedly" . . . This affirmation contains an entire dialogical theory of how to construct the program content of education, which cannot be elaborated according to what the *educator* thinks best for his students.[115]

When Paulo Freire referred to the "fundamental aspect of Mao's Cultural Revolution," it was in support of his assertion:

> The pedagogy of the oppressed, as a humanist and libertarian pedagogy, has two distinct stages. In the first, the oppressed unveil the world of oppression and through the praxis commit themselves to its transformation. In the second stage, in which the reality of oppression has already been transformed, this pedagogy ceases to belong to the oppressed and becomes a pedagogy of all men in the process of permanent liberation. In both stages, it is always through action in depth that the culture of domination is culturally confronted.[116]

The new progressive pedagogy of Paulo Freire emerged from the upheaval of South American revolutions, which, in part, included the borrowing of Marxist ideas to plan for the liberation of Indigenous and peasant populations. Marxist rhetoric was used in the 1952 Bolivian National Revolutionary Movement, the 1953 to 1959 Cuban Revolution, the revolutionary projects of Che Guevara, the 1960 overthrow of the Venezuelan government, the 1963 creation of the Venezuelan Armed Forces of National Liberation (FALN), and the 1961 Nicaraguan insurgency led by the Sandinista National Liberation Front.[117]

An important influence on Freire was the Cuban literacy crusade that took place after Fidel Castro's guerilla forces overthrew the dictatorship of Fulgencio Batista on January 1, 1959. Castro feared that if a revolutionary education stressing critical and dialectical thought was not initiated, then the Cuban people would never be free because of the hegemony of colonial masters. He stated that education should "prevent cultural colonization from surviving economic colonization."[118] Similar to Mao and Latin American Marxists, Castro emphasized the importance of relating theory to practice and schooling to work. He envisioned attaching schools to workplaces. Liss summarized Castro's educational ideas as follows:"People do not learn by indoctrination, by having their heads filled with bits and pieces of theory. They learn by thinking, analyzing, and searching history for lessons and answers. In Castro's ideal revolutionary society, people go to school to learn, dissect, to understand."[119]

Following the revolution, Che Guevara declared that society must become a "gigantic" school. Referring to the literacy crusade, Che wrote in 1965 that the state should give direct political instruction to the people: "Education takes hold among the masses and the foreseen new attitude tends to become a habit. The masses continue to make it their own and to influence those who have not yet educated themselves. This is the indirect form of educating the masses, as powerful, as the other, structured, one."[120]

Freire was exposed to the ideas of the Cuban literacy campaign when he went to Chile in 1964 after being exiled following a coup d'état by the Brazilian military elite. During his exile, Freire's socialist philosophy and instructional methods crystallized, and he wrote *Pedagogy of the Oppressed*. In 1964, Chile was in a political ferment, which would eventually result in the first elected Latin American Marxist government in 1970 under the leadership of Salvador Allende. In the charged atmosphere of Chilean politics, Freire met socialists from many Latin American countries, including Cuba. It was here that he read Che Guevara's statement that "the true revolutionary is guided by great feelings of love." In reference to the Cuban presence and Guevara's statement on love, Freire wrote, "The Cubans showed that changes could be made . . . Guevara's capacity for love was there."[121] In *Pedagogy of the Oppressed*, he used the quote on love from Guevara to justify the statement, "Dialogue cannot exist, however, in the absence of a profound love for the world and for men. The naming of the world, which is an act of creation and re-creation, is not possible if it is not infused in love."[122] He used Guevara's quote to footnote the following statement: "I am more and more convinced that true revolutionaries must perceive the revolution, because of its creative and liberating nature, as an act of love."[123]

In *Pedagogy of the Oppressed*, Freire emphasized the lessons he learned in the Chile. He criticized educators who "approach the peasant or urban masses with projects which may correspond to their own view of the world, but not to that of the people."[124] Interestingly, he supported this conclusion with a lengthy footnote from the writings of Mao Zedong, which ended, "There are two principles here: one is the actual needs of the masses rather than what we fancy they need, and the other is the wishes of the masses, who must make up their own minds instead of our making up their minds for them."[125] Freire believed that a dialogical interaction with peasants, Indigenous peoples, and the urban workers was the key to their involvement in social transformation.

Obviously, there is a lot more to say about the sources Freire borrowed from in developing his educational theory. There is also the question of how many borrowed from Freire. Even today Freire's ideas are influential in the liberation theology movement (which I discuss in more detail in Chapter 6). By the end of the

1970s, wars of liberation in Nicaragua and El Salvador sparked literacy crusades that reflected the influence of liberation theology and Paulo Freire's pedagogical methods. Both countries were composed of ruling elites, impoverished peasants, and Indigenous peoples. In 1961, the Sandinista National Liberation Front was formed in Nicaragua, which overthrew the dictatorship of the Somoza dynasty in 1979. In neighboring El Salvador, the Farabundo Marti National Liberation Front was formed in 1980 resulting in a decade of civil war with major areas of the country captured by the Liberation Front in 1989. In both countries, literacy crusades were considered fundamental parts of the revolutionary movement.[126]

Schriewer and Martinez's previously cited quantitative study of the international progressive education movement includes an example of the spread of Freire's ideas. One of their data analyses used citations from the 1994 *International Encyclopedia of Education*. Paul Freire ranked twenty-third in the number of citations. Not bad considering that UNESCO was second, OECD was fifth, the World Bank was ninth, and John Dewey was thirty-first.[127] Also, Freirian educational methods still operate as a counterpoint to the human capital model. In a detailed study, which my brief description does not do justice, Lesley Bartlett describes two competing literacy projects in Brazil. One is funded by the World Bank and the other by liberation theologists in the Brazilian Catholic Church using Freirian methods.[128]

Conclusion: Corporatization of Global Education, English, and the Rejection of Consumerist Economics

Corporatization of education is resulting from the selling of products and services by the multinational education industry. What I mean by corporatization of education is the domination of school policies by global industries that see schools as a place to sell products and services and train corporate workers. These corporate interests also support school policies that will yield profits from the sale of tests, software, computer hardware, and other products, including for-profit schools. Education policy becomes a profit opportunity.

Corporatization extends to the standardization of world Englishes for use in global businesses and trade. Language testing by international organizations like ETS and the treatment of English as a lingua franca is contributing to this standardization. I would argue that the goal is standardizing global English usage around the needs of corporations or, as stated earlier in this chapter, teaching "the English words your boss wants to hear."

Some INGOs are interconnected with corporate interests and provide business interests with a positive public image. They can be accused of "humanitarian imperialism" and serving "global capitalist interests." Some are part of a network connected to such institutions as the World Bank.

Culturalists point to the various forms of progressive education as a dissenting global force to human capital education. Human rights and environmental

INGOs use progressive education methods to teach social activism. This sets them apart from human capital education, which stresses educating conformist workers and not political and social activists. Some environmental INGOs reject the basic premises of consumer-industrial societies and call for a new form of economic system that considers humans as one species among other species, rejects commodification of human activities and goods, and values a holistic view of the interrelationship between humans and the environment.

In summary, there is tension between education corporatization and INGOs teaching social activism and rejection of the current global economic structure. However, I would argue, for-profit education corporations are contributing to global uniformity of national school policies and practices along with promoting the growth of a corporatized form of English. In this framework, schools will educate compliant workers who use English as a lingua franca that is stripped of political meaning. Workers can talk about work with each other but may lack the words to protest working conditions, unfair labor practices, and economic inequalities.

Notes

1 Aziz Choudry and Dip Kapoor, editors, *NGOization: Complicity, Contradictions and Prospects* (New York: Zed Books, 2013).

2 Stephen J. Ball, *Global Education Inc.: New Policy Networks and the Neo-Liberal Imaginary* (London: Routledge, 2012), pp. 71, 92.

3 Janine Wedel, *Shadow Elite: How the World's New Power Brokers Undermine Democracy, Government, and the Free Market* (New York: Basic Books, 2009).

4 Ball, *Global Education Inc.*, p. 9.

5 Ibid.

6 Ibid., p. 92.

7 Anthony G. Picciano and Joel Spring, *The Great American Education-Industrial Complex: Ideology, Technology, and Profit* (New York: Routledge, 2013), pp. 22–33.

8 Amplify, "Company." Retrieved from www.amplify.com/company on November 20, 2013.

9 Picciano and Spring, *The Great American Education-Industrial Complex*, pp. 25–28.

10 Ball, *Global Education Inc.*, p. 71.

11 Ibid., p. 70.

12 Ibid., p. 74.

13 Ibid., p. 75.

14 Ibid., p. 93.

15 Samuel Trosow and Kirsti Nilsen, *Constraining Public Libraries: The World Trade Organization's General Agreement on Trade in Services* (Lanham, MD: Scarecrow Press, 2006).

16 Ibid., p. 89.

17 Ingram, "About Ingram Content Group." Retrieved from www.ingramcontent.com/pages/company.aspx on November 26. 2013 .

18 Coutts, "Services for Academic and Professional Libraries." Retrieved from www.ingramcontent.com/Pages/Academic-library.aspx on November 26, 2013.

19 Bertelsmann, "Corporate Divisions." Retrieved from www.bertelsmann.com on July 8, 2007; HCIRN, "Human–Computer Interaction Resource Network." Retrieved from

www.hcirn.com on July 13, 2007; HCIRN, "Kluwer Academic Publishers"; Informa, "About." Retrieved from www.informa.com on July 14, 2007; Informa, "Divisions: Taylor and Francis"; Holtzbrinck Publishers, "Who We Are." Retrieved from www. holtzbrinck.com/ on July 13, 2007; Pearson Education, "About Pearson Education." Retrieved from www.pearsoned.com on July 16, 2007; Reed Elsevier, "About Us." Retrieved from www.reed-elsevier.com on July 17, 2007; The McGraw-Hill Companies, "Education. Financial Services. Information & Media." Retrieved from www. mcgraw-hill.com on July 13, 2007.

20 Verlagsgruppe Georg Von Holtzbrinck, "The Company." Retrieved from www.holtz brinck.com/artikle/778433&s=en on January 7, 2008.

21 Holtzbrinck Publishers, "Employment Opportunities." Retrieved from www.holtz brinckusa-jobs.com on January 7, 2008.

22 Informa, "Divisions: Taylor and Francis." Retrieved from www.informa.com/corpo rate/divisions/academic_scientific/taylor_francis.htm on July 14, 2007.

23 Pearson, "Pearson at a Glance." Retrieved from www.pearson.com/about-us/pear son-at-a-glance.html on November 26, 2013.

24 Pearson, "Education." Retrieved from www.pearson.com/about-us/education.html on November 26, 2013.

25 Ball, *Global Education Inc.*, pp. 126–127.

26 McGraw-Hill Education, "About Us." Retrieved from www.mheducation.com/ about/about-us on November 26, 2013.

27 Ibid.

28 Ibid.

29 Springer Science+Business Media, "Developing Countries Initiatives." Retrieved from www.springer-sbm.com on July 23, 2007.

30 Pearson, "About Pearson VUE: History." Retrieved from www.pearsonvue.com/ about/history/ on November 26, 2013.

31 Pearson VUE, "About: Markets." Retrieved from www.pearsonvue.com/about/mar kets/ on November 26, 2013.

32 Ruby Chua, "Pearson VUE Testing." E-mail received on February 5, 2008 from Technology Training Center, Queens College.

33 Ibid.

34 Thomas Wailgum, "Testing 1,2, 3: Kurt Landgraf of ETS Has All the Right Answers," *Continental* (January 2008), p. 59.

35 ETS, "About: Who We Are." Retrieved from https://www.ets.org/about/who/ on November 26, 2013.

36 Ibid.

37 English as a Lingua Franca, "6th Annual Meeting of English as a Lingua Franca." Retrieved from http://host.uniroma3.it/eventi/elf6/information.php on November 27, 2013.

38 Barbara Seidlhofer, "English as a Lingua Franca," *ELT Journal* (October 4, 2005). Retrieved from http://host.uniroma3.it/eventi/elf6/information.php on November 27, 2013.

39 Ibid., p. 338.

40 Ibid., p. 339.

41 Philip Altbach, "The Imperial Tongue: English as the Dominating Academic Language," *International Higher Education* (Fall 2007) No. 49, pp. 2–5. Retrieved from www.bc.edu/ bc_org/avp/soe/cihe/newsletter/Number49/p2_Altbach.htm on December 19, 2007.

42 Ibid., p. 2.

43 Ibid., pp. 2–4.

44 Ibid., p. 3.

45 Ibid., p. 4.

46 Ibid., p. 5.

47 John Boli and George M.Thomas, editors, *Constructing World Culture: International Non-governmental Organizations since 1875* (Palo Alto, CA: Stanford University Press, 1999).

48 John Boli, Thomas A. Loya, and Teresa Loftin, "National Participation in World-Polity Organization," in *Constructing World Culture*, p. 53.

49 Ibid.

50 Ibid., p. 56.

51 Aziz Choudry and Dip Kapoor, "Introduction," in *NGOization: Complicity, Contradictions and Prospects*, p. 4.

52 Ibid.

53 Ibid., p. 5.

54 Aziz Choudry, "Saving Biodiversity, for Whom and for What? Conservation NGOs, Complicity, Colonialism and Conquest in an Era of Capitalist Globalization," in *NGOization: Complicity, Contradictions and Prospects*, p. 25.

55 World Bank, "The World Band and Civil Society." Retrieved from http://web.world bank.org/WBSITE/EXTERNAL/TOPICS/CSO/0,,contentMDK:20092185~menu PK:220422~pagePK:220503~piPK:220476~theSitePK:228717,00.html on November 29, 2013.

56 Ibid.

57 World Bank, "Civil Society Organizations." Retrieved from http://web.worldbank. org/WBSITE/EXTERNAL/TOPICS/CSO/0,,contentMDK:20127718~menuPK: 288622~pagePK:220503~piPK:220476~theSitePK:228717,00.html on November 27, 2013.

58 Dana Burde, "International NGOs and Best Practices: The Art of Educational Lending," in *The Global Politics of Educational Borrowing and Lending* , edited by Gita Steiner-Khamsi, (New York: Teachers College Press, 2004), p. 174.

59 Ibid., p. 183.

60 Ibid.

61 Akira Iriye, *Global Community: The Role of International Organizations in the Making of the Contemporary World* (Berkeley: University of California Press, 2002).

62 Ibid., p. 3.

63 Ibid., p. 14.

64 "INGOs and the Organization of World Culture," in *Constructing World Culture: International Nongovernmental Organizations Since 1875*, edited by John Boli and George M. Thomas, (Palo Alto: Stanford University Press, 1999), p. 23.

65 Margaret E. Keck and Kathryn Sikkink, *Activists Beyond Borders* (Ithaca, NY: Cornell University Press, 1998), p. 11.

66 Joel Spring, *How Educational Ideologies Are Shaping Global Society: Intergovernmental Organizations, NGOs, and the Decline of the Nation-State* (Mahwah, NJ: Lawrence Erlbaum, 2004), pp. 68–71.

67 Canadian Human Rights Foundation, *Module: The Global Human Rights Context* (Montreal: Canadian Human rights Foundation, 2002), p. 10.

68 Ibid., p. 14.

69 Ibid., p. 16.

70 Ibid., p. 19.

71 Ibid., p. 23.

72 Ibid., p. 25.

73 Betty Reardon, *Educating for Human Dignity: Learning about Rights and Responsibilities: A K-12 Teaching Resource* (Philadelphia: University of Pennsylvania Press, 1995).

74 Ibid., pp. 189–191.

75 Ibid., p. 192.

76 Ibid.

77 Ibid., p. 193.

78 Ibid., p. 194.

79 Ibid., pp. 33–35.

80 Ibid., p. 35.

81 *Human Rights Here & Now: Celebrating the Universal Declaration of Human Rights* (Minneapolis, MN: Human Rights Educators' Network, Amnesty International USA, Human rights Resource Center, 1998). The copy of the book I used is available online at www.hrusa.org/hrh-and-n/ and has unnumbered pages.

82 Second World Conservation Strategy Project, *Caring for the Earth: A Strategy for Sustainable Living* (Gland, Switzerland: The World Conservation Union/United Nations Environment Programme/World Wide Fund For Nature, 1991), p. 77.

83 Paul Pace, "From Belgrade to Bradford—20 Years of Environmental Education," in *A Sourcebook for Environmental Education: A Practical Review Based on the Belgrade Charter*, edited by W. Leal Filho, Z. Murphy, and O'Loan (Pearl River, NY: Parthenon, 1996), p. 18.

84 Ibid., p. 19.

85 The Global People's Forum, "Civil Society Declaration" (24 August–3 September 2002). Retrieved from www.staff.city.ac.uk/p.willetts/NGOS/WSSD/GPF-DECL. HTM on November 27, 2013.

86 Ibid.

87 Ibid.

88 EELink: A Project of the North American Association for Environmental Education, "Perspectives: Foundations of EE." Retrieved from http://eelink.net/perspectives foundationsofee.html on January 5, 2005.

89 A four-part table of the World Wildlife Fund's emerging forms of education is given in William B. Stapp, Arjen E.J. Wals, and Sheri L. Stankorb, *Environmental Education for Empowerment: Action Research and Community Problem Solving* (Dubuque, IA: Kendall/Hunt, 1996), p. 6. This publication is copyrighted by the Global Rivers Environmental Education Network.

90 WWF, "What Does WWF Do?" Retrieved from http://wwf.panda.org/what_we_do/ on November 27, 2013.

91 Rebecca A. Martusewicz, Jeff Edmundson, and John Lupinacci, *EcoJustice Education: Toward Diverse, Democratic, and Sustainable Communities* (New York: Routledge, 2011), p. 80.

92 Ibid.

93 Earth First!, "About Earth First." Retrieved from http://earthfirstjournal.org/about/ on November 27, 2013.

94 Edward Abbey, *The Monkeywrench Gang* (New York: Perennial, 2000).

95 Earth First!, "Taking a Monkey Wrench to Climate Change: Renegade Naturalist Doug Peacock on Saving Ourselves from a Bleak Future by Elizabeth Miller / Boulder Weekly." Retrieved from http://earthfirstjournal.org/newswire/2013/06/07/taking-a-monkey-wrench-to-climate-change/ on November 27, 2013.

96 Dave Foreman and Bill Haywood, *ECODEFENSE: A Field Guide to Monkeywrenching* (Chico, CA: Abbzug Press, 1993).

97 Quoted in Christopher Manes, *Green Rage: Radical Environmentalism and the Unmaking of Civilization* (Boston: Little, Brown and Company, 1990), p. 167.

98 Ibid., p. 170.

99 Ibid., p. 190.

100 Ingrid Newkirk, "Week 4: Veganize Your Cafeteria" in *Animal Rights: Weekend Warrior* (New York: Lantern Books, 2003).

101 Ingrid Newkirk, "Week 11: Cut Out Dissection," in *Animal Rights: Weekend Warrior.*

102 Ingrid Newkirk, "Week 2: Make a Library Display," in *Animal Rights: Weekend Warrior.*

103 Elizabeth Becker, "Animal Rights Group to Sue Fast-Food Chain," *New York Times* (July 7, 2003), p. A11.

104 Ibid.

105 See Barry Keenan, *The Dewey Experiment in China: Educational Reform and Political Power in the Early Republic* (Cambridge, MA: Harvard University Press, 1977); and the story of the Soviet use of the Dalton method and Stalin's reaction in the 1930s can be found in Larry Holmes, *Stalin's School: Moscow's Model School No. 25, 1931–1937* (Pittsburgh, PA: University of Pittsburgh Press, 1999).

106 The Portuguese manuscript was completed in 1968, and it was published in the United States as Paulo Freire, *Pedagogy of the Oppressed* (New York: Herder and Herder, 1970).

107 Jürgen Schriewer and Carlos Martinez, "Constructions of Internationality in Education," in Gita Steiner-Khamsi, *The Global Politics of Educational Borrowing and Lending,* pp. 29–52.

108 Ibid., p. 45.

109 Ibid.

110 For a general study of the internationalization of progressivism and other educational ideas, see Joel Spring, *Pedagogies of Globalization: The Rise of the Educational Security State* (Mahwah, NJ: Lawrence Erlbaum, 2006).

111 Keenan, *The Dewey Experiment in China,* pp. 30–33.

112 As quoted in Ibid., p. 78.

113 See Philip Short, *Mao: A Life* (New York: Henry Holt and Company, 1999), pp. 1–133.

114 Freire, *Pedagogy of the Oppressed,* p. 40.

115 Ibid., p. 82.

116 Ibid., p. 40.

117 The best general summary of global wars of liberation is Daniel Moran's *Wars of National Liberation* (London: Cassell, 2001).

118 Sheldon Liss, *Fidel! Castro's Political and Social Thought* (Boulder, CO: Westview Press, 1994), p. 137.

119 Ibid., p. 139.

120 Che Guevara, "Socialism and Man in Cuba," *Global Justice: Liberation and Socialism* (Melbourne, Australia: Ocean Press, 2002), p. 35. This book was published in cooperation with Che Guevara Studies Center in Havana, Cuba.

121 Paulo Freire, *Pedagogy of Hope: Reliving Pedagogy of the Oppressed* (New York: Continuum, 2004), p. 43.

122 Freire, *Pedagogy of the Oppressed,* p. 77.

123 Ibid.

124 This is footnote #10 on p. 83 of Freire's *Pedagogy of the Oppressed,* which is cited as "From the *Selected Works of Mao-Tse-Tung,* Vol. III. 'The United Front in Cultural Work' (October 30, 1944) (Peking, 1967), pp. 186–187."

125 Freire, *Pedagogy of the Oppressed,* p. 83.

126 See Sheryl Hirshon with Judy Butler, *And Also Teach Them to Read: The National Literacy Crusade of Nicaragua* (Westport, CT: Lawrence Hill & Company, 1983); and John L. Hammond, *Fighting to Learn: Popular Education and Guerilla War in El Salvador* (New Brunswick, NJ: Rutgers University Press, 1998).

127 Schriewer and Martinez, , "Constructions of Internationality in Education," p. 43.

128 Lesley Bartlett, "World Culture or Transnational Project? Competing Educational Projects in Brazil," in *Local Meanings, Global Schooling: Anthropology and World Culture Theory*, edited by Kathryn Anderson-Levitt, (New York: Palgrave Macmillan 2003), pp. 183–197.

6

RELIGIOUS AND INDIGENOUS EDUCATION MODELS

A Clash of Civilizations?

Many religious and Indigenous peoples disagree with the values that world culture theorists believe are part of a growing global uniformity. Some religious and Indigenous groups are major dissenters to the world culture model and the materialism embodied in the human capital and progressive models of education. There is also an argument about a "clash of civilizations" resulting from religious differences. Religious and Indigenous viewpoints have created tensions within global educational superstructure. Also, religious and Indigenous groups often resist and change global models when they are used in local-level communities.

By religious knowledge I mean those modes of learning, perceptions, beliefs, and forms of reasoning associated with organized religions. Most, if not all, organized religions have some educational program to propagate their particular form of knowledge. Indigenous knowledge has two sources. One is local forms of knowledge that are different from those embedded in world culture and world education culture. The second are knowledges associated with Indigenous peoples. In Chapter 1, I identified Indigenous peoples (sometimes referred to as First Nations, Indigenous ethnic minorities, native minorities, and tribes) as those recognized as such by the United Nations and that have as a key characteristic close attachment to ancestral territories and their natural resources.

As I discuss in this chapter, religious and Indigenous perspectives add a conflictual dimension to what I have called the global superstructure of education. As Eduardo Mendieta asserts, "A theory of globalization that makes no room for religion has major theoretical flaws."[1] Some religious groups reject what they believe are the central values of globalization, namely secularization, individual autonomy, and freedom. In a similar vein, the editors' introduction to *Indigenous Knowledges in Global Contexts* expresses concern that "for indigenous peoples, the 'crisis of knowledge' can be seen in . . . fragmentation of traditional values and beliefs; erosion of spirituality; distortions in local, regional, and national ecosystems and economies; and tensions related in cultural revitalization and reclamation."[2]

The Existence of Knowledges

The concept of knowledges, in contrast to a single knowledge, assumes the existence of multiple ways of seeing and knowing the world. The organization and networks I have so far discussed believe that schools will educate from the perspective of a single world knowledge. However, progressive education, as I discussed in Chapter 5, involves recognition of other ways of thinking and knowing the world. Paul Wangoola, the founder of Mpambo, the African Multiversity in Uganda, explains the importance of understanding the existence of multiple world knowledges, "A *multi*versity differs from a *uni*versity insofar as it recognizes that the existence of alternative knowledges is important to human knowledge as a whole."[3] Why are Indigenous knowledges important? Wangoola argues that the "problems human kind today cannot be resolved by modern scientific knowledge alone, or by indigenous knowledge alone. More durable solutions will be found in new synthesis between indigenous knowledges and modern scientific knowledge."[4] One group of defenders of the knowledges of Indigenous peoples assert, "Increasingly within [Indigenous] communities, refreshing critical voices are emerging to question the processes of knowing and validating knowledge and disseminating it across national and global spaces."[5]

Cross-cultural psychologists have provided a wealth of evidence on differences in ways of knowing and seeing the world. It is certainly beyond the scope of this book to review all of their findings. One cross-cultural psychologist, Richard Nisbett, discusses these findings in *The Geography of Thought: How Asians and Westerners Think Differently . . . and Why.*[6] Nisbett's book highlights differences in ways of knowing by comparing results of psychological experiments in the United States and in Confucian-based countries (China, Japan, and the Republic of Korea). The assumption is that there is a difference between the brain (organic) and the mind (organic + experience). Every person has the same basic physical brain, which interacts with different environments resulting in a variety ways of thinking and knowing the world. Nisbett provides a complex argument about the growth of differing ways of knowing. He highlights the following differences:

1. Regard the self as part of a larger interdependent whole (Confucian)/Regard the self as a unitary free agent (Western);
2. Regard the world as complex, interrelated, constantly changing (Confucian)/ Regard the world as divided into discrete and separate parts (Western);
3. Desire for blending harmoniously with the group (Confucian)/Desire for individual distinctiveness (Western);

4. Attuned to feelings of others and striving for interpersonal harmony (Confucian)/More concern with knowing one's own feelings (Western);
5. Value success and achievement because it reflects well on the group (Confucian)/Value success and achievement because it makes the individual look good (Western);
6. Preference for societies governed by social obligations (Confucian)/Preference for societies governed by the rule of law (Western);
7. Preference for judging behavior according to the situation (Confucian)/Preference for judging behavior according universal rules (Western).

Nisbett's work challenged the assumption that there was only a single way of knowing. At the time of publication, it was a groundbreaking book in cross-cultural psychology. Renowned psychologist Robert Sternberg asserted, "Nisbett shows conclusively that laboratory experiments limited to American college students or even individuals from the Western Hemisphere simply cannot provide an adequate understanding of how people, in general, think."[7] Anthropologist and human development expert at the University of Chicago Richard Shweder contends, "*The Geography of Thought* challenges a fundamental premise of the Western Enlightenment—the idea that modes of thought are, ought to be, or will become the same wherever you go—east or west, north or south—in the world."[8] Multiple intelligence guru Howard Gardner describes Nisbett's work "as a research-based challenge to the assumption, widespread among cognitive scientists, that thinking the world over is the same."[9]

Nisbett's work indirectly confirmed research that found different ways of knowing among Indigenous peoples. For example, Marlene Brant Catellano's research among the First Nations of Canada found very distinct differences between Indigenous and Western ways of knowing. She divides the distinctive features of First Nations peoples' way of knowing into "Sources of Knowledge" and "Characteristics of Aboriginal Knowledge." Under sources of knowledge, Catellano identifies three sources of knowledge: traditional knowledge, which is handed down from generation to generation; empirical knowledge based on careful observation in contrast to the use of the scientific method; and revealed knowledge "acquired through dreams, visions, and intuition that are understood to be spiritual in nature."[10] Of course, spiritualism, as I discuss later in this chapter, is a central ingredient in religious knowledge and religious education.

What are the "Characteristics of Aboriginal Knowledge"? Catellano states that aboriginal knowledge is based on personal experience and "lays no claim to universality."[11] As Nisbett points out, Western thought assumes the existence of universal truths that are identified through reason or scientific method; whereas, with aboriginal knowledge, even though two people might have contradictory experiences of the same event, both are accepted as valid. In First Nations, there is no contest to see who is correct. Group discussion and consensus building determine the validity of an interpretation of an event. Or, as Catellano states, "Knowledge is validated through collective analysis and consensus building."[12]

Similar to the Confucian-based societies described by Nesbitt, First Nations people see the world in holistic terms in contrast to seeing it as divided into discrete and separate parts. Catellano quotes a First Nations elder: "There are only two things you have to remember about being Indian. One is that everything is alive, and the second is that we are all related."[13] The first part of the statement about "everything is alive" reflects a spiritual view. Everything is permeated by spirits. In reference to the holistic thought, she writes, "The holistic quality of knowledge implies that isolating pieces of experience and trying to make sense of them apart from the environment that gave rise to them flies in the face of reality and is bound to lead to frustration."[14]

In "Updating Aboriginal Traditions of Knowledge," Marlene Castellano writes about holistic thinking among the First Nations of Canada: "The holistic quality of knowledge implies that isolating pieces of experience and trying to make sense of them apart from the environment that gave rise to them flies in the face of reality and is bound to lead to frustration."[15] For Castellano, the medicine wheel symbolizes holistic knowledge with the circle of the wheel representing the circle of life, which "contains all experience, everything in the biosphere—animal, vegetable, mineral, human, spirit—past, present and future."[16] Paul Wangoola, in discussing the African Multiversity, offers a similar image of humans linked to a great chain of being: "At the center of African spirituality was the unshakeable belief that humans were but a weak link in the vast chain of nature, which encompassed the many animals, plants, birds, insects, and worms, and indeed inanimate things such as stones and rocks."[17] Peruvian anthropologist Mahia Maurial uses the term holisticity to describe Indigenous thought and states, "The holistic basis of indigenous knowledge is produced and reproduced within human relationships as well as in their relationship with nature."[18]

Writing about Indigenous peoples in sub-Saharan Africa, George J. Sefa Dei argues that differences in knowledges should not be thought of as being opposites but should be thought of as being at opposite ends of a scale with hybrid knowledges in between. He writes, "Different knowledges represent different points on a continuum; they involve ways that people perceive the world and act on it."[19] On this continuum, Indigenous knowledges on one end of the scale are oriented toward the metaphysical and physical, and at the other end toward science and modernity. The in-between points on the continuum represent a blending of traditional knowledge and modernity. Dei states, "Through daily practice, societies 'import' and 'adapt' freely whatever from 'outside' will enrich their accumulated knowledge. In this sense, 'modernity' is embedded in indigenous knowledges."[20]

What are Indigenous knowledges in Africa? While claiming there is no "essentialized" Africa because of the variety of Indigenous peoples and localities, Dei identifies what he considers to be shared characteristics of sub-Saharan African ways of knowing the world. Shared with Confucian-based societies and First Nations of North America is a holistic view of the world: "the wholeness of relationships in a world that today is fragmented, polarized, and destructive of people and their social aspirations."[21] Embedded in this worldview is an orientation to communal solidarity and community responsibility. Consequently, rather than being driven by a desire to accumulate wealth like Westernized humans, traditional societies were oriented toward sharing wealth. The concept of "poverty" did not exist in traditional societies because of community sharing. Traditional Indigenous peoples, Dei claims, did not share the image with the modern world "of the competitive, isolated individual who lives in fear of others and is protected from them by the state or community."[22] In traditional societies the image was of the cooperative individual who was enriched by his ties to the community.

What about differences in religious knowledges? I will elaborate on some of these differences later in this chapter when exploring religious models of education. It is beyond the scope of this book to review the knowledges of all world religions, which can range from the individualistic faith of modern Christian Protestantism to the emphasis on community responsibility in Islamic thought.

A general description of religious thought might include knowledge of a spiritual world that cannot be explained by modern science. Therefore, a deeply religious person might view the world and its interactions as a mystery that can only be partially understood through science and the exercise of human reason. Life being a mystery, religious people might seek understanding of existence through a belief in a god or gods and some form of theology. Religions offer a spiritual answer to the meaning of life and the mystery of what happens after death. This way of knowing the world is quite different from one that believes that science can provide all answers to life's questions and that human behavior should be guided by a science of ethics rather than faith. The result is a clash between many religious knowledges and a secularized world where the major goal is economic growth and increasing consumption of the material products.

In summary, religious and Indigenous knowledges are often different from the concept of knowledge embodied in human capital and progressive models of education. In the human capital model, life is considered as knowable through science, and the end goal of human life is the accumulation of wealth and economic growth. Knowledge is considered an aid in achieving an economic goal, while most religions see knowledge as a means of following the wishes of a god or gods. Progressive models of education promise to educate people to take charge of the reconstruction of society to achieve social justice. Most Indigenous cultures and religions would consider this goal as naive and impossible. How can people reconstruct a world that is, from the perspective of many religions and Indigenous peoples, unknowable and spiritual? How can social justice be defined outside the context of a religious theology. Does social justice mean providing everyone with an equal chance to accumulate wealth, or does it mean the opportunity to enjoy a strong community life that is directed by spiritual ethics?

There are also differences in knowledges between collectivist and individualist societies such as the previously described differences found by Nisbett between Western and Confucian-based societies. Cross-cultural psychologists suggest that these differences in knowledges involve different values regarding human actions,

TABLE 6.1 Basic Character Traits in Individualist and Collectivist Cultures

Individualist	Collectivist
Hedonism, stimulation, self-direction	Tradition and conformity
Good opinion of self (self-enhancing)	Modest
Goals fit personal needs	Goals show concern with needs of others
Desire for individual distinctiveness	Desire for blending harmoniously with the group
Value success and achievement because it makes the individual look good	Value success and achievement because it reflects well on the group
More concerned with knowing one's own feelings	Attuned to feelings of others and striving for interpersonal harmony
Exhibits "social loafing" or "gold bricking"—trying to minimize work in group efforts	No social loafing in group efforts
Less sensitive to social rejection	More sensitive to social rejection
Less modest in social situations	More modest in social situations
Less likely to feel embarrassed	More likely to feel embarrassed

which, as Dei contends, should be considered as opposite ends of a spectrum with blended variations in between. In "Individualism and Collectivism: Past, Present, and Future," Harry C. Triandis provides a summary of differing character traits valued in the two types of society, which I have complied in Table 6.1. Certainly, any model of education must consider outcomes related to character traits. Human capital educational models are supportive of individualist character traits, while progressive models tend to support collectivist character traits.[23]

Recognizing the various differences in knowledges leads to the question of what it means for the phenomenon of globalization, particularly the globalization of educational practices. Will these differences continue into the future, or will they converge into a common way of knowing the world? Or will these knowledge differences lead to a continuous clash over the goals and content of education?

The Clash of Civilizations and the Role of Religion

The existence of differing knowledges raises important doubts about globalization leading to a uniform global culture and common educational policies and practices. Also, differences in religious knowledges highlight the importance of religious models of education. Strong objections to growing global uniformity were raised by Samuel P. Huntington in his 1996 book *The Clash of Civilizations and the Remaking of World Order*.[24] The very title of the book suggests that world cultural uniformity will not occur in the immediate future or may never occur. Huntington's hypothesis is that future world conflicts will not be economic or ideological but will be cultural. The main conflicts will be between civilizations. As Huntington uses the term, civilizations exist across nation-states and represent groups of people that share cultural values. Huntington writes, "Civilization and culture both refer to the overall way of life of a people, and a civilization is a culture writ large. They both involve the 'values, norms, institutions, and modes of thinking to which successive generations in a given society have attached primary importance'."[25]

Like Nisbett, Huntington identifies Sinic (Confucian based) and Western as two of the possibly eight world civilizations. Huntington uses the term Sinic to indicate Chinese civilization in which Confucianism is a major element. Regarding other civilizations, he tentatively refers to Africa (sub-Saharan) as a civilization but recognizes problems in identifying a cohesive culture because of the impact of European imperialism and existing divisions between Islamic and Christian groups. However, he does argue that Africa maybe forming a separate civilization. Huntington contends, "Throughout Africa tribal identities are pervasive and intense, but Africans are increasingly developing a sense of African identity, and conceivably sub-Saharan could cohere into a distinct civilization with South Africa possibly being its core state."[26] The other four civilizations, according to Huntington, are Japan, Hindu, Islamic, Orthodox, and Latin America. He identifies Japan as a separate civilization even though might be an offshoot of Chinese civilization.

Religion is a defining quality of what Huntington identifies as civilizations. Some of these religions contain elements referred to as "strong religion" or "fundamentalist."[27] The existence of conflicting religious fundamentalisms supports Huntington's vision of a clash of civilizations. For instance, Japan has strong nationalist religious movements associated with Shintoism and new religions such as Soka Gakkai, Agon-shu, and Aum Shinrikyo.[28] In 1995, the Aum Shinrikyo (Supreme Truth) released nerve gas in a Japanese subway killing a dozen people and injuring thousands of others.[29] Hinduism he identifies as the core of civilization of the Indian Subcontinent.[30] Within modern Hinduism is an extremely militant and at times violent group of Hindu fundamentalists identified with the nationalist Hindu teachings in V. D. Savarkar's 1923 book *Hindutva*, which considers Christianity, Buddhism, and Islam major enemies of Hinduism.[31] Islam also has militant factions that believe modernity, and particularly the secular state, was causing defections from Islamic religions. Some want to establish a theocratic state with the Islamic Sharia as the governing law.[32]

What Huntington calls Orthodox civilization is centered in Russia and is distinguished from Western Christianity, which has its roots in the Roman Catholic Church. Russia and others within the Orthodox civilization identify with the Byzantine Church. In this conceptualization, the Russian Orthodox Church developed during the Middle Ages with little contact with the Roman Church. Today, the Russian Orthodox Church is associated with the rise of Russian nationalism, which has added another tension to world politics.[33] At the core of Western civilization are forms of Western Christianity including both Roman Catholic and Protestant churches. Each of these forms of Western Christianity contains types of militant fundamentalists who have killed and attacked scores of people.[34]

Huntington considers Latin America to be a separate civilization with roots in Western civilization but also tied to Indigenous civilizations. Huntington writes about Latin America that it "has evolved along a very different path from Europe and North America. It has had a corporatist, authoritarian culture, which Europe had to a much lesser degree and North America not at all."[35] There have been many militant Indigenous religious movements, including the Ecuadorian fundamentalists the Puruha.[36] There are also other militant Indigenous movements such as the Zapatista of Mexico and the supporters of the first Indigenous president of Bolivia, Evo Morales.[37]

Huntington's troubling vision hardly suggests a world moving toward cultural unity. Also, the revolt of Indigenous peoples against previous colonialism embodies a rejection of a uniform global society.

In an issue of *Foreign Affairs*, Fouad Ajami, professor of Middle Eastern Studies at Johns Hopkins wrote, "But Huntington is wrong. He has underestimated the tenacity of modernity and secularism."[38] Robert Bartley, editor of the *Wall Street Journal*, recognized the possibility that the twenty-first century might demonstrate that Huntington is correct. However, Bartley believes in the triumph of Western values in the global arena: "The dominant flow of historical forces in the 21st century could well be this: economic development leads to demands for democracy and individual (or familial) autonomy; instant worldwide communications reduces power oppressive governments; the spread of democratic states diminishes the potential for conflict."[39] In responding to Huntington's article, former U.S. ambassador to the United Nations Jeane Kirkpatrick claimed that Western values will be grafted onto other cultures: "But he [Huntington] . . . knows how powerful is the momentum of modern, Western ways of science, technology, democracy and free markets. He knows that the great question for non-Western societies is whether they can be modern without being Western."[40]

The most triumphant support of the West came from Gerard Piel, former chairman of Scientific American Inc., in his response to Huntington titled "The West is Best." Piel writes about the world's people, "They all aspire to the Western model . . . As they proceed with their industrialization, they progressively embrace . . . 'Western ideas' . . . of individualism, liberalism, constitutionalism, liberalism, human rights, equality, liberty, the rule of law, democracy, [and] free markets." He claims, "Mass education, which comes with Westernizing industrialization, makes its contribution as well."[41]

An important thing about these responses is that they all assume that the West will continue to be dominant in global cultural change. In this framework, it is Western civilization versus all other civilizations. They also assume that Western civilization will provide the best benefits to the rest of the world and that the values of Western civilization will triumph over religious and Indigenous values. But will they?

In assuming the triumph of Western values over civilizational clashes, there is also an assumption of the triumph Western secular schooling over religious and Indigenous education models. Militant religious groups see materialistic Western values as antithetical to their beliefs. Even militant Christian groups worry about the secularization of Western nations. Given their historical experiences, many Indigenous peoples see the West as the cultural enemy.

In summary, many religious and Indigenous education models are in direct conflict with the human capital model of education. Issues of spirituality, the purpose of life, the meaning of wisdom, and traditional knowledge are in conflict with human capital economics that defines the welfare of humans as a function of economic development. I will explore this issue in the next two sections on religious and Indigenous educational models.

Religious Educational Models: A Rejection of Secular Modernity?

First, I want to make clear that I am unable within the limits of this book to cover all forms of religious education. Besides the wide variety of world religions there are also many splinter groups within each religious tradition. The world's largest religions—Hinduism, Buddhism, Christianity, and Islam—contain many groups claiming to be the authentic voice of their religions. So my approach will be to highlight common elements of religious education and differences regarding acceptance or rejection of modernity.

In Chapter 1, I provided the following generalized model of religious education.

Religious Education World Models

1. Study of traditional religious texts;
2. Study and practice of religious rites;
3. Emphasis on spirituality;
4. Emphasis on instilling moral and ethical standards;
5. Rejection of secularism.

Most religious instruction involves learning a religion's rites, studying a religion's core texts, developing ethical or moral standards from religious texts, and learning how a god or gods manifest themselves in the world. These elements vary considerably between religions and within religions. Secular public education is sometimes seen as the greatest threat. For example, writing about Protestant (a branch of Christianity) religious education in the United States and Germany, Richard Osmer and Friedrich Schweitzer state, "The advocates of the secularization of public education may not have imagined that this would hinder or diminish religious education in the family or in religious communities; nevertheless, *the secularization of the school has been accompanied by a gradual weakening of most traditional forms of religious education* [author's emphasis]."[42]

Religious Content in National School Systems

Some countries have included elements of religious instruction in national school systems in which the overall curriculum is secular in orientation. In the West, this has been difficult because of support for a secular state and religious liberty. For instance in the United States, public schools in the nineteenth century were often called Protestant schools, as contrasted with the privately operated Catholic educational system, because of the Protestant-orientation of public school textbooks, the teaching of a secular form of Protestant morality, and religious instruction in the form of school prayer and readings from the Christian Bible. When the U.S. Supreme Court in the 1960s declared school prayer and Bible reading unconstitutional, many Christian-oriented parents protested by withdrawing their children from public schools and either homeschooled them or sent them to private religious schools.[43]

In some nations, the adoption of Western forms of education has included a continuation of religious instruction through state-operated schools. As previously stated, world culture theorists argue that the spread of the Western concept of the nation-state and constitutional government was accompanied by the spread of mass schooling. However, this does not mean the spread of secular mass schooling. For instance, Article 13 of the Constitution of Saudi Arabia includes the support of religion as a goal of mass schooling: "Education will aim at instilling the Islamic faith in the younger generation, providing its members with knowledge and skills and preparing them to become useful members in building of their society, members who love their homeland and are proud of its history."[44] In the Saudi Arabian Constitution, citizens are required to have allegiance to the Qur'an. The Saudi Arabian Constitution states:

> Article 6: Citizens are to pay allegiance to the King in accordance with the Holy Koran and the tradition of the Prophet, in submission and obedience, in times of ease and difficulty, fortune and adversity."
>
> Article 26: The state protects human rights in accordance with the Islamic Shari'ah.[45]

The integration of religious instruction into government-operated school systems has been a major goal of some Islamic nations that have adopted Western forms of mass schooling including the Western educational ladder of primary, middle, secondary, and higher education. The merger of Islamic religious education, Western science and technology, Arab nationalism, and education for economic planning is exemplified by the curriculum for Egyptian primary schools (grades 1–5). The greatest numbers of class periods in the curriculum are devoted to religious education, Arabic language, and mathematics.

Egyptian Primary Curriculum, 1990–91

> Religious Education
> Arabic Language
> Mathematics
> Social Studies
> Science & Health
> Observation of Nature
> Technical Education (industrial subject,
> agriculture, or home economics)
> Physical Education
> Music and/or Art
> Practical/Technical Training[46]

Religious study in Egyptian primary schools focuses on traditional religious values and students' obligations to society and duties to the government.[47] These religious textbooks contain quotes from the Qur'an along with vocabulary lists and summaries. Stories are used to illustrate proper behavior according to Islamic traditions and, of course, to ensure an orderly society. Textbooks contain lists of religious-behavioral rules to be memorized for examinations.[48] The problem for some Islamic leaders is that this type of religious instruction in Western-style schools can be perfunctory.

Education and Religious Nationalism

Some religious leaders object to the limited inclusion of religion in schools and to the secularization of national school systems. These groups want young people to receive traditional forms of religious instruction. One example is the schools established in India by the Vishva Hindu Parishad (V.H.P.). V.H.P. represents religious nationalism where attempts are made to link a feeling of national spirit to a religion: "The objective of the V.H.P. is to organize—consolidate the Hindu society and to serve—protect the Hindu Dharma . . . The Impact of V.H.P.: An increased expression of Hindu pride & unity in the society."[49] At the top of the V.H.P. website is a pulsating: "Unite Hindus—Save Humanity."[50]

This effort exists in many other countries, such as in the United States where some Christians as represented by Pat Robertson's Christian Coalition insist that Christianity is part of the ideal of American nationalism and in Israel where the Gush Emunim associated the destiny of Judaism with Israeli nationalism.[51] Even the U.S. military takes on the trappings of Christianity in a country noted for multireligious population. In 2008, a controversy developed at the U.S. Naval Academy over the dipping of the American flag in front of a Christian altar in the academy's chapel. Neela Banerejee reported in the *New York Times* about the controversy:

> Evangelical Christians and their critics alike assert that the academy had
> to reconsider after an outcry by congregants and alumni. "I think the cer-
> emony is fully representative of the highest traditions of our country," said
> Bob Morrison, who has attended the 11 a.m. service for 12 years and who
> heads an internship program at the Family Research Council, a conservative
> Christian group. "It basically says that our country is one nation under God
> and the nation-state is not the highest authority in the world."[52]

Organized in 1964, V.H.P. was a product of the strong religious nationalism accompanying the resistance to British colonization of India. An influential book was V. D. Savarkar's *Hindutva*, which linked Hinduism to national unity and rebellion against British colonizers and religiously imposed doctrines of Christianity and Islam. An early section of the book celebrates the "fall of Buddhism" in India and links race, nationalism, and religion: "the political consequences of Buddhistic expansion [had] been so disastrous to the national virility and even the national existence of our race."[53] Representative of Savarkar's religious nationalism is the claim that Muslim and Christian Indians should not be considered as Hindus in the context of the "fatherland." He claims they owe their religious allegiance to the lands from which their religions were born.

> That is why in the case of some of our Mohammedan or Christian country-
> men who had originally been forcibly converted to a non-Hindu religion
> and who consequently inherited along with Hindus, a common Fatherland
> and a greater part of the wealth of a common culture—language, law, cus-
> toms, folklore and history—are not and cannot be recognized as Hindus . . .
> Their holy land is far off in Arabia or Palestine.[54]

In recent years, the V.H.P. has been associated with violent attacks on Christian churches and mosques and the killing of Christians and Muslims. These actions sparked increased religious tensions particularly between Hindus and Muslims.[55]

As I have suggested, religious nationalism can lead to internal conflicts within countries. For example in Sri Lanka, the national government has struggled against the independence movement led by the Tamil Tigers who are mainly Hindu and Christian and represent an ethnic minority. The Sri Lankan government is officially Buddhist. While claiming to protect the rights of other religions, the Sri Lankan Constitution states: "CHAPTER II—BUDDHISM: The Republic of Sri Lanka shall give to Buddhism the foremost place and accordingly it shall be the duty of the State to protect and foster the Buddha Sasana, while assuring to all religions the rights granted by Articles 10 and 14(1)(e)."[56] Inevitably, religion became a focal point of conflict in Sri Lanka. For example, in 2006 a giant white statue of Buddha was erected on a five-foot-high concrete platform near the market in a small Sri Lankan town. The Tamils considered this a provocative act by the ruling Sinhalese. The leader of the Tamil protest against the statute was killed while going to the bank. The bodies of 5 Tamil youths were found on a beach. In response, a bomb was set off in the market killing 16 people. Then Sinhalese Buddhists torched Tamil-owned stores, homes, and schools. The Tamil Tigers then set off a bomb in the capital, and the Sinhalese Buddhist government responded with air strikes on Tamil villagers killing dozens.[57] The religious and ethnic violence continues in Sri Lanka.

Sarvodaya: The Welfare of All

In contrast to the religious nationalism of the V.H.P. and the materialist goals of human capital doctrines, Indian leader Mohandas Gandhi offered a different vision of Hinduism and education based on pacifism and a rejection of industrialism. Gandhi led the struggle against British colonialism, social class differences, and the discriminatory distinctions of the Hindu caste system. Of particular concern to Gandhi was the plight of untouchables. In 1948, Gandhi was killed by a Hindu nationalist because of his willingness to seek reconciliation with Muslims. Unlike Hindu religious nationalists, Gandhi believed that there was a unity to all world religions. Gandhi wrote, that the "study of other religions besides one's own will give one a grasp of the rock-bottom unity of all religions and afford a glimpse also of the universal and absolute truth which lies beyond the 'dust of creeds and faiths'."[58]

Gandhi's religious ideas are still attractive to large numbers of the world's Hindu population and are considered an alternative to the religious nationalism preached in the *Hindutva*.[59] His doctrine of *Sarvodaya*, or the welfare of all, rejects the emphasis of human capital education on technological development and economic growth. Gandhi made a distinction between "standard of living" and "standard of life." Increases in the "standard of living," he argued, simply means increased income and acquisition of material goods. Income and material goods are not indicators of the quality of life. In contrast, the concept of "standard of life" represents a major deviation from the dominant global commitment to economic growth as improving human lives. Gandhi wrote that "a rise in the standard of living might even lower the standard of life, by reducing man's physical, moral, intellectual and spiritual standards. Hence, the progressive development of Nature must be consistent with rise in the standard of life, and not of living."[60]

The "craze for machinery," as Gandhi referred to industrialism, he believed was primarily driven by greed. Consequently, the result has overworked laborers being exploited by the few owners of factories. "Scientific truths and discoveries," he asserted, "should first of all cease to be mere instruments of greed. Then laborers will not be over-worked and machinery, instead of becoming a hindrance will be a help."[61] From Gandhi's perspective, the goal of technological and economic development should be improving the standard of life for all people rather than improved industrial efficiency to profit the owners of production. Consequently, a major result of industrialism, Gandhi asserted, was resulting greater social and economic inequality.

Gandhi's educational plan involved "*Sarvodaya* workers" reforming village life. Included in the agenda of *Sarvodaya* workers was making the spinning wheel and agriculture the center of the productive and community life of villages. This was to be part of what Gandhi called "nation-building" as part of the remedy for the destructive effects of previous British colonialism. *Sarvodaya* workers were to be models of self-denial, voluntary poverty, and temperance. They were to be acquainted with all aspects of cloth making including the use of spinning wheels. They were to be interested in the plight of untouchables. In this manner, *Sarvodaya* workers were to be models to guide the spiritual and moral life for villagers.

Sarvodaya workers were also teachers. First, Gandhi saw them spreading knowledge about sanitation and health which certainly is an important aspect of increasing "the standard of life." Second, they were to impart orally useful information before actually teaching reading. Gandhi stated, "Lots of useful information on current affairs, history, geography, and elementary arithmetic can be given by word of mouth before the alphabet is touched. The eyes, the ears and the tongue come before the hand."[62] In Gandhi's curriculum, reading was to be taught before writing and drawing before learning the alphabet. However, the role of the scholar-teacher was to be secondary to being a model village worker: "He will not pose as a litterateur buried in his books, loath to listen to details of humdrum life. On the contrary, the people whenever they see him, will find him busy with the tools—spinning wheel, loom, adze, spade, etc.—and always responsive to their meanest inquiries."[63]

Gandhi's educational goal was self-governing and independent villages, or what he called complete republics. Villages were to be the basic governing unit of society. In these village republics, activities were to be cooperative endeavor. The focus on cloth production would ensure, Gandhi hoped, economic independence for the villages. Education to the final basic course would be compulsory. Economic and social inequality would be banished, including discrimination against untouchables. "Here," Gandhi declared, "there is perfect democracy based upon individual freedom. The individual is the architect of his own government. The law of non-violence rules him and his government."[64]

In summary, Gandhi and his followers believe a truly spiritual life would be fostered by small villages focused on a simple life of farming and cloth making. The goal is a spiritual life based on nonviolence and social and economic equality. Education would provide knowledge of sanitation, literacy, and basic knowledge of geography, current events, and history. Rather than seeking the good life through raising material standards of living, Gandhi stressed the importance of measuring the quality of living by a "standard of life." The value of technology would be determined by its contribution to the "standard of life" and not by how it might increase a company's profits or stimulate economic growth. By suggesting that all world religions shared similar spiritual messages, Gandhi avoided the conflictual religious nationalism expressed *Hindutva*.

Gandhi's form of Hinduism rejects the material goals of human capital theory. It also rejects the assumption of many progressive educators that education should promote equality of economic goods without ensuring that material goods will really contribute to a "standard of life" including spiritual well-being. Reflecting an antimaterialist bias against the West, Gandhi proclaimed: "People in the West generally hold that the whole duty of man is to promote the happiness of the majority . . . and happiness is supposed to mean only physical happiness and economic prosperity. If the laws of morality are broken in the conquest of this happiness [economic prosperity], it does not matter very much."[65] From Gandhi's perspective, "The consequence [*sic*] of this line of thinking are writ large on the face of Europe."[66]

Education and Liberation Theology

Similar to Gandhi's proposals, liberation theology seeks to free humans from the spiritual vacuum caused by political and economic oppression. While liberation theology has been widely discussed and in some situations condemned by the leadership of the Roman Catholic Church, it has been primarily practiced in Central and South America. As Samuel Huntington suggests, "Latin America" can be considered a civilization where the role of Christian churches has been different from those in Europe and North America. In Europe, Marxist ideology was primarily atheist in its orientation. In Central and South America, Marxist ideology was integrated into the doctrines of Christian Catholicism. Jose Mariátegui was a leading figure in the integration of Marxism and Christianity. Often identified as the originator of South American Marxism, Mariátegui was born on July 14, 1894, and grew up in the small southern Peruvian coastal town of Moquegua. His work would influence the development of Marxism in South and Central America, including the thinking of Che Guevara, Fidel Castro, and leaders of the Sandinistas. Marc Becker asserts, "He is widely regarded as being the first truly creative and original Latin American Marxist thinker."[67] In *Marxist Thought in Latin America*, Sheldon B. Liss concluded, "No Latin American Marxist receives more acknowledgments of intellectual indebtedness from fellow thinkers than José Mariátegui."[68]

Raised in poverty by his devout Catholic mestiza mother, Mariátegui, by giving a role for the Catholic Church in his Marxist theories, provided an intellectual justification for liberation theology. Many Marxists in South and Central America blended socialist ideas with their religious faith. Liberation theology was formally proclaimed at the 1968 Medellín Bishops Conference, which committed the Church to helping the poor and protecting human rights. Following the proclamation, a movement started called Christians for Socialism, which believed, as stated by the bishop of Cuernavaca, Mexico, Sergio Arceo, that "only socialism can give Latin America the authentic development it needs . . . I believe that a socialist system is more in conformity with the Christian principles of brotherhood, justice, and peace."[69]

Besides being an early advocate of liberation theology, Mariátegui called for the mass political education of peasants and Indigenous peoples as a necessary condition for the growth of Marxism in South America. Literacy, he argued, should be taught with political content. Mass political education, Mariátegui believed, was necessary for adapting Marxism to South American conditions, particularly for the recruitment of peasants and Indigenous peoples. Mariátegui argued, "The problem of Indian illiteracy goes beyond the pedagogical sphere. It becomes increasingly evident that *to teach a man to read and write is not to educate him* [my emphasis]."[70] He contended that Marxism should be adapted to South America's social and political conditions, which included a large peasant population and Indigenous tribes.

Mariátegui believed that praxis was necessary for creating a free as opposed to an authoritarian Marxist society. He defined praxis as a "dialectic interrelation between objective and subjective conditions."[71] In other words, people were to understand how their subjective beliefs determined their interpretation of the objective world and how the objective world informed their subjective views. This form of education, Mariátegui stated in a manner similar to Freire's later use of consciousness as a liberating force, would "spark the revolutionary consciousness that would accelerate the socialist revolution, and thus help to compensate for the underdeveloped nature of the nation."[72]

Mariátegui, who was of Inca ancestry, believed that Marxism could be adapted to Indigenous cultures. He envisioned the creation of an "Indo-American" socialism. In his most widely read and translated book, *Seven Interpretive Essays on Peruvian Reality*, Mariátegui rejected industrialization as a necessary condition for a socialist revolution among the Inca people and called for recognition of a traditional Inca-communist society. He argued that traditional Inca society was socialist. "Faith in the renaissance of the Indian is not pinned to the material process of 'Westernizing' the Quechua [Inca] country," he asserted. "The soul of the Indian is not raised by the white man's civilization or alphabet but by the myth, the idea, of Socialist revolution."[73] After noting how Chinese and Hindu societies were able to incorporate socialist ideas, he questioned those who did not see Indigenous cultures as incorporating Marxist ideas: "Why should the Inca people, who constructed the most highly-developed and harmonious communistic system, be the only ones unmoved by the worldwide emotion? The consanguinity of the Indian movement with world revolutionary currents is too evident to need documentation."[74] Quoting Indigenous peoples' advocate González Prada, Mariátegui emphasized the importance of revolution for changing the conditions of Native Americans: "the condition of the Indian can improve in two ways: either the heart of the oppressor will be moved to take pity and recognize the rights of the oppressed, or the spirit of the oppressed will find the valor needed to turn on the oppressors."[75]

Mariátegui's ideas provided the initial stimulus for members of the Catholic Church to look more closely at South America's social conditions and plan an educational and social program for uplifting peasant and Indigenous populations. This work coalesced at the 1968 Conference of Latin American Bishops in Medellín, Columbia, which proposed educational programs to carry out the work of liberation theology. Medellín Conference's declaration "Justice and Peace" stated, "The lack of political consciousness in our countries makes the educational activity of the Church absolutely essential, for the purpose of bringing Christians to consider their participation in the political life of the nation as a matter of conscience and as the practice of charity in its most noble and meaningful sense for the life of the community."[76]

The spirit of the conference was captured by the words one of the participants, Franic Split:

> If the workers do not become in some way the owners of their labor, all structural reforms will be ineffective. [This is true] even if the workers receive a higher salary in an economic system but are not content with these raises. They want to be owners, not sellers, of their labor . . . At present the workers are increasingly aware that labor represents a part of the human person. A person, however cannot be bought; neither can he sell himself. Any purchase or sale of labor is a type of slavery.[77]

The documents issued by the Medellín Conference supported Paulo Freire's educational methods by emphasizing the importance of protecting cultures and by advocating "Concientización." The documents rejected violent revolution for peaceful methods. Similar to Freire, they advocate a cultural revolution through education. This idea was reiterated in a section titled "Information and Concientización."

> We wish to affirm that it is indispensable to form a social conscience and a realistic perception of the problems of the community and of social structures. We must awaken the social conscience and communal customs in all strata of society and professional groups regarding such values as dialogue and community living within the same group and relations with wider social groups (workers, peasants, professionals, clergy, religious, administration, etc.).[78]

The Medellín Conference announced that the Church would actively work to raise the level of people's consciousness: "This task of 'Concientización' and social education ought to be integrated into joint pastoral action at various levels."[79]

In addition to recognizing the educational role of the Church in raising political consciousness, "Justice and Peace" stressed the importance of recognizing cultural differences. "The lack of socio-cultural integration," the declaration argued, "in the majority of our countries, has given rise to the superimposition of cultures. In the economic sphere systems flourished which consider solely the potential of groups with great earning power. This lack of adaptation to the characteristics and to the potentials of all our people, in turn, gives rise to frequent political instability and the consolidation of purely formal institutions."[80]

Participants at the Medellín Conference believed that overcoming social and economic oppression was necessary for achieving Christian peace. The Medellín Conference refused to support armed revolution while recognizing that continued economic inequalities would disrupt peaceful relationships. "In the face of the tensions which conspire against peace, and even present the temptation of violence," the Medellín Conference declaration stated, "we believe that the Latin American Episcopate cannot avoid assuming very concrete responsibilities; because to create a just social order, without which peace is illusory, is an eminently Christian task."[81] The declaration went on to stress that pastoral work should include education, defending the rights of the poor and oppressed, denouncing economic inequalities, creating grassroots organizations, ending the arms race, and denouncing the unjust actions of world powers. Regarding education, it was declared, "To us, the Pastors of the Church, belongs the duty to educate the Christian conscience, to inspire, stimulate and help orient all of the initiatives that contribute to the formation of man."[82]

Liberation theology included a criticism of the ongoing efforts at economic "development." At the 1969 Campine, Switzerland, meeting of the World Council of Churches, Peruvian theologian Gustavo Gutiérrez raised the question of "Why development? Why not liberation?" These ideas were later incorporated in Gutiérrez's 1971 book *A Theology of Liberation*.[83] "But it is not enough that we be liberated from," Gutiérrez wrote, "oppressive socio-economic structures; also needed is a personal transformation by which we live with profound inner freedom in the face of every kind of servitude, and this is the second dimension or level of liberation."[84] Finally, he argued there was liberation from sin as defined by the Catholic Church.

Similar to many other radicals, Gutiérrez urged the development of a social theory adapted to the special needs of Central and South America. He asserted that "one of the most creative and fruitful efforts implemented in Latin America is the experimental work of Paulo Freire, who has sought to establish a 'pedagogy of the oppressed'."[85] Gutiérrez cited the work of José Carlos Mariátegui who, as I previously discussed, urged the adaptation of Marxist theories to the needs of the Indigenous peoples of South and Central America. "We must bring Indo-American socialism," Gutiérrez quoted Mariátegui, "to life with our own reality, in our own language."[86] Quoting Che Guevara, Gutiérrez emphasized the importance of a new theoretical approach: "One of the great dangers which threaten the building of socialism in Latin America—pressed as it is by immediate concerns— is the lack of its own solid theory, and this theory must be Latin American, not to satisfy a desire for originality, but for the sake of elementary historical realism."[87]

The educational efforts of advocates of liberation theology were primarily carried out by Base Ecclesial Communities (BECs). The formation of BECs were advocated by the bishops attending the 1968 Medellín meeting, which called for "small communities," "grass-roots organizations," and "collaboration . . . with non-Catholic Christian Churches and institutions dedicated to the task of restoring justice in human relations."[88] In his history of liberation theology, Christian Smith offered this summary of the BECs' work: "BECs offered not only a solution to the lack of clergy but also, for the liberation theology movement, a means of educating the masses at the grass roots. Pastoral workers, utilizing Paulo Freire's method of conscientization, taught community members how to do critical social analysis."[89]

Liberation theology's educational programs were practiced by the Sandinista National Liberation Front in Nicaragua, which overthrew the dictatorship of the Somoza dynasty in 1979, and in neighboring El Salvador by the Farabundo Marti National Liberation Front, which after a decade of civil war captured the government in 1989. The official director of the Nicaraguan Literacy Crusade was liberation theologian Father Fernando Cardenal who proclaimed at the beginning of the crusade: "Literacy is fundamental to achieving progress and it is essential to the building of a democratic society . . . You learn to read and write so you can identify the reality in which you live, so that you can become a protagonist of history rather than a spectator."[90]

In El Salvador, sociologist John Hammond concluded that liberation theology played major roles in supporting the armed struggle. In Hammond's words, "During the 1970s a political movement arose in the Salvadoran countryside that led to the decade-long revolt of the 1980s. Innovative church people inspired by liberation theology formed Christian base communities in rural parishes, and from these a new political consciousness emerged."[91] In one typical situation, Hammond described the use of the Bible as the thematic representation used to explore local political and economic injustices.

In summary, liberation theology is sharply different from religious nationalism. Liberation theologists believed they were preaching universal religious values that were not linked to any particular nation. However, liberation theology did share with religious nationalism a concern that contemporary social movements were placed in a traditional religious context. For instance, both the V.H.P. and liberation theology combined religion and economic improvement in their educational campaigns. In the next section, I will examine a more traditional form of religious education.

State-Supported Islamic Education

Islamic education will be my example of the various supports given by governments to religious studies. While Islamic education can be associated with religious nationalism such as in Iran, I will focus on traditional elements in the passing on of Islamic religious knowledge. I would also like to remind the reader that my goal is to illustrate religious education models that are in potential conflict with human capital and progressive education models. In other words, religious education can counter the growth of uniform global education policies and practices. Also, in possible competition with global English, Islamic education requires learning Qur'anic Arabic to read the Qur'an.

In general, Islamic education has a holistic vision of knowledge and education. This holistic view of the world is different from that of many Indigenous peoples. For Islam, holistic knowledge is directly related to the unity of God's knowledge. As the Creator, God's knowledge permeates humanity and the surrounding natural world. Consequently, a study of nature can lead to knowledge about God. "A holistic education," writes Zahra Al Zeera, author of *Wholeness and Holiness in Education: An Islamic Perspective*, "should lead its followers through observation and reflection on nature to apprehend the unity that connects God's creation. A holistic education integrates and unites the spiritual and the physical."[92] As Al Zeera points out that the Islamic concept of holistic knowledge is sharply different from that of Western support of human capital education and Western paradigms of knowledge. As she emphasizes, all the major paradigms in vogue in Western universities (positivist, postpositivist, critical theory, and constructivist) do not contain a spiritual dimension, and they are grounded in secular and materialist reality.[93] From her perspective, Western education lacks not only a holistic understanding of the interrelationship between God and the material world, but any clear direction about how the world "ought to be." Driven by the quest for economic expansion and conquest of nature through science, Western education, in contrast to Islamic education, denies the ability of God's knowledge to enlighten humans and provide humans with a moral compass.

Consequently, Al Zeera supports a concept of holistic education, which is quite different from most of those supported under the progressive models of education. Progressive models stress a holistic approach as a means of understanding the interrelationships between academic subjects. In contrast, a holistic approach to education within the Islamic model stresses the interrelationships between God, nature, and humans. She writes, "A holistic education should lead its followers through observation and reflection on nature to understand the unity that connects God's creation."[94] From this perspective, spirituality is a key component of holistic education: "A holistic education integrates and unites the spiritual and the physical."[95]

Despite this vision of holistic education, as described earlier in this chapter, the curricula of many state-supported schools in Islamic countries separate subjects by disciplines including special courses on Islam. On the other hand, some countries support separate Islamic institutions. A description of traditional Islamic educational institutions provides background for understanding current government support of Islamic religious schools in contrast to requiring special courses on Islam in government-supported schools offering a general curriculum.

Between roughly 1000 and 1500 CE, Islamic madrasas were the primary sources of religious thought and education. They might be considered "colleges" in contrast to primary schools called *kuttabs*. In *kuttabs*, students recited and memorized the Qur'an. For most of these early years, there were no printed texts, and instruction relied on oral instruction with students writing on slates. The first printed book used in Egyptian schools appeared in 1834. It was a printed version of an eight-century legal commentary.[96] Memorization of the Qur'an can create a mental framework for interpreting life's events. A recalled verse of the Qur'an can serve to guide people in their social interactions and as a reminder of their duty to God.

A primary goal of madrasas of this period was to determine how to live a just and godly life by studying the Qur'an, which required learning Arabic. Therefore the subjects studied in these traditional madrasas were Qur'anic recitation, Arabic grammar, Qur'anic interpretation, jurisprudence, the sources of Sharia (Islamic canonical law), and moral instruction. Nonreligious subjects in some madrasas included arithmetic, astronomy, medicine, and poetry.[97] According to Robert Hefner, "A generation ago, historians of Islamic education concluded that the madrasa's classrooms, degrees (ijaza), professorships, and endowed properties were proof that madrasas were the Muslim equivalent of the medieval West's universities."[98]

Islamic scholars in these early madrasas focused their scholarship on theology and law. The Qur'an called for the creation of a society based on community, socio-economic justice, and human egalitarianism. The goal of scholars was to achieve this type of society by formulating laws based on the Qur'an and the Hadith. The Qur'an was the very Word of God, while the Hadith was a collection of the sayings of Mohammed. Religious and legal scholars consulted both the Qur'an and the Hadith to determine how human relationships should be regulated.

In their search for just laws and a just society, madrasa scholars wrote commentaries on the Qur'an and the Hadith, as well as commentaries on the commentaries. Fazlur Rahman argues that this involved a deductive form of scholarship using the following method: "First one must move from the concrete case treatments of the *Qur'an*—taking the necessary and relevant social conditions of that time into account—to the general principles upon which the entire teaching converges. Second, from this general level there must be a movement back to specific legislation, taking into account the necessary and relevant conditions now obtaining."[99] This scholarship formed the Sharia or sacred law, which in the twentieth century was included in the constitutions of many Arab nations.

While under pressure from European colonialism and influence in the nineteenth century, Islamic scholars worried about how to protect Islamic values. One of these scholars, Muhammad Abduh (1849–1905 BCE) had the greatest influence over Arab education. In Egypt, he stressed that the true goal of education was the cultivation of human character according to the principles of Islam.

He objected to the foreign schools in Egypt with declaration: "Let parents refrain from sending their children to foreign schools that tend to change their habits and religious faith."[100] Muhammad Abduh argued that national education systems should include religious education. Regarding Egyptian national education, Abduh wrote, "If one seeks to educate and improve the Egyptian nation without religion, it is as if a farmer would try to sow seed in unsuitable soil . . . his efforts will be in vain."[101]

Of particular importance for Abduh was the use of Arabic as the medium of classroom instruction. While foreign schools used Euro-American languages as the medium of instruction, many Arab schools used Turkish because of the influence of the Ottoman Empire. Abduh advocated the use of Arabic for religious and nationalist reasons. First, knowledge of Arabic was essential for reading the Qur'an. Second, since culture and language were intimately bound together, preservation of Arab culture against the inroad of Euro-American culture required the preservation of the Arab language.[102]

Indonesia and Malaysia provide examples of government support of contemporary madrasas. They represent attempts to combine human capital goals with Islamic morality. In 1997, Indonesia, the nation with the largest Islamic population, had in 1,770,760 students enrolled in Islamic *pesantrens* and 5,698,143 studying in madrasas out of a total national primary and secondary student population of 44,067,090.[103] Traditionally, *pesantrens* were three- to four-year boarding schools beginning at the ages of 11 or 12 for educating mosque leaders (imam) and religious teachers. However, government-mandated reforms in the 1970s required *pesantrens* to include general education subjects (English, history, and mathematics). For private madrasas, the Indonesian government requires students to take 70 percent of their studies in general education and 30 percent in Islamic religious studies.[104] Madrasas exist as a subsystem to the general government educational system. In 1989, a government regulation defined madrasas as a "general school with an Islamic identity."[105]

In Malaysia, madrasas became centers for resistance against British colonialism. In 1908, the first madrasa was established in Malaysia, and these madrasas eventually offered curricula in Malay, English, and Arabic. After World War II, religion became a central issue as nationalist groups worked to finalize independence for the British. The 1957 constitution made Islam the official religion of Malaysia. Regarding educational institutions, the constitution declared, "Every religious group has the right to establish and maintain institutions for the education of children and provide therein instruction in its own religion."[106] One special clause allowed for government funding of Islamic schools: "Federal law or State law may provide for special financial aid for the establishment or maintenance of Muslim institutions or the instruction in the Muslim religion of persons professing that religion."[107] Following the adoption of the constitution, the government made Islamic religious instruction compulsory for all Muslim students.

Islamic morality is now part of the Malaysian primary and secondary school curriculum. Islamic morality is embodied in the 1987 New Education Philosophy report issued by the Malaysian government: "Education in Malaysia is an on-going effort towards further developing the potential of individuals . . . based on a firm belief in and devotion to God."[108] Under the New Education Philosophy, the teaching of Islamic values served the secular purpose of social control by the state. The school system was to educate good citizen with the following values:

1. Have a firm belief in and obedience to God;
2. Be knowledgeable;
3. Possess living skills;
4. Possess high moral standards;
5. Be responsible to his self, society, and nation;
6. Contribute to the well-being of society and nation;
7. Have a balanced personality.[109]

Saudi Arabia is an example of Islamic nation that provides government support to universities to counter Western influence. The three Islamic-oriented universities established by the Saudi government are the Islamic University of Medina, the Imam Muhammad ibn Sa'ud Islamic University in Riyadh, and the Umm al-Qura University in Mecca. Saudi royal decree at the founding of the Islamic University of Medina illustrates the religious intent of these institutions: "The formation of scholars ('ulama) specializing in the Islamic and Arabic sciences . . . and equipped with the forms of knowledge that would enable them to call others to Islam and to solve the problems that confront Muslims in their religious and worldly matters in accordance with the Book [of God], the normative example [of the Prophet] and the practices of the pious forbears."[110]

In Pakistan, the lack of government schools aided the steady and rapid growth of madrasas since 1947.[111] Another important factor in the growth of Pakistani madrasas is that they provide free room and board, textbooks, and instruction through a combination of government subsidies and community. The Pakistani madrasas are famous throughout the Islamic world. They attract foreign students associated with fundamentalist Islamic movements including those who participate in the Taliban movement in Afghanistan.[112] The free room and board is particularly attractive to low-income families. Nayyar writes,

> Madrasahs, unlike formal schools, are attractive because they are invariably boarding houses, providing free boarding and lodging, free books, and often even clothing . . . This is an important, perhaps, overriding, factor for many from the lower and lower-middle classes. Not only does it go to reduce the burden on the tight family budget, it also keeps the children away from loitering and street crime.[113]

Pakistani education developed quite differently from that of Arab nations. The madrasas movement in nineteenth-century India provided the model for later madrasas in Pakistan. A.H. Nayyar states, regarding the madrasa revival in late nineteenth-century British India, "The founders of *madrasahs* were strongly anti-imperialist, and communicated this spirit to their students . . . They viewed the imperialism of the West more as that of Christendom, and the modern technology brought in by the imperialists as a tool in the hands of adversarial religious force."[114] The Pakistani madrasas focus on memorization of the Qur'an and discussion of the Hadith. They now serve the Islamic world in educating students for continued resistance to Western Christian values.

In summary, religious educational models offer striking contrasts to human capital and progressive educational models. However, religious content added to national systems of education might be nested in a more general goal of human capital development and used primarily as means of social control. On the other hand, spiritual teachings often run counter to the material desires needed to maintain an industrial consumer society. From that standpoint, Gandhi's *Sarvodaya* represents a radical break with assumptions that material prosperity is key to a higher standard of life. Liberation theology provides a spiritual attempt to overcome the oppression of economic and political systems. Religious nationalism, as exemplified in this section by *Hindutva*, lends support to Huntington's contention that present and future events will involve a clash of civilizations.

KEY POINTS: TYPES OF RELIGIOUS EDUCATION

1. Religious content in national schools
   a. Religious values translated into secular values for public school instruction
   b. Used as a form of social control to ensure "good" behaviors among citizens, which often occurs in public schools in Christian and Islamic countries
   c. Religious courses included in general curriculum of public schools
2. State-supported religious schools
   a. Schools devoted to religious instruction
   b. Schools with religious instruction plus government-mandated general curriculum
3. Religious nationalism
   a. Nationalism and religion believed to be closely related, such as Hindu fundamentalism, some forms of Christianity in the United States, and religious groups in Japan
   b. Education involves creating a belief of the inseparability of religion from the identity of a particular nation

4. Globalized religious education
   a. Education to create international religious communities
   b. Often associated with the missionary work of Christians and Islamic forms of conversion
5. Religion and education for social justice
   a. Exemplified by Gandhi's *Sarvodaya* and the Christian Catholic Church's liberation theology

Indigenous Models of Education

As discussed in Chapter 1, the world's 370 million Indigenous peoples are identified by a number of characteristics, including long-term occupancy of the land, tribal organization, and subsistence-oriented production. Indigenous groups have a social and cultural identity distinct from dominant national societies. Similar to discussion of world religions, it is not within the scope of this book to discuss all of the world's Indigenous peoples. In Chapter 1, I provided a generalized model of Indigenous education.

Indigenous Education World Models

1. Indigenous nations control their own educational institutions;
2. Traditional Indigenous education serves as a guide for the curriculum and instructional methods;
3. Education is provided in the language of the Indigenous nation;
4. Education reflects the culture of the Indigenous nation.

Most Indigenous peoples have been subjected to attempts to eradicate their cultural traditions by colonial powers in the Americas, Europe, Russia, Australia, New Zealand, Africa, and the South Pacific. Some have faced cultural domination by an often hostile surrounding society such as in the Americas, Russia, China, Japan, and India. As a result, many Indigenous groups have attempted to rescue their educational traditions as a means of protecting or restoring their cultural traditions. In 2007, after many years of seeking United Nations' protection, this international body ratified the United Nations Declaration of the Rights of Indigenous Peoples. This declaration specifies educational rights that are often in conflict with human capital, progressive, and religious global models. Article 14 of the UN declaration states:

1. Indigenous peoples have the right to establish and control their educational systems and institutions providing education in their own languages, in a manner appropriate to their cultural methods of teaching and learning.
2. Indigenous individuals, particularly children, have the right to all levels and forms of education of the State without discrimination.

3. States shall, in conjunction with indigenous peoples, take effective measures, in order for indigenous individuals, particularly children, including those living outside their communities, to have access, when possible, to an education in their own culture and provided in their own language.[115]

Numbers 1 and 3 of Article 14 are designed to protect and restore Indigenous educational methods and languages. Number 2 of Article 14 is supposed to ensure that Indigenous peoples have access to a nation's public school system.

Earlier in this chapter, I outlined some of the basic characteristics of Indigenous knowledges. Again, I should warn the reader that there is a danger in assuming that all Indigenous peoples share the same educational and cultural characteristics. However, most attempts to summarize Indigenous knowledge and educational practices emphasize the importance of holistic knowledge and educational practices. In the conclusion to the previous section, I suggested that Islamic thought and Indigenous thought differed in their concepts of holistic knowledge and education. While both see all things permeated by the spiritual, Muslim people rely for guidance on the Qur'an and they believe that creation is linked to a single God. In contrast, Indigenous people tend to rely on guidance from nature, dreams, and intuition and often see the spiritual world as composed of many gods.

In contrast to Indigenous knowledges, monotheistic religions consider humans a central focus of natural existence. Indeed, some world religions, including Judaism, Christianity, and Islam, believe only humans have souls and not other animals. Many Indigenous peoples, however, see humans as just one species among many others. For instance, "Islam sees man as the vice regency of God on earth … Gifted with intelligence in the true sense of the term, he alone of all creature is capable of knowing."[116] In contrast, Hinduism and Buddhism by believing in reincarnation see other animals as part of the same life cycle as humans. Consequently, many forms of Hinduism and Buddhism practice vegetarianism.

Giving humans a privileged place in the natural order justifies human exploitation of other animals and nature. The assumption that only humans have souls leads to a supposition that all of earth was created by a god to benefit humans. Many Indigenous peoples see themselves as sharing a spiritual life with animals and nature. Consequently, Indigenous peoples are often romanticized in environmentalist literature. Indigenous animism can lead to seeking signs about the meaning of past, present, and future events in nature and often in dreams or visions.[117]

Learning through experience, traditional practices, and the wisdom of elders is the basis for many forms of Indigenous education. Examples of the many forms of Indigenous education can be found in Maenette Benham and Joanne Cooper's *Indigenous Educational Models for Contemporary Practice: In Our Mother's Voice*.[118] Many of these educational practices, in contrast to the use of the scientific method, study nature through careful observation and the learning of traditional knowledge. Knowledge of human social interactions utilizes accumulated wisdom about relationships, which is passed on from generation to generation.

Consequently, elders, who embody their own life experiences, are the keepers of tradition and assume the role of tribal educators.

The United Nations Declaration of the Rights of Indigenous Peoples gives Indigenous peoples the right to control their own education and protection against the loss of language. Of course, all tribal groups have been affected by outside forces and the influences of the world's knowledges. For many Indigenous peoples, the hope is to preserve and restore languages and cultures while integrating influences from the global flow of cultures. Obviously, particularly after the ravages of colonialism and imposition of outside religions, Indigenous peoples will never be able to restore their lives to the state that existed prior to the invasion of these outside forces. However, for the purpose of this book's argument, Indigenous movements are not only part of the global flow of educational practices and ideas, but also often critical of the crass materialism and exploitation of nature embodied in the goals of human capital education.

KEY POINTS: CHARACTERISTICS OF INDIGENOUS EDUCATION

1. Learning of traditional knowledge
   a. Usually taught by elders
   b. Elders' wisdom based on accumulated knowledge from the past
   c. Elders' wisdom based on accumulated personal experience
2. Careful observation of
   a. Nature
   b. Human interaction with nature
   c. Human interaction with other humans
3. Learning from spirits, dreams, and other prophetic signs
   a. Interpretation usually taught by elders
4. Holistic view of humans, nature, and spiritual world
5. Instruction of the interrelationship and interdependence of all humans, nature, and the spiritual world

---

Conclusion: Rejecting the Industrial-Consumer Paradigm?

The existence of different knowledges suggests that there are global educational variations despite global educational similarities in curricula and grade structures. Religion remains a central part of many people's lives and will continue to influence the way they think about the world and the values they hold. The spiritual nature of religions creates a tension with the materialistic values embedded in human capital theory with its emphasis on economic growth and increasing personal income or, in the words of Gandhi, on raising the "standard of living." Not only are there inherent tensions between religion and a consumer-oriented secular society, but there are also conflicts between religions, which reduce the possibility of a uniform world culture. Religious nationalism and religious rejection of Western secular values gives support to Huntington's contention that the future involves a clash of civilizations rather than the sharing of common global values.

Those championing the restoration or maintenance of Indigenous knowledges and culture cast a wary eye on the fruits of Western science and industrialization. Countering the influence of the secular-scientific global culture, Indigenous educational programs stress the learning of traditional knowledge, careful observation of nature and human relations to others and nature, respect for the wisdom of elders, and the importance of the world of spirits. The hope is that Indigenous education programs, as recognized by the United Nations Declaration of the Rights of Indigenous Peoples, will maintain Indigenous cultures and languages while, at the same time, select from the world's knowledges useful information that will aid in the growth of the "standard of life."

Will the globalization of educational practices and policies erode religious values and undermine Indigenous cultures? Or is there some middle ground between education for human capital development and religious or traditional values? Will there be a continuing clash of civilizations, or will all people adopt the similar ways of knowing and seeing the world?

Notes

1 Eduardo Mendieta, "Society's Religion: The Rise of Social Theory, Globalization, and the Invention of Religion," in *Religions/Globalizations: Theories and Cases*, edited by Dwight N. Hopkins, Lois Ann Lorentzen, Eduardo Mendieta, and David Batstone (Durham, NC: Duke University Press, 2001), p. 47.

2 George J. Sefa Dei, Budd L. Hall, and Dorothy Goldin Rosenberg, "Introduction," in *Indigenous Knowledges in Global Contexts: Multiple Readings of Our World*, edited by George J. Sefa Dei, Budd L. Hall, and Dorothy Goldin Rosenberg (Toronto: University of Toronto Press, 2000), p. 4.

3 Paul Wangoola, Mpambo, "The African Multiversity: A Philosophy to ReKindle the African Spirit," in Indigenous Knowledges, p. 273.

4 Ibid.

5 Dei, Hall, and Goldin Rosenberg, "Introduction," in *Indigenous Knowledges in Global Contexts*, p. 3.

6 Richard Nisbett, *The Geography of Thought: How Asians and Westerners Think Differently . . . and Why (New York: Free Press, 2003)*.

7 Ibid., Quote from unnumbered front matter.

8 Ibid.

9 Ibid.

10 Marlene Brant Castellano, "Updating Aboriginal Traditions of Knowledge," in *Indigenous Knowledges in Global Contexts*, pp. 23–24.

11 Ibid., p. 26.

12 Ibid.

13 Ibid., p. 29.

14 Ibid., p. 30.

15 Ibid.

16 Ibid.

17 Wangoola, "The African University . . . ," p. 265.

18 Mahia Maurial, "Indigenous Knowledge and Schooling: A Continuum Between Conflict and Dialogue," in *What Is Indigenous Knowledge? Voices from the Academy*, edited by Ladislaus M. Semali and Joe L. Kincheloe (New York: Falmer Press, 1999), p. 63.

19 George J. Sefa Dei, "African Development: The Relevance and Implications of 'Indigenousness'," in *Indigenous Knowledges in Global Contexts*, p. 73.

20 Ibid.

21 Ibid., p. 74.

22 Ibid., p. 75.

23 For a summary of character traits in individualist and collectivist societies, see Harry C. Triandis, "Individualism and Collectivism: Past, Present, and Future," in *The Handbook of Culture and Psychology*, edited by David Matsumoto (New York: Oxford University Press, 2001), pp. 35–50.

24 Samuel P. Huntington, *The Clash of Civilizations and the Remaking of World Order* (New York: Simon & Schuster, 1996).

25 Ibid., p. 41.

26 Ibid., p. 47.

27 Gabriel Almond, R. Scott Appleby, and Emmanuel Sivan, *Strong Religion: The Rise of Fundamentalisms Around the World* (Chicago: University of Chicago Press, 2003).

28 Mark Juergensmeyer, "The Global Rise of Religious Nationalism," in *Religions/Globalizations: Theories and Cases*, pp. 73–74.

29 Almond, Appleby, and Sivan, *Strong Religion*, p. 91.

30 Huntington, *The Clash of Civilizations and the Remaking of World Order*, p. 45.

31 V. D. Savarkar, *Hindutva Second Edition* (New Delhi: Hindi Sahitya Sadan, 2005). Also see Almond, Appleby, and Sivan, *Strong Religion*, pp. 135–140.

32 Almond, Appleby, and Sivan, *Strong Religion*, pp. 40–45.

33 For an introduction to current strand of Russian nationalism, see Andrew Meier, "Putin's Pariah," *New York Times Magazine* (March 2, 2008). Retrieved from www.nytimes.com/2008/03/02/magazine/02limonov-t.html?pagewanted = all on March 3, 2008.

34 For examples of violent religious confrontations including Western Christianity, see Almond, Appleby, and Sivan, *Strong Religion*, pp. 145–191.

35 Huntington, *The Clash of Civilizations and the Remaking of World Order*, p. 46.

36 Almond, Appleby, and Sivan, *Strong Religion*, p. 114.

37 Regarding the Zapatista movement, see Lois Ann Lorentzen, "Who Is an Indian? Religion, Globalization, and Chiapas," in *Religions/Globalizations: Theories and Cases*, pp. 84–102. Regarding the Indigenous political movement in Bolivia, see Simon Romero, "Protestors in Bolivia Seek More Autonomy," *New York Times* (December 16, 2007). Retrieved from www.nytimes.com/2007/12/16/world/americas/16bolivia.html on March 3, 2008.

38 Fouad Ajami, "The Summoning: 'But They Said, We Will Not Harken'," in *Samuel P. Huntington's The Clash of Civilizations? The Debate* (New York: Council on Foreign Relations, 1996), p. 27.

39 Robert L. Bartley, "The Case for Optimism," in *Samuel P. Huntington's The Clash of Civilizations* , p. 44.

40 Jeane Kirkpatrick, "The Modernizing Imperative," in *Samuel P. Huntington's The Clash of Civilizations*, p. 53.

41 Gerard Piel, "The West Is Best," in *Samuel P. Huntington's The Clash of Civilizations*, p. 55.

42 Richard Osmer and Friedrich Schweitzer, *Religious Education between Modernization and Globalization: New Perspectives on the United States and Germany* (Grand Rapids, MI: William Eerdmans, 2003), p. 11.

43 See Joel Spring, *The American School: From the Puritans to No Child Left Behind Seventh Edition* (New York: McGraw-Hill, 2008), pp. 110–115, 459–478.

44 "Saudi Arabia—Constitution." Retrieved from www.the-saudi.net/saudi-arabia/saudi-constitution.htm on March 4, 2008.

45 Ibid.

46 Leslie S. Nucho, editor, *Education in the Arab World Volume I: Algeria, Bahrain, Egypt, Jordan, Kuwait, Lebanon, Morocco* (Washington, DC: AMIDEAST), p. 150.

47 Gregory Starrett, *Putting Islam to Work: Politics and Religious Transformation in Egypt* (Berkeley: University of California Press, 1998), p. 78.

48 Ibid., pp. 131–132.

49 Vishva Hindu Parishad, "Swagatam." Retrieved from http://vhp.org/swagatam on November 30, 2013.

50 Vishva Hindu Parishad. Retrieved from http://vhp.org/ on November 30, 2013.

51 Almond, Appleby, and Sivan, *Strong Religion*, pp. 140–142, 156–157.

52 Neela Banerjee, "Clashing over Church Ritual and Flag Protocol at the Naval Academy Chapel," *New York Times* (March 8, 2008). Retrieved from www.nytimes.com/2008/03/08/us/08chapel.html on March 8, 2008.

53 Savarkar, *Hindutva*, p. 18.

54 Ibid., p. 113.

55 See Human Rights Watch, "'We Have No Orders to Save You': State Participation and Complicity in Communal Violence in Gujarat." Retrieved from www.hrw.org/reports/2002/india/ on March 7, 2008.

56 Sri Lanka: The Constitution, "Chapter II-Buddhism." Retrieved from www.priu.gov.lk/Cons/1978Constitution/Chapter_02_Amd.html on March 8, 2008.

57 Somini Sengupta, "Sri Lankan City Mired in Ethnic Violence," *New York Times* (May 15, 2006). Retrieved from www.nytimes.com/2006/05/15/world/asia/15lanka.html?pagewanted = all on March 8, 2008.

58 M.K. Gandhi, *Sarvodaya: The Welfare of All* (Ahmedabad, India: Jovanji Dahyabhai Desai Navajivan Press, 1954), p. 27.

59 For instance, see Viniti Vaish's discussion of Gandhi and Sarvodaya in Viniti Vaish, *Biliteracy and Globalization: English Language Education in India* (Clevedon, England: Multilingual Matters, 2008).

60 Gandhi, *Sarvodaya*, p. 194.

61 Ibid., p. 43.

62 Ibid., p. 128.

63 Ibid.

64 Ibid., p. 132.

65 Ibid., p. 7.

66 Ibid.

67 For a study of his lasting influence, see Marc Becker, *Mariátegui and Latin American Marxist Theory* (Athens: Ohio University Center for International Studies, 1993).

68 Sheldon B. Liss, *Marxist Thought in Latin America* (Berkeley: University of California Press, 1984), p. 129.

69 Ibid., p. 284.

70 José Carlos Mariátegui, *Seven Interpretive Essays on Peruvian Reality* (Austin: University of Texas Press, 1971), p. 122.

71 Becker, *Mariátegui and Latin American Marxist Theory*, p. 38.

72 Ibid., p. 37.

73 Mariátegui, *Seven Interpretive Essays*, p. 28.

74 Ibid., p. 29.

75 Ibid., p. 25.

76 Medellín Conference, *Medellín Conference Documents: Justice and Peace* (1968), p. 3. Retrieved from www.shc.edu/theolibrary/resources/medjust.htm on April 21, 2014. November 20, 2004.

77 Quoted in Paulo Freire, *Pedagogy of the Oppressed* (New York: Herder and Herder, 1970), pp. 139–140.

78 Ibid., pp. 3–4.

79 Ibid.

80 Ibid., p. 1.

81 Ibid., p. 10.

82 Ibid.

83 Christian Smith, *The Emergence of Liberation Theology: Radical Religion and Social Movement Theory* (Chicago: University of Chicago Press, 1991), pp. 15–21.

84 Gustavo Gutiérrez, *A Theology of Liberation; 15th Anniversary Edition* (Maryknoll, NY: Orbis Books, 1988), p. xxxviii.

85 Ibid., p. 57.

86 Ibid., p. 56.

87 Ibid.

88 Smith, *The Emergence of Liberation Theology*, p. 19.

89 Ibid., p. 107.

90 Quoted in Sheryl Hirshon with Judy Butler, *And Also Teach Them to Read: The National Literacy Crusade of Nicaragua* (Westport, CT: Lawrence Hill & Company, 1983), p. 5.

91 John L. Hammond, *Fighting to Learn: Popular Education and Guerilla War in El Salvador* (New Brunswick, NJ: Rutgers University Press, 1998), p. 25.

92 Zahra Al Zeera, "Paradigm Shifts in the Social Sciences in the East and West," in *Knowledge across Cultures: A Contribution to Dialogue among Civilizations*, edited by Ruth Hayhoe and Julia Pan (Hong Kong: Comparative Education Research Center, 2001), p. 70.

93 Ibid., pp. 25–23.

94 Ibid., p. 68.

95 Ibid.

96 Gregory Starrett, *Putting Islam to Work: Politics and Religious Transformation in Egypt* (Berkeley: University of California Press, 1998), p. 27.

97 See Robert Hefner, "Introduction: The Culture, Politics, and Future of Muslim Education," in *Schooling Islam: Culture and Politics of Modern Muslim Education*, edited by Robert Hefner and Muhammad Qasim Zaman (Princeton, NJ: Princeton University Press, 2007), pp. 1–39.

98 Ibid., p. 8.

99 Fazlur Rahman, *Islam & Modernity: Transformation of an Intellectual Tradition* (Chicago: University of Chicago Press, 1982), p. 20.

100 A.L. Tibawi, *Islamic Education: Its Traditions and Modernizations into Arab National Systems* (London: Luzac & Company, 1972), p. 71.

101 Bassam Tibi, *Arab Nationalism: Between Islam and the Nation-State* (New York: St. Martin's Press, 1997), p. 93.

102 Tibawi, *Islamic Education*, p. 74.

103 Azyumardi Azra, Dina Afrianty, and Robert Hefner, "Pesantran and Madrasa: Muslim Schools and National Ideals in Indonesia," in *Schooling Islam: Culture and Politics*, pp. 178–179.

104 Ibid., p. 186.

105 Ibid., p. 187.

106 "Constitution of Malaysia Ratified on August 31, 1957," Retrieved from www.slideshare.net/mbl2020/constitution-of-malaysia on April 21, 2014. 2005.

107 Ibid.

108 Rosnani Hashim, Educational Dualism in Malaysia: Implications for Theory and Practice (Oxford: Oxford University Press, 1996), p. 130.

109 Ibid., p. 131.

110 Muhammad Qasim Zaman, "Epilogue: Competing Conceptions of Religious Education," in *Schooling Islam: Culture and Politics*, p. 253.

111 A.H. Nayyar, "Madrasah Education Frozen in Time," in *Education and the State: Fifty Years of Pakistan*, edited by Pervez Hoodbhoy (Karachi: Oxford University Press, 1998), pp. 228, 229, and 232.

112 Ibid., p. 230.

113 Ibid., p. 233.

114 Ibid., p. 226.

115 United Nations General Assembly, *Report of the Human Rights Council: United Nations Declaration on the Rights of Indigenous Peoples, Article 14* (New York: United Nations, 2007), p. 6.

116 Al Zeera, "Paradigm Shifts in the Social Sciences in the East and West," p. 71.

117 See Joel Spring, *How Educational Ideologies Are Shaping Global Society: Intergovernmental Organizations, NGOs, and the Decline of the Nation-State* (Mahwah, NJ: Lawrence Erlbaum, 2004), pp. 100–130.

118 For examples of Indigenous forms of education, see Maenette Benham and Joanne Cooper, editors, *Indigenous Educational Models for Contemporary Practice: In Our Mother's Voice* (Mahwah, NJ: Lawrence Erlbaum, 2000).

7

A GLOBAL WORKFORCE

Migration and the Talent Auction

Envisioning a global workforce, global corporatization has resulted in a world migration of workers accompanied by a migration of refugees. Global migration results in culture and language issues for both migrants and host countries. There are rural to urban migrations resulting in the majority of the world's peoples living in urban centers. In part, global and rural to urban migrations are prompted by hopes of better economic opportunities. Often, skilled and educated workers migrate from poorer to wealthier nations. This migration raises serious issues related to the effect on poorer nations of the loss of skilled and educated workers and how these migrant workers are integrated into the labor force of host nations. Global migration has made multicultural education and language instruction important issues for national school systems. What policies should public school systems adopt for the education of immigrant children who do not speak the dominant or national language? What cultural and language policies should national and local schools adopt when global migration results in multicultural populations?

I will first describe the current pattern of global migration and the migration from rural to urban areas, which includes issues of *brain drain, brain gain, brain waste,* and *brain circulation.* I will examine the educational issues facing the children of global migrants. Migration involves the movement of educated and skill workers from low-income nations and rural areas to more prosperous nations and/or urban centers, which often results in *brain drain.* Some countries experience a *brain gain* by attracting immigrants with high levels of educational achievement. Sometimes migrants to other countries or urban areas are not able to obtain employment commensurate with their educational qualifications. This is called *brain waste.* Some migrants return to their home countries or become transnational with homes in different countries. This phenomenon is captured in the phrase *brain circulation*. Global migration and rural to urban migration have a direct effect on national supplies of educated workers and national school policies.

KEY POINTS: GLOBAL, INTERNATIONAL, AND RURAL TO URBAN MIGRATION

1. Global Migration
   a. Between 1960 and 2013, the number of international migrants more than doubled with 232 million in 2013.
   b. The largest migration patterns are from poorer to wealthier nations.
   c. A small number of countries host 75 percent of the world's international migration.
   d. Immigrant populations have higher rates of unemployment due to:
      i. Lack of networks to find jobs in host country;
      ii. Lack of knowledge about the labor market in host country;
      iii. Discrimination on basis of country of origin.
2. Rural to Urban Migration
   a. In 2008 the majority of the world's population lived in urban centers.
   b. By 2050, 80 percent of the world's population growth will be in urban centers.
   c. In developing countries, the poor constituted about half of the urban population.
3. Brain Drain
   a. Many developing nations are experiencing a migration of their post-secondary educated populations.
      i. This seriously affects health and education services and reduces the tax base in developing nations.
   b. Many migrants are overqualified for the jobs resulting in brain waste.

Global Migration: International and National

Migration is both international and national. Migrations of populations within a country primarily involve population movement from rural to urban centers. International global migration has increased, and apparently it will continue to do so. The largest migration patterns are from poorer to wealthier nations. While wealthier nations have only 16 percent of the world's workers, they have more than 60 percent of global migrants.[1] The report of the Global Commission on International Migration, *Migration in an Interconnected World: New Directions for Action*, declared: "International migration has risen to the top of the global policy agenda . . . In every part of the world, there is now an understanding that the economic, social and cultural benefits of international migration must be more effectively realized, and that the negative consequences of cross-border movement could be better addressed."[2] Phillip Martin provided an official description of global migrants for the Commission: "Migrants are defined by the United Nations as people outside their country of birth or citizenship for 12 months or more."[3]

The United Nations Population Division reported, "More people than ever are living abroad. In 2013, 232 million people, or 3.2 per cent of the world's population, were international migrants, compared with 175 million in 2000 and 154 million in 1990."[4] Most of these migrants are from poorer to richer nations: "The new estimates include breakdowns by region and country of destination and origin, and by sex and age. The North, or developed countries, is home to 136 million international migrants, compared to 96 million in the South, or developing countries. Most international migrants are of working age (20 to 64 years) and account for 74 per cent of the total. Globally, women account for 48 per cent of all international migrants."[5]

In 2013, the following world regions hosted international migrants:

1. Europe—72 million
2. Asia—71 million
3. North America—53 million
4. Africa—19 million
5. Latin America and the Caribbean—9 million
6. Oceania—8 million[6]

The pattern of global migration becomes clearer when it is broken down by country. A small number of countries host 51 percent of the world's international migrants. In 2013, the United States had the largest number of international migrants with 46 million, about equal to 19.8 percent of the total world migrants.[7] Second was the Russian Federation with 11 million. It is important to note that the high percentage of global migrants in the Russian Federation is a result of the 1991 disintegration of the Union of Soviet Socialist Republics (USSR). This is an example of how political changes can affect citizenship. The high number in the Russian Federation is a result of the reclassification of citizens after the dissolving of the USSR. Prior to 1991, there were large numbers of internal migrants who moved from former parts of the USSR to what is now the Russian Federation. After 1991, these formerly internal migrants were reclassified as international migrants.[8]

What countries are the sources of the world migrants? The United Nations Population Division distinguishes between migrants moving to developing countries and migrants moving to developed nations. For example, in 2013, 3.2 million migrated from Bangladesh to India with both being considered developing countries. Afghanistan had the largest total number migrating to developing countries with 2.3 million going to Pakistan and 2.3 million going to Iran.[9]

The complicated nature of global migration is exemplified by migrants to the oil-rich United Arab Emirates. The United Arab Emirates hosts the second largest movement of migrants to a developing country with 2.9 million migrating from India mainly as guest workers.[10] There are also migrants from other countries to the United Arab Emirates as illustrated in the following story involving multiple migrations. In 2013, 29-year-old American citizen Shezanne Cassim was arrested in Dubai for helping to produce a video that poked fun at the Dubai government. In 1976, Cassim's parents had migrated from Sri Lanka to Dubai, "because it was a land of opportunity 'where you could go and make your fortune'."[11] His mother worked for an airline, and his father was an advertising executive, while his two siblings were educated in private British schools. In the early part of the twenty-first century, the family moved to the United States and became American citizens. After attending the University of Minnesota, Cassim, now a U.S. citizen, returned to Dubai to work for a subsidiary of Emirates airline and later as a consultant to PricewaterhouseCoopers before his arrest. Cassim's family's migrations are a good example of brain circulation.

The largest number of migrants going to a developed country in 2013 was the 13 million migrating from Mexico to the United States. Other top sources of immigrants to the United States were China, 2.2 million; India, 2.1 million; and the Philippines, 2.0 million. The top European Union countries were Germany with 1.5 million from Turkey and France with 1.5 million from Algeria.[12]

Refugees

A refugee is defined by the Office of the United Nations High Commissioner for Refugees as: "someone who 'owing to a well-founded fear of being persecuted for reasons of race, religion, nationality, membership of a particular social group or political opinion, is outside the country of his nationality, and is unable to, or owing to such fear, is unwilling to avail himself of the protection of that country'."[13]

In *The State of the World's Refugees 2012*, the UN Office of Refugees reported: "Current trends in forced displacement are testing the international system like never before. Some 33.9 million people were 'people of concern' to UNHCR at the start of 2011, an increase from 19.2 million in 2005."[14]

Rural to Urban Migration

Concurrent with increasing international migration is internal migration from rural to urban areas—the majority of humans now live in cities. A 2008 UN report predicted that "during 2008, the population of the world will become, for the first time in human history, primarily urban, and is likely to continue to urbanize substantially over the coming decades."[15] The UN report also claimed that "the shift of population from relatively low-productivity rural areas to higher productivity urban areas has been a major aspect if not a driver of economic progress."[16]

The following is a list of facts reported by the United Nations regarding global urbanization:

- Almost all of the world's population growth to 2050 will occur in urban areas of developing countries;
- In developing countries the poor constituted about half of the urban population;
- For a majority of developed countries, urban growth is a result of natural growth rather than rural–urban migration;
- Most of the urban population growth is in small cities (under 500,000);
- Large cities are growing at a relatively slow pace;
- The number of poor people is increasing faster in urban areas;
- Urbanization concentrates a large part of the population on a small surface of the earth;
- About 80 percent of the world's population growth to 2050 will be in urban areas in Asia and Africa;
- The growth of the world's rural population is expected to be negative by 2018;
- In 2007, 50 percent of all rural dwellers in the world lived in Asia, primarily in China, India and Indonesia.[17]

The report also noted that the rural to urban migrants tend to be young and to be better educated and have more skills than the rest of the rural population. In other words, there is a brain drain from rural to urban centers. In addition, as noted previously, in developing countries the poor constitute half the urban population. This has strained social services including the provision of public education. Many of the rural to urban migrant poor have been forced "to invade and settle ("squat") on marginal lands, such as under bridges, on floodplains or on steep slopes."[18]

Illegal Migrants

There is also the tragedy of illegal migration. National borders and passport controls can lead to tragedy as some people try to illegally enter countries to gain employment. The following are just a few examples of the tragedies associated with attempts to illegally cross national borders:

- In 2001 in Britain, 58 illegal Chinese migrants died when they were crammed into a sweltering tomato truck.
- In 2002, Spanish authorities found the bodies of 5 illegal immigrant African men in the back of a refrigeration truck carrying vegetables from Morocco.
- In 2003, 19 Latin American migrants died from overheating and suffocation inside a trailer truck as they illegally entered the United States.

- In 2008, Thai authorities reported the death of 37 women and 17 men being illegally smuggled from Myanmar to work in resorts serving foreign tourists in Phuket. The deaths resulted from 121 people being shipped inside an airtight seafood container that measured just 20 feet long and 7 feet wide. These deaths were in addition to those in 2007 that included 22 illegal immigrants found floating in the ocean near the West Coast of Thailand and 11 illegal immigrants killed in truck crash as they were being smuggled.[19]

The Children of Global Migrants in OECD Countries

OECD uses three classifications when discussing the children of immigrants:

1. Foreign-born who migrated at a young age (first generation);
2. Native-born children of foreign-born parents (second generation);
3. Native-born children with one foreign-born parent.

For foreign-born immigrant children, a major issue is differences between the educational systems in the country of origin and the host countries. Is it easy for the school-age child to make the transition into the school system of the new country? Is there a similarity in the curricula between the two nations? Has the child received an education in several other countries before arriving in the new host country? What are the language issues for the new immigrant child? Does the host country have educational provisions for helping immigrant children learn the language used in local schools? The previous questions are important for considering the integration of migrants into the social and economic system of their host country. In OECD countries, these questions are imperative because of the large percentage of youth ages 20 to 29 with migrant backgrounds who are in the labor market. For instance, persons with migrant backgrounds account for almost 45 percent of the 20- to 29-year-olds in Australia. In Canada, the figure is close to 35 percent. In the United States, the figure is about 25 percent, and in France it is around 24 percent.[20]

In general, first-generation children do not obtain the same level of educational achievement as native-born children. The educational achievement of both the first and second generations is related to the educational achievement of their parents. Variations in achievement are related to the immigration policies of the host country. For instance, Australia and Canada select immigrants based on their education qualifications and the needs of their countries' labor markets. In these two countries, the educational achievement of second-generation children is about the same or higher than other native-born children. In contrast, Germany and Belgium recruit low-skilled foreign workers. The educational achievement of the second generation in these two countries is significantly lower than that of other native-born children. In some countries, when the socio-economic status of immigrant parents is taken into account, second-generation children still have lower educational achievement levels compared to other native-born children, particularly in Germany, Belgium, Switzerland, and Austria.[21]

There are significant gender differences in educational achievement among immigrants. Usually, women have lower levels of educational achievement among foreign-born and non-school-age immigrants to developed OECD countries. However, this significantly changes for the second generation. This represents the cultural impact on family dynamics and female status. According to the OECD, "In all countries with the exception of the United States, native-born women with foreign-born parents have a higher educational attainment than their male counterparts."[22] In the United States, educational attainment is almost equal between second-generation men and women.[23]

Except for Canada, the United States, and Australia, first- and second-generation immigrants have higher rates of unemployment relative to native-born workers. Unemployment differences remain high even when the second generation has comparable educational attainment as other native-born workers. OECD provides the following reasons for the higher rates of unemployment:

- Lack of networks: OECD found that a significant proportion of jobs are found through friends and relatives;
- Lack of knowledge about the functioning of the labor market in host country;
- Discrimination on basis of country of origin.[24]

Language is the other factor affecting school achievement and employment opportunities. I will discuss language policies in more detail later in this chapter. However, there are important questions to consider regarding the language usage of first- and second-generation immigrants. Did the immigrant family know the language of the host country before immigrating? Do host countries have educational programs to help first-generation children learn the language of the host country? Do immigrant families continue to speak their mother tongues when at home? According to OECD, "One factor specific to children of immigrants is that they often speak a language at home which differs from that of the host country. Such children tend to have lower [educational achievement] outcomes than other children with a migration background."[25] Does the educational system in the host country try to maintain the languages of their immigrant populations?

The Knowledge Wars: Brain Drain, Gain, and Circulation

The 2011 book *The Global Auction* captures the current national and corporate competition to attract the best workers. The book's authors coin the term "knowledge wars" and write about "the growing emphasis on attracting foreign workers to meet the needs of the national economy. The knowledge wars were extended from a competition for quality jobs to include competition for the most talented workers."[26] They claim that the global war for talent began in the United States and has become an important factor in global politics.[27]

The knowledge wars have resulted in the global migration of skilled and educated workers. The term "brain drain" was first used in the United Kingdom to describe the influx of Indian scientists and engineers.[28] In this situation, the United Kingdom had a brain gain while India lost educated workers. Now there is also focus on brain circulation where skilled and professional workers move between wealthy nations or return to their homelands after migrating to another country.

The report of the Global Commission on International Migration provided a justification for dropping brain drain in favor of brain circulation:

> Given the changing pattern of international migration, the notion of 'brain drain' is a somewhat outmoded one, implying as it does that a migrant who leaves her or his own country will never go back there. In the current era, there is a need to capitalize upon the growth of human mobility by promoting the notion of 'brain circulation', in which migrants return to their own country on a regular or occasional basis, sharing the benefits of the skills and resources they have acquired while living and working abroad.[29]

Brain circulation is aided by national efforts to bring back educated workers lost in the brain drain. In China, returning knowledge workers are called "turtles" as explained in a 2007 issue of the *China Daily*: "Enticed by more opportunities in a blossoming economy, many overseas Chinese—or 'turtles'—are swimming home."[30] The Chinese government is offering special benefits to encourage turtles. Malaysia has developed a national strategy to bring scientists home.[31]

There is a great deal of debate about the effect of the movement of highly educated populations on the knowledge economies of nations. As Brown, Lauder, and Ashton write regarding the global auction for talent, "The brain drain of talent from emerging countries, such as doctors, nurses, teachers, and IT workers can also have negative consequences for the countries they leave behind."[32] They give as an example South Africa, which in 2008 experienced a shortage of 400,000 nurses as the country's supply of nurses migrated to countries offering higher incomes.[33] There are many other examples of the effects of the global auction for talent, such as the fact that "many Central American and island nations in the Caribbean had more that 50 percent of their university-educated citizens living abroad in 2000."[34] Nearly 40 percent of tertiary-educated adults have left Turkey and Morocco, while Africa has lost 30 percent of its skilled professionals.[35]

The problem of brain drain resulting from the global talent auction is serious when you consider the statistics for other nations. In 2000, the number of post-secondary educated citizens emigrating from Guyana, Grenada, and Jamaica was 89 percent, 85.1 percent, and 85.1 percent, respectively. The numbers emigrating from these countries is small because of their small populations. However, the problem is more serious for these countries when considered as a percentage of the total population. Sub-Saharan Africa, a region struggling with poverty, health problems, and wars has lost its educated population: Ghana (46.9%), Mozambique (45.1%), Sierra Leone (52.5%), Kenya (38.4%), Uganda (35.6%), Angola, (33.0%), and Somalia (32.7%). The same pattern is occurring in developing countries in Asia, such as Lao Peoples Democratic Republic (37.4%), Sri Lanka (29.7%), Vietnam (27.1%), Afghanistan (23.3%), and Cambodia (18.3%).[36]

A loss of such high percentages of educated workers from developing countries has devastating effects on health and education services. In part, this is a result of losses to the tax base as high-paid professional workers migrate overseas.[37] For instance, 85 percent of Filipino nurses work overseas with many having migrated to the United Kingdom, Saudi Arabia, Ireland, and Singapore. Over half the graduates of Ghana's medical schools left the country within five years of graduation. Only 360 doctors out of 1,200 doctors educated in Zimbabwe in the 1990s remained in 2001. Twenty-one thousand doctors have left Nigeria to practice in the United States. Similar examples of the loss of medical personnel can be found for other developing countries.[38]

Another way of considering the brain drain is in terms of the figures regarding the percentage of educated immigrants in a particular country, such as the United States. For instance, 83 percent of the migrants over 25 years old from Nigeria to the United States have some form of postsecondary education. Other examples of the percentage of immigrants from a particular country to the United States who are over 25 with postsecondary education are India (80%), Indonesia (75%), Egypt (78%), Sri Lanka (72%), and Pakistan (67%).[39]

If a country invests money in educating a worker and that worker migrates to another country, then the country that provided the original education has lost its investment. For example, training a worker in India to be a data processing specialist in 2001 cost the Indian government from US$15,000 to $20,000. If that worker migrates to another country, then India loses the cost of the training plus the worker's potential contribution to the Indian economy estimated at $2 billion.[40] This fact is important when one considers that in the 1970s, 31 percent of the graduates of one of India's most prestigious schools, Indian Institute of Technology Mumbai, migrated overseas. The overseas migration rate for graduates from India's most prestigious medical school, All India Institute for Medical Sciences, was 56 percent between 1956 and 1980 and 49 percent in the 1990s.[41] This represents a tremendous loss of talent and educational investments for India.

Some researchers claim positive effects for countries experiencing brain drain. One positive effect is the remittances sent home.[42] Also, some researchers are suggesting the migration results in demands for greater government spending on education (brain gain) by populations in less developed countries wanting to migrate.[43] These researchers believe that this can result in a "net brain gain [for countries losing educated workers], that is, a brain gain that is larger than the brain drain; and a net brain gain raises welfare and growth."[44]

The argument that there is a net brain gain as a result of pressures for expanded educational opportunities might only apply to larger nations. The net brain gain argument does not apply to small developing countries that have difficulty maintaining their educational systems because of the loss of educational workers. Also, in the most recent study for the World Bank, Schiff concluded that previous studies had been overly optimistic about the positive effects of brain drain on countries experiencing the loss of educated workers. His conclusion for the World Bank study was that "the brain drain on welfare and growth is likely to be significantly greater, than reported.[45] Frustrated by the difficulty of determining the economic consequences of brain circulation, Vinokur argues that the debate over "who wins, who loses and how much" in brain circulation as being "irresolvable— analytically and empirically."[46]

Brain circulation is not always beneficial for developed nations such as members of OECD. In some cases, jobs migrate rather than educated workers, with low- and high-skilled jobs moving to developing countries. For instance, Brown and Lauder found software companies relocating from the United States and the European Union to India. In the United States, according to Brown and Lauder, software developers earned in 1997 from $49,000 to 67,500 as compared to $15,700 to 19,200 in India.[47] The implication of these findings is that rather than India experiencing a brain drain, they could be experiencing a gain in brain-related jobs. Or, in other words, the United States could experience a loss of jobs requiring highly skilled workers to countries with lower wages and an increasing number of college graduates.

What are the effects of educated and skilled migrants and foreign students on the destination country? Researchers find contradictory effects. In the most recent research for the World Bank, it was concluded that reducing the flow of students and skilled workers to the United States would have a strong negative impact on innovation. Raising the number of foreign graduate students by 10 percent would increase the number of patent applications by 4.7 percent.[48] On the other hand, researchers have found no significant increases in wages for college graduates in developed countries, such as the United States and Great Britain, except for those few entering at the top of the wage scale.[49] Two possible implications of these finding are that developed countries are experiencing an oversupply of college graduates, which would reduce wages, and that the brain gain from migration might be depressing wages for college graduates.

Brain Waste

Is there a global oversupply of college graduates? Do host countries utilize the educational qualifications of their immigrants? Is there a global "brain waste"? According to OECD findings, well-educated immigrants have difficulty utilizing their educational training in OECD countries for the following reasons:

- Problems with the recognition of degrees in the country of origin;
- Lack of human and social capital specific to the host country, such as proficiency in the language of the host country;
- Local labor market conditions;
- Various forms of discrimination.[50]

Not surprisingly, given the previously mentioned factors, OECD statisticians found that more immigrants were overqualified for their jobs than native-born workers. The overqualification of immigrants varied between countries. In survey data for 2003–2004 for workers aged 15 to 64, the highest percentages of foreign-born workers who were overqualified were in Spain (42.9%), Greece (39.3%), Australia (24.6%), and Ireland (23.8%). The countries with the smallest percentages of overqualified foreign-born workers were Luxembourg (9.1%), Hungary (9.7%), Czech Republic (10.0%), and Switzerland (12.5%). In the United States, which as previously stated has 19.8 percent of the total global migrants, the percentage of overqualified foreign-born workers was 18.1 percent.[51]

Examining similar statistics for the World Bank, Caglar Ozden stresses the importance of immigration laws and the nature of the labor market in determining the percentage of overqualified foreign-born workers:

> Despite the relatively large share of migrants from developing countries, migrants to the United States are relatively more educated. This selection effect might be the result of the relative ease with which highly educated people can migrate to the United States. The labor market and migration policies seem to favor the more educated in the United States, especially when compared to Europe.[52]

What about native-born workers? Is there brain waste or an overeducated population? Of course, education has other benefits to the person and society than those related to employment. OECD provides national statistics on native-born workers who are overeducated for their jobs. Keep in mind that in every nation a higher percentage of foreign-born workers are overqualified for their jobs as compared to native-born workers. The countries that have the most native-born workers who are overqualified for their jobs are Spain (24%), Australia (19%), Ireland (15.7%), Belgium (15.6%), and the United Kingdom (15.3%).[53]

One measure of labor market discrimination against immigrant workers is the difference between the percentages of native-born workers who are overqualified for their jobs as compared to immigrant workers. If there is no difference, then immigrant workers are being treated the same as native-born workers in the labor market. The greater the disparity in qualifications between the two, the greater the degree of discrimination or difficulties for foreign workers entering the labor market. The highest ratios between overqualified native-born workers and overqualified foreign-born workers are in Greece, Italy, Luxembourg, Sweden, Austria, and the Czech Republic. In other words, these national labor markets are the most difficult for immigrants to find employment that utilizes their skills and education.[54]

A critical evaluation of the issue of brain waste might claim that large corporations are pressuring national governments to raise the educational attainment of their populations as a means of ensuring a cap or lowering of wages for educated workers. For instance, an oversupply of college graduates might reduce wages for the college educated. This would benefit the employer but not the employee. This argument is supported by the findings of Phillip Brown and Hugh Lauder. Regarding college graduates in the United States, they conclude that since 1973 "the vast majority of college graduates have received no additional 'premium' on their investments in their human capital (as promised by those arguing for human capital education for the knowledge economy) compared to college graduates in the 1970s."[55] For the United Kingdom, they argue that "the first jobs taken by young people today may have less income and status associated with them than when their fathers entered the labor market."[56]

There will be variations in the actual economic outcomes for individuals swept up in the rhetoric of human capital education. The paradigm of human capital education drives people to go to school to get well-paid jobs, which might not exist after they graduate. Caught up in the global flow of well-educated migrant workers, the graduate might suffer the emotional pain of cultural change, loss of social and family relations, and a sense of being homeless. As I discussed in Chapter 6, Gandhi warned that there is a difference between a "standard of living" and a "standard of life." The human capital model of education promises but frequently does not deliver a higher standard of living. There is no promise about improving the standard of life. Some global migrants might experience a declining standard of life through cultural and geographical dislocation and the possibility of being overeducated for jobs in their host countries.

Remittances and Unskilled Labor

Global migration creates interdependence in the global economy particularly as a result of the money (remittances) immigrants send back to their home countries. Economists suggest that countries experiencing brain drain to wealthier countries benefit from remittances. This has been particularly true for legal and illegal immigrants from Central and South America to the United States. Most of the migrant workers are unskilled, and their families that have been left behind depend on their remittances. However, the amounts of remittances are directly affected by economic conditions in the host country. This became starkly clear in 2008 when the United States economy began to erode and remittances began to decline to Central and South America. In 2008, the Inter-American Development Bank reported that 50 percent of Latin American adults living in the 50 states and the District of Columbia in the United States sent remittances on a regular basis to their families. This percentage was lower than the 73 percent reported in 2006. This was after a steady growth in remittances since 2000. Normally, unskilled workers from Latin America earn an average of $1,600 a month and send an average of $160 of that pay back to their homelands. Remittances reached $1 billion in 10 of the states of the United States with the largest coming from Nevada, Colorado, Washington, Massachusetts, and California.[57]

In 2013, according to the *Los Angeles Times* article "Remittances to Latin America Rebound—Except in Mexico": "The amount of money U.S. immigrants send to their families in Latin America has more than doubled since 2000, and the cash flow home—except to Mexico—has recovered from a considerable drop during the Great Recession, a 13-year survey of remittance trends shows."[58] The *Business News Americas* also reported on the recovery of remittances in a 2013 article titled "Remittances to Guatemala Well on Track to Surpass 2012 Inflow."[59] In summary, the global brain circulation is accompanied by a global flow of money.

Global Migration and Multicultural Education

A main concern of the Global Commission on International Migration is how nations maintain social cohesion with increasing multicultural populations. This is an important educational problem for wealthier nations facing an influx of immigrant cultures. The commission declares the existence of nations containing a single cultural population a thing of the past:

> International migration is increasing not only in scale and speed, but also in terms of the number of countries and the range of people involved. Throughout the world, people of different national origins, who speak different languages, and who have different customs, religions and patterns of behavior are coming into unprecedented contact with each other. As a result, the notion of the socially or ethnically homogeneous nation state with a single culture has become increasingly outdated. Most societies are now characterized by a degree (and often a high degree) of diversity.[60]

Consequently, global migration is confronting national school systems with the problem of educating multicultural and multilingual populations. The Global Commission on International Migration is concerned that unless immigrants are integrated into the social structures of their host societies, nations will face problems of social cohesion resulting in increased cultural conflicts between native-born and foreign-born populations. The commission stresses under the heading "Strengthening Social Cohesion through Integration" in its six "Principles of Action" that the integration of immigrants to national life "should be actively supported by local and national authorities, employers and members of civil society, and should be based on a commitment to non-discrimination and gender equity. It should also be informed by an objective public, political and media discourse on international migration."[61]

The problem of social cohesion resulting from global migration has stimulated many national responses to the issue of multicultural education. Multiculturalism also involves language issues. Sometimes national school systems provide little help in maintaining immigrant languages and either neglect language issues facing immigrant children or are primarily focused on ensuring that they learn the dominant language of the host country. Also, some government leaders worry that the global use of English will undermine their national language. For example, worried about the effects of globalization, the Thai Ministry of Culture felt compelled to issue a small booklet of traditional nicknames compiled with help from language experts at the Royal Institute, the official authority on Thai language. The concern was that parents were no longer giving their children Thai nicknames like Shrimp, Chubby, and Crab but were using English nicknames such as Mafia or Seven—as in 7-Eleven—Tom Cruise, Elizabeth, Army, Kiwi, Charlie, and God. Vira Rojpojchanarat, the permanent secretary of the Thai Ministry of Culture, declared that the booklet was necessary: "It's important because it's about the usage of the Thai language. We worry that Thai culture will vanish." On the other hand, Manthanee Akaracharanrya, a 29-year-old real estate contractor, whose nickname is the English word "Money," said that English nicknames were practical because foreigners had a hard time pronouncing Thai words.[62]

It is not possible in this book to describe all national forms of multicultural education. If readers are interested in particular national approaches to multicultural education, there are a number of works that can be consulted.[63] While I cannot describe all national multicultural educational programs, I can indicate international covenants related to multicultural education and provide a general outline of differing approaches. For instance, in Chapter 6, I discussed the United Nations' Declaration of the Rights of Indigenous Peoples, which protects the educational methods and languages and cultures of these peoples. The United Nations' 1960 Convention against Discrimination in Education in Article 5, Section C provides clear protection of cultural and language minorities, which would include immigrant children. Article 5, Section C states:

> (C) It is essential to recognize the right of members of national minorities to carry on their own educational activities, including the maintenance of schools and, depending on the educational policy of each State, the use or the teaching of their own language, provided however:
>   1. That this right is not exercised in a manner which prevents the members of these minorities from understanding the culture and language of the community as a whole and from participating in its activities, or which prejudices the national sovereignty;
>   2. That the standard of education is not lower than the general standard laid down or approved by the competent authorities; and
>   3. That attendance at such schools is optional.[64]

The first thing to note in Article 5, Section C of the United Nations' 1960 Convention against Discrimination in Education is the assertion that national minorities should have the right to control and maintain their own schools in an effort to protect minority cultures and languages. If nations were to act on this aspect of the 1960 convention, then immigrant minorities would be given the ability by governments to protect their immigrant cultures and languages. Of course, there is the danger that recognition of this right might result in children being excluded from the language and the culture of the host country. This could lead to discrimination. Consequently, Section C contains Clause 1, which stresses that this right should not result in the child not learning the majority language and culture. In other words, the protection of cultural and language rights of minority children should not result in them being excluded from the language and the culture of the majority. Also, attendance at schools operated by language and cultural minorities is presented as a right but not a requirement as stated in Section C, Clause 3.

What about cultural differences that include religious differences? A model for this issue can be found in the 1950 European Convention, which was incorporated into the Treaty for the European Union. The convention declares that "the State shall respect the right of parents to ensure such education and teaching in conformity with their own religious and philosophical convictions."[65] If this right were followed by all national governments, then religious rights in education would be protected.

A world-famous crusader for language rights, Tove Skutnabb-Kangas, has argued that languages are disappearing as quickly as living species. In part, she argues this a result of the spread of English, an issue I have discussed in previous chapters. It is also a result of nations not protecting minority languages and not using them as a medium of instruction in their educational systems. Skutnabb-Kangas proposes "A Universal Covenant of Linguistic Human Rights" to protect the languages of national minorities and global migrants:

Everybody Has the Right

- To identify with their mother tongue(s) and to have this identification accepted and respected by others
- To learn the mother tongue(s) fully, orally (when physiologically possible) and in writing
- To education mainly through the medium of their mother tongue(s), and within the state-financed educational system
- To use the mother tongue in most official situations (including schools)

Other Languages

- Whose mother tongue is not an official language in the country where s/he is resident ... to become bilingual (or trilingual, if s/he has 2 mother tongues) in the mother tongue(s) and (one of) the official language(s) (according to her own choice)

The Relationship between Languages

- Any change ... [in] mother tongue ... [being] voluntary (includes knowledge of long-term consequences) ... [and] not imposed

Profit from Education

- To profit from education, regardless of what her mother tongue is[66]

Tove's language rights convention tackles a number of issues. First is the problem of educational equality when classroom instruction is presented in a language that is different from the family language of the student. In this circumstance, the student is at a disadvantage compared to pupils whose home language is the same as the language of instruction. Tove's proposal would guarantee that children could receive their education in their mother tongue. Of course, if students only learn their minority languages, then they could be excluded or discriminated against in the political and economic system. To correct this situation, Tove stresses that children should learn the dominant language of the society in which they are living. Therefore, she argues, these children should become bilingual or trilingual.

In *Globalization and Educational Rights*, I proposed language and cultural rights articles that I believe should be included in national constitutions.[67] My intention in proposing these was to protect the language and cultures of national minorities and immigrants. My list of cultural and language rights in education is based, in part, on existing human rights conventions. Contrary to many others, I stress the importance of protecting religious cultures and religious languages. My list of cultural and language rights in education includes the following:

- Everyone has a right to an education using the medium of their mother tongue within a government-financed school system when the number of students requesting instruction in that mother tongue equals the average number of students in a classroom in that government-financed school system.
- Everyone has the right to learn the dominant or official language of the nation. The government-financed school system will make every effort to ensure that all students are literate in the dominant or official language of the country.
- Everyone has the right to instruction in a language used for religious purposes, such as Qur'anic Arabic or Hebrew, within a government-financed school system when the number of students requesting instruction in that language equals the average number of students in a classroom in that government-financed school system.
- The duty and right to an education includes the right to a secular or religious education financed by the government. No student will be forced to receive a religious education.

- The right of the parents to choose a government-financed school based on their philosophical convictions and/or cultural values includes the right for their philosophical convictions and/or cultural values to be reflected in the content and methods of instruction.[68]

In summary, there are several international covenants protecting the linguistic and cultural rights of minority groups within nations including those of immigrants. However, many nations, including many within OECD, are more concerned with assimilating minority and immigrant populations into the mainstream of their societies. The fear is often of violence between dominant and minority groups and the loss of a sense of national community. On the other hand, some countries, such as Singapore, have reduced cultural tensions by creating an educational system where parents can choose to send their children to schools where classes are taught in the family's mother tongue. A sense of national community is supposedly achieved through a nationalistic curriculum and the learning of a common language, in addition to the mother tongues of its citizens, namely English.[69] In the next section, I will explore the range of possible national responses to multicultural and multilingual populations.

Educational Responses to Multicultural and Multilingual Populations

There are a variety of possible educational responses by national governments to increasing multicultural and multilingual populations resulting from global migration. I am placing these responses on a scale from no effort by the educational system to preserve minority languages and cultures to strong effort to preserve them. This scale is not meant to be judgmental with one end of the scale being considered negative and the other end positive. Of course, my proposal for an amendment to national constitutions indicates my own preference for preserving languages and cultures.

However, I am also realistic about special historical conditions that complicate multicultural issues. For instance, in Malaysia, former British colonizers discriminated against Malay culture and language while importing workers from India and China. Today, the Malaysian government is trying to rectify this historical condition by giving special preferences to Malay language and culture over protests from the Indian and Chinese minorities. Complicating the issue in Malaysia are increased demands to learn English for global commerce.[70] The debates over language and cultural policies in Malaysia highlight the difficulty of developing any single multicultural educational plan for every nation. Each country must work out its own solutions to fit the particular conditions. My hope is that all national school systems in trying to resolve multicultural issues will keep in mind the global efforts to protect cultures and languages.

With the previous qualifications to my scale, I would put at one end national school systems that provide no special help to linguistic and cultural minorities.

In this situation, minority and immigrant students are immersed in the culture and language of the country without receiving any help. Now this might be a planned approach, or, on the other hand, it could result from a lack of concern by educational leaders. If planned, then national leaders might have adopted a sink or swim attitude with the hope that minority cultures and languages will disappear. Students might be discouraged from speaking their mother tongues.

At the next step on the scale, government schools could provide special programs and classes to help minority and immigrant cultures assimilate to the dominant culture. This educational approach might be called planned assimilation. Students could be assisted in learning the national language including using bilingual education programs. These bilingual programs would not be for the purpose of preserving minority languages and cultures. The programs would only assist students to learn the majority language.

A variation to the previous assimilation scenario might be a curriculum that stresses teaching about other cultures in hopes that this will result in fewer cultural conflicts. Teaching about other cultures is not the same as trying to maintain different cultures. The purpose would not be to preserve minority cultures but to maintain social cohesion and reduce social tensions. The goal would be to maintain the dominant position of the majority culture and language.

The next step on the scale might involve educational attempts to maintain minority cultures and languages while at the same time creating unity through a shared culture and language. In this situation, bilingual education would be for the purpose of maintaining minority languages while also teaching the national language. Parents could have the choice of sending their children to schools where the family's mother tongue is used in classroom instruction. The schools using the mother tongue of the parents for instruction would center the curriculum on the cultural background of the students. Instruction would also be required in the national language, and the curriculum would introduce students to the country's history, government, and cultures. This approach might be called unity through diversity where everyone feels united by sharing a learned national language and an understanding of the nation's attempt to maintain a multicultural society.

One variation to the previous scenario would be government support of religious schools where parents have a choice to send their children to a particular religious school. Consider a society with Buddhist, Christian, Hindu, and Muslim populations. One might assume that cultural traditions of the population are reflected in their religious practices. Choice of school based on religion might be a means of ensuring a multicultural society. Of course, language is still an issue. Would each religious school use the language of its particular religious culture for instruction? The answer is dependent on the circumstances of the various religions and whether there are cultural and language differences within each religious group.

The next step on the scale might involve cultural groups controlling their own schools and using their languages for instruction and traditional educational methods. This is the United Nations' proposal for protecting the rights of

Indigenous peoples. The school curriculum would reflect the culture of the group in control and would make every effort to maintain cultural traditions including religious traditions. In this scenario, the goal of the educational system is to maintain a multicultural and multilingual society.

Embodied in some of the previously discussed scenarios is the idea of choice, such as parents choosing to send their children to a school using their mother tongue or associated with their religious beliefs. Should educational choice be financially supported by the government? In most cases, choices can only be meaningful if parents have the economic freedom to send their child to a particular type of school. Financed by the government, educational choice might be one way for schooling to maintain multilingual and multicultural societies.

There is also the issue of control. Should national governments control the content of instruction, or should that be left to the school or local community? For Indigenous groups, the stress is on tribal control. What about religious schools? In Indonesia, the reader will recall from Chapter 6, the government mandates a general curriculum for its religious schools. On the other hand, should the religious community associated with the school determine the curriculum?

Another option is what might be called education for cosmopolitanism. Rather than educating for submission to the will of a nation, students might be educated as global citizens where they learn to move easily among the world's peoples with an acceptance of differences in cultures and languages. In this case, education would not attempt to ensure allegiance to a particular nation-state but would instead try to create an allegiance to humanity and a concern for the welfare of all people.

National discussions of multicultural education are beset with issues involving choice, local versus national control, the role of religion in education, and the desire by the majority to ensure that their language and culture remain dominant. How this will work out in the future is not clear. Those believing in the development of a global education culture would argue that national policies will eventually become uniform regarding multilingual and multicultural populations. However, the differences in national histories and conditions would suggest that there may not be a single policy that can fit all circumstances. Each nation may have to find its own path in resolving the multicultural education issues in a world of mass global migrations.

Conclusion: A World in Motion

The globalization of the workforce has resulted in increasing migration, or, as it is now stated, greater brain circulation. Education plays an important role in this process. Increasing schooling can result in brain drain from poorer countries. The skilled and well educated in developing countries are increasingly moving to countries where they can have higher incomes. This phenomenon can cause an imbalance in the distribution of the world's educated population. Brain drain is matched by brain gain in richer countries. This type of global migration could exasperate the disparities between the rich and poor. In addition, rural to urban migrations in developing countries are increasing the plight and size of the urban poor while depleting rural areas of their educated populations. As a consequence, rural and developing nations are suffering a shortage of educated personnel in vital areas, such as health care and education.

Global migration is pushing the issue of multicultural education to the forefront of school agendas. Embedded in the issue of multicultural education is the preservation of the power of national elites. Dominant elites can feel threatened by minority cultures that continue to use their minority languages. Sometimes elites feel that their power will be protected if the schools protect their language and culture while trying to eradicate other languages and cultures. On the other hand, minority groups often demand some recognition and protection of their cultures and languages in schools. As I suggested previously, there is no single solution for the issue of multicultural education because of the peculiar historical and cultural circumstances of each nation. Maybe this issue will be resolved in the future with a form of cosmopolitan education where each student is taught to hold allegiance to humanity rather than a nation-state.

KEY POINTS: DIFFERENT FORMS OF MULTICULTURAL EDUCATION IN A WORLD OF MASS MIGRATIONS

1. Immersion of children of minority cultures into the dominant culture and language of the nation
   a. No special help for linguistic and cultural minority students
   b. Minority students are discouraged from speaking their mother tongues
   c. Language of the classroom is the language of the majority population
   d. The curriculum reflects the history and culture of the majority population
2. Planned assimilation
   a. Special classes and programs to help students learn the majority language
   b. Bilingual programs to help students learn the majority language but not for the purpose of preserving minority languages and cultures
   c. Teaching about other cultures for purpose of maintaining social cohesion
3. Unity through diversity
   a. Educational efforts to maintain minority cultures and languages
   b. Classroom instruction using the mother tongue of the family

    c. The teaching of a shared culture and language
    d. Curriculum materials that include a variety of cultural perspectives
4. Religious schools
    a. Parents given choice of religious school
    b. Each religious school reflects the culture and language of the local members of that religion
5. Each national cultural group controls its own schools
    a. Each cultural group determines the content and methods of instruction
    b. Each cultural group determines the language of instruction

Notes

1 See Phillip Martin, "Migrants in the Global Labor Market"; and John Parker, "International Migration Data Collection." Both papers were prepared for the policy analysis and research program of the Global Commission on International Migration, Geneva, and were utilized in the report of the Global Commission on International Migration, *Migration in an Interconnected World: New Directions for Action* (Geneva: Global Commission on International Migration, 2005).
2 Global Commission on International Migration, *Migration in an Interconnected World*, p. vii.
3 Martin, "Migrants in the Global Labor Market," p. 7.
4 United Nations, Department of Economic and Social Affairs, Population Division, "232 Million International Migrants Living Abroad Worldwide—New UN Global Migration Statistics Reveal." Retrieved from http://esa.un.org/unmigration/wall chart2013.htm on December 2, 2013.
5 Ibid.
6 United Nations, Department of Economic and Social Affairs, Population Division, Fact Sheets, "The Number of International Migrants Worldwide Reaches 232 Million." Retrieved from http://esa.un.org/unmigration/wallchart2013.htm on December 2, 2013.
7 Ibid.
8 Ibid.
9 United Nations, Department of Economic and Social Affairs, Population Division, Fact Sheets, "International Migration 2013: Migrants by Origin and Destination." Retrieved from http://esa.un.org/unmigration/wallchart2013.htm on December 5, 2013.
10 Ibid.
11 Ben Hubbard, "Arrests over Satirical Video Lay Bare Emirati Sensitivities," *New York Times* (December 5, 2013). Retrieved from www.nytimes.com/2013/12/06/world/middleeast/united-arab-emirates-satirical-video.html?ref=world&_r=0&pagewanted=print on December 6, 2013.
12 United Nations, Department of Economic and Social Affairs, Population Division, Fact Sheets, "International Migration 2013: Migrants by Origin and Destination."
13 Office of the United Nations High Commissioner for Refugees, "Refugees." Retrieved from www.unhcr.org/pages/49c3646c125.html on December 5, 2013.

14 Office of the United Nations High Commissioner for Refugees, *The State of the World's Refugees 2012*. Retrieved from www.unhcr.org/publications/4-introduction-trends-in-forced-displacement.html#more-4 on December 5, 2013.

15 United Nations, Department of Economic and Social Affairs, Population Division, *United Nations Expert Group Meeting on Population Distribution, Urbanization, Internal Migration and Development New York, 21–23 January 2008* (New York: United Nations, 2008), p. 3.

16 Ibid.

17 Ibid, pp. 3–4.

18 Ibid., pp. 5–9.

19 Seth Mydans, "Migrants Perish in Truck to Thailand," *New York Times* (April 11, 2008). Retrieved from www.nytimes.com/2008/04/11/world/asia/11thai.html?pagewanted=print on January 13, 2014; and Emma Daly, "World Briefing: Spain: Immigrants Found Dead in Truck," *New York Times* (October 12, 2002). Retrieved from www.nytimes.com/2002/10/12/world/world-briefing-europe-spain-immigrants-found-dead-in-truck.html on January 14, 2014.

20 OECD, *International Migration Outlook: Annual Report 2007 Edition* (Paris: OECD, 2007), p. 79.

21 Ibid. pp. 79–80.

22 Ibid., p. 81.

23 "Annex Table I.A1.3: Education Levels for Immigrants, the Second Generation, and Other Native-Born, 20–29 and Not in Education, by Gender, Latest Available Year," in OECD, *International Migration Outlook*, pp. 92–93.

24 Ibid., p. 85.

25 Ibid., p. 80.

26 Phillip Brown, Hugh Lauder, and David Ashton, *The Global Auction: The Broken Promises of Education Jobs, and Incomes* (Oxford: Oxford University Press, 2011), p. 22.

27 Ibid., p. 88.

28 Annie Vinokur, "Brain Migration Revisited," *Globalisation, Societies and Education* 4(1) 2006, pp. 7–24.

29 Global Commission on International Migration, *Migration in an Interconnected World*, p. 31.

30 R. Jiaojiao, "The Turning Tide," *China Daily* (May 30, 2007), p. 20.

31 Susan Robertson, "Editorial: Brain Drain, Brain Gain and Brain Circulation," *Globalisation, Societies and Education* 4(1) 2006, pp. 1–5.

32 Brown, Lauder, and Ashton, *The Global Auction*, p. 92.

33 Ibid.

34 Caglar Ozden and Maurice Schiff, "Overview," in *International Migration, Remittances & the Brain Drain*, edited by Caglar Ozden and Maurice Schiff (Washington, DC: The World Bank, 2006), p. 11.

35 Robertson, "Editorial," pp. 1–5.

36 Frederic Docquier and Abdeslam Marfouk, "International Migration by Educational Attainment, 1990–2000," in *International Migration*, pp. 175–185.

37 See Devesh Kapur and John McHale, *Give Us Your Best and Brightest: The Global Hunt for Talent and Its Impact on the Developing World* (Washington, DC: Center for Global Development, 2005).

38 Ibid., pp. 25–29.

39 Ibid., p. 17.

40 Vinokur, "Brain Migration Revisited."

41 Kapur and McHale, *Give Us Your Best and Brightest*, pp. 21–22.

42 Richard Adams, "Remittances and Poverty in Guatemala" in *International Migration*, pp. 53–80; and Jorge Mora and J. Edward Taylor, "Determinants of Migration, Destination, and Sector Choice: Disentangling Individual, Household, and Community Effects," in *International Migration*, pp. 21–52.

43 O. Stark, "Rethinking the Brain Drain," *World Development* 32(1) 2004, pp. 15–22.

44 Maurice Schiff, "Brain Gain: Claims about Its Size and Impact on Welfare and Growth Are Greatly Exaggerated," in *International Migration*, p. 202.

45 Ibid., p. 203.

46 Vinokur, "Brain Migration Revisited," p. 20.

47 Phillip Brown and Harold Lauder, "Globalization, Knowledge and the Myth of the Magnet Economy," *Globalisation, Societies and Education* 4(1) 2006, pp. 25–57.

48 Gnanaraj Chellaraj, Keith Maskus, and Aadotya Mattoo, "Skilled Immigrants, Higher Education, and U.S. Innovation," in *International Migration*, pp. 245–260.

49 Lawrence Mishel and Jared Bernstein, *The State of Working America 2002/2003* (Ithaca, NY: Cornell University Press, 2003).

50 OECD, *International Migration Outlook*, p. 132.

51 Ibid., p. 137.

52 Caglar Ozden, "Educated Migrants: Is There Brain Waste?" in *International Migration*, pp. 236–237.

53 OECD, *International Migration Outlook*, p. 137.

54 Ibid.

55 Brown and Lauder, "Globalization, Knowledge and the Myth of the Magnet Economy," p. 37.

56 Ibid.

57 Inter-American Development Bank, "Fewer Latin Americans Sending Money Home from the United States, Survey Finds" (April 30, 2008). Retrieved from www.iadb.org/en/news/news-releases/2008–04–30/fewer-latin-americans-sending-money-home-from-the-united-states-survey-finds,4595.html on December 5, 2013.

58 Carol J. Williams, "Remittances to Latin America Rebound—Except in Mexico," *Los Angeles Times* (November 15, 2013). Retrieved from www.latimes.com/world/worldnow/la-fg-wn-remittances-latin-america-study-20131114,0,2874353.story#ixzz2miVwVQXY on December 6, 2013.

59 Ulric Rindebro, "Remittances to Guatemala Well on Track to Surpass 2012 Inflow," *Business News Americas* (December 5, 2013). Retrieved from www.bnamericas.com/news/banking/remittances-to-guatemala-well-on-track-to-surpass-2012-inflow on December 6, 2013.

60 Global Commission on International Migration, *Migration in an Interconnected World*, p. 42.

61 Ibid., p. 4.

62 T. Fuller, "In Thai Cultural Battle, Name-Calling Is Encouraged," *New York Times* (August 23, 2007). Retrieved from www.nytimes.com/2007/08/29/world/asia/29nickname.html?_r=0 on December 6, 2013.

63 For global perspectives on multicultural education, see James Banks, editor, *Diversity and Citizenship Education: Global Perspectives* (New York: Jossey-Bass, 2007); Carl Grant and Joy Lei, editors, *Global Constructions of Multicultural Education; Theories and Realities* (Mahwah, NJ: Lawrence Erlbaum, 2001); Iris Rotberg, editor, *Balancing Change and Tradition Global Education Reform* (Lanham, MD: Scarecrow Education, 2004); Stephen Stoer and Luiza Cortesao, "Multiculturalism and Educational Policy in a Global

Context," in *Globalization and Education: Critical Perspectives*, edited by Nicholas Burbules and Carlos Torres (New York: Routledge, 2000), pp. 253–274.

64 "Convention against Discrimination in Education, 1960," in *Basic Documents on Human Rights Third Edition*, edited by Ian Brownlie (New York: Oxford University Press, 1994), pp. 320–321.

65 "European Convention on Human Rights and Its Five Protocols," in *Basic Documents*, p. 342.

66 See Tove Skutnabb-Kangas, *Linguistic Genocide in Education or Worldwide Diversity and Human Rights?* (Mahwah, NJ: Lawrence Erlbaum, 2000), pp. 567–638.

67 Joel Spring, *Globalization and Educational Rights* (Mahwah, NJ: Lawrence Erlbaum, 2001).

68 Ibid., pp. 161–162.

69 For a discussion of Singapore and a general picture of multiculturalism in a global society, see Joel Spring, *How Educational Ideologies are Shaping Global Society* (Mahwah, NJ: Lawrence Erlbaum, 2004), pp. 1–28.

70 For an introduction to the problems caused by the multicultural legacy of British colonialism, including Malaysia, see Joel Spring, *Pedagogies of Globalization: The Rise of the Educational Security State* (Mahwah, NJ: Lawrence Erlbaum, 2006), pp. 152–189.

8

GLOBALIZATION AND COMPLEX THOUGHT

Is There a Theory of Educational Globalization?

Throughout this book, I have provided examples supporting a number of theoretical perspectives regarding the globalization of education, including world education culture, postcolonial/critical, world system, and culturalist. Are they all right? I would argue, "No!" Are they all of wrong? Again my answer is, "No!" How can theories be both right and wrong?

I think people can be trapped by a form of techno-rational thought that assumes that humans can find, or that they have found, a theory to explain human behavior including interactions between humans in social settings. What we actually have are theories that serve as explanations for behaviors in certain contexts. In other words, the discussed theories are true for the examples provided but not for all other situations. The problem is that people sometimes assume that if they find a number of instances when a theory is true, then it is true for all cases.

In the twenty-first century, scholars continue to grasp at theories that will open the door to truth. However, complex thinking suggests that life is filled with the unexpected and that we can only guess at the future. Scholars often forget that human actions are more driven by emotions and fantasies than by reason. French sociologist and philosopher Edgar Morin states, "We are infantile, neurotic, frenzied beings and yet we are rational. That is truly the stuff that human beings are made of."[1]

Humans, he argues, often live in a world of fantasy and imagination combined with self-deception. Humans are often captured by the demonic, which drives them to folly and madness. This description of humanity applies to scholarly work, which is a complex activity that might involve rational, infantile, neurotic, imaginative, self-deceptive, and demonic thought processes. Such a view of scholarly work and humanity leads to what Morin calls the "principle of rational uncertainty." Uncertainty and unpredictability are the conditions of humanity.

Despite using elaborate strategies to plan for the future, we can never be certain of the outcome of our actions. Morin refers to the desire for certainty and predictability as "an illness of our minds."[2] The principle of rational uncertainty, which Morin believes should be part of the education of children, means that rationality "must recognize the contributions of emotions, love, repentance" and that humans "must remain open to everything that disputes it; otherwise it closes itself into a doctrine and becomes rationalization."[3]

Human capital theory applied to education is a good example of an attempt to add certainty to the workings of society. Economists, who are the major proponents of human capital theory, are often inaccurate in their economic predictions. Morin states that "economics, the most mathematically advanced social science is the most socially, humanly backward science because it has abstracted itself from the social, historical, political, psychological and ecological conditions inseparable from economic activity."[4] Consequently, economists have a poor track record about predicting and managing economies. Can we know what the labor market will be 12 to 16 years after a child enters school? Is there certainty about the skills needed for entering a future labor market? Will people want to work in the type of economy predicted by human capital theorists, or will their emotions and imagination cause them to drop out of society? Is it possible or desirable to plan an educational system to school workers into an unknown economy?

Morin suggests that our thinking is guided by blinding paradigms, or what I have called wheels in the head.[5] The blinding paradigm gives privilege to particular logical operations and sets of assumptions in interpreting human action discourse. The blinding paradigm, according to Morin, "grants validity and universality to its chosen logic. Thereby it gives the qualities of necessity and truth to the discourse and theory it controls."[6]

The concept of blinding paradigms helps us to understand differences in interpretations of the globalization of education. World education culture theorists see globalization of education as a process originating in the spread of Western educational ideas and sustained by national leaders selecting best practices and research from a global flow of educational ideas. This spread of mass schooling, according to world culture theorists, is accompanied by Western ideas of human rights, democracy, free markets, and constitutional government. Schooling is thought of as a source of economic improvement and social advancement.

In contrast, world system and postcolonial/critical theorists work from the perspective that societies are in a constant struggle between the haves and have-nots. These theorists consider the central figures behind globalization to be those seeking the domination of the rich over the poor or the powerful over the powerless and those resisting this domination. As a result, these theorists contend, globalization is increasing inequalities between and within nations. Rather than considering the globalization of education as a positive spread of Western ideals, like the world education culture theorists, these theorists see it as a continuation of the exploitation by the few of the many. Consequently, the national adoption of an educational reform is often interpreted as another triumph for the power of the rich rather than, as world culture theorists might argue, adoption of a positive idea supported by concepts of justice and school improvement.

These differences in interpretation can be highlighted by a couple of quotes. In *National Differences, Global Similarities: World Culture and the Future of Schooling*, world educational theorists David Baker and Gerald LeTendre conclude, after reviewing the global spread of mass schooling, the growing uniformity of schooling, and the common use of educational research, "As the trends have led us to do throughout this book, we take a particularly bullish perspective on the future of mass education in general. Bullish in the sense that the institution, in a relatively short time, has become so dominant in most places in the world that we see little to suggest that it will not continue to be so into the near future."[7]

What is the blinding paradigm represented by the previous quote? First, there is the assumption that mass schooling is good for humanity. Second, it is assumed that the common use of globally available educational research, which represents a form of techno-rational thought, will improve education and the lives of the world's peoples. This blinding paradigm leads world education cultural theorists to focus on examples of the spread of mass schooling and the development of global educational reform without considering the possibility that mass schooling might actually be bad for a society and that educational research and reform might actually be serving the interests of the rich and powerful and not the interests of the global poor and downtrodden.

Another part of this blinding paradigm is the assumption that people act in a rational manner. Educational research is viewed as a rational process in search of truth, and it is assumed that national education policy leaders think logically in selecting educational reform ideas and research from the global flow. Educational research embodies techno-rational thought where the belief is that research findings can be used to engineer the best learning situations. Students are viewed as brains on sticks to be manipulated to learn more and it is assumed that learning more will improve the person and society.

My focus is on the blinding paradigm, and, consequently, I am avoiding the obvious questions about educational research, such as what is to be learned and for what purpose. Educational researchers, like other people, are also subject to the power of emotions and their own blinding paradigms. Emotions, desire for status and money, academic politics, and sources of funding play a fundamental role in shaping the nature and results of educational research. While they espouse techno-rational approaches to education, educational researchers often act to serve their own interests and those of their financial supporters, and like others, they can be dominated by emotions rather than reason. The same argument can be made about those who see national educational leaders as making logical choices about the best educational practices. National political leaders are often driven by a lust for power and greed.

Secularism is another aspect of the blinding paradigm of world education theorists. This blindness to the importance of religion and the issue of religious education is shared by postcolonial/critical and world system theorists. Earlier in this book, I quoted Eduardo Mendieta: "A theory of globalization that makes no room for religion has major theoretical flaws."[8] The lack of consideration of the role of religion in the globalization of education is a major deficit when wars of religion seem to have dominated global politics and social movements since the late twentieth century. Often those trapped by techno-rational thought and secularism believe that religion stands in the way of social progress. Consequently, they think that religious beliefs are something that will disappear with the spread of mass schooling or that religion can serve the purpose of regulating people's morality and act as a form of social control. World culture theorists do not spend time examining education for the purpose of maintaining religious beliefs or the role of the spiritual in education and society.

In summary, the blinding paradigm of world culture theorists that obscures their worldview includes the assumption that mass schooling is good, that mass schooling will result in a better society, that educational research is based on a techno-rational process, that national leaders utilize techno-rational processes in planning school systems, and that religious considerations are unimportant for educational planning.

Secularism is a value shared by world education cultural, postcolonial/critical, and world system theorists. When religion is discussed by postcolonial/critical and world system theorists, it is often treated as another instrument of domination by the rich and powerful or as a problem in maintaining a secular state. Exemplifying this flaw is the lack of any chapters on religion in the three major texts by postcolonialist/critical theorists on education and globalization, namely Nicholas Burbules and Carlos Torres (Eds.), *Globalization and Education: Critical Perspectives*; Michael Apple, Jane Kenway, and Michael Singh (Eds.), *Globalizing Education: Policies, Pedagogies, & Politics*; and Hugh Lauder, Phillip Brown, JoAnne Dillabough, and A.H. Halsey (Eds.), *Education, Globalization & Social Change*.[9]

The secular blindness to religion as a global education issue is exemplified not only by the lack of any chapters dealing with religion in the book edited by Burbules and Torres, but also by the total lack of discussion of the topic in *any* of the chapters. In the book edited by Apple, Kenway, and Singh, a discussion does appear in Michael Apple's chapter "Are Markets in Education Democratic? Neoliberal Globalism, Vouchers, and the Politics of Choice."[10] Apple's discussion demonstrates the tendency of only mentioning religion when it is a threat to secularism or when it supports an economic ideology. Regarding the threat to secularism, Apple refers to "religious fundamentalists and conservative evangelicals who want a return to (their) God in all of our institutions."[11] Referring to free market economics, he writes, "Still others will take the market road [supporting free markets] because for them God has said that this is 'His' road."[12] The issue is not that Apple is right or wrong in his comments—I tend to agree with him—but that these are the only comments in a book on globalization when the world has experienced centuries of religious struggles. In the book edited by Lauder, Brown, Dillabough, and Halsey, the only article that I could find that discusses religion focuses on the threat to the secular state by Muslim women wearing head scarves to school.[13]

Secularism represents only one element of the blinding paradigm of post-colonial/critical theorists. Another is derived from the thinking of Adam Smith and Karl Marx. The assumption is that human actions can be explained as a self-interested pursuit of material rewards. Other human actions such as spiritualism, a return to Indigenous cultural patterns, and rejection of industrialism are simply dismissed as delusional or a product of false consciousness. In fact, postcolonial/critical theorists often share the same assumptions as business leaders regarding human capital education. Business leaders are concerned that schools supply them with cheap labor. Postcolonial/critical theorists worry about human capital economics promoting greater economic inequality. These theorists want to ensure that schools promote economic equality. Both business leaders and postcolonial/critical theorists support an industrial consumer society and the material rewards it promises. The difference is in how the rewards are distributed.

The blinding paradigms of both world education culture and postcolonial/critical theorists might obscure the possibility that some people reject human capital theory because it despiritualizes humans and treats them as bloodless cogs to be fitted into the corporate and industrial global machinery. In discussions of human capital theory in my college classes, there are usually several students who react in abhorrence to the concept of humanity embedded in human capital theory—a concept of people that makes them simply natural resources to be molded by education to serve the economic system. World education culture theorists might applaud human capital education because it is supported by two organizations, the World Bank and Organization for Economic Cooperation and Development (OECD), which they consider engines of progress. On the other hand, the support by the World Bank and OECD might lead postcolonial/critical theorists to reject human capital economics because they see these two institutions as instruments that primarily serve the world's rich nations and people. However, there is little or nothing in the literature of these theorists about human capital education that expresses concern about the transformation of the traditional spiritual view of humanity or the effort to turn human society into a well-oiled machine or to reduce human action to a techno-rational process.

Culturalists, such as the anthropologists and comparative education scholars discussed in Chapter 1, provide a broad and complex view of globalization. Anthropologists search for ways in which cultures change as they interact with other cultures. Rather than seeing a developing uniformity to national and local schools, they see hybridity and new forms of education evolving. They also see competing educational models vying for dominance in the global arena. Missing from their work is the concern with economic inequalities and injustice that haunts the work of postcolonial/critical theorists. Their approach seems to blind them to the importance of power, wealth, and exploitation in shaping global culture. The borrowing and lending rhetoric of comparative educators creates a view of education as one of exchange rather than imposition, though many comparative educators do recognize the educational impositions of former colonial powers. They also give recognition to the role of power and wealth in determining national policies. However, the traditional approach of comparative educators is a comparison of national school systems to find ways by which school systems might be improved. Is the blinding paradigm of comparative educators the assumption that mass schooling operates for the benefit of humanity?

In summary, I think future research into the globalization of education should operate from Morin's principle of rational uncertainty. The world is a holistic and complex system that, at least at this point in time, cannot be encompassed in any single theory. Any theory of human action is only applicable to the examples that are used to prove it. The future is unpredictable. We can only make guesses because humans are at the same time rational, emotional, and maniacal, and the effects of human interactions within the biosphere are uncertain. In other words, we should examine our own blinding paradigms as we try to describe the globalization of education.

Future research on the globalization of education should embrace Morin's principle of rational uncertainty. In Chapter 2, I examined the policies and networks of the World Bank. Will future research show that the World Bank's educational efforts had positive effects on local communities, or will it, as I would suspect, show a mixed bag of results? In doing research on both the World Bank and OECD, scholars must carefully examine their own assumptions about what a "good education" means. Chapters 2 and 3 demonstrate how the educational policies of the World Bank, OECD, and the United Nations are linked to the development of Internet learning, games, and television programs. In the future, will the Internet, video games, and television contribute to a global uniformity of educational policies and practices? In Chapter 4, I examined the growth of the international marketing of tests, learning materials, and schools. Will these contribute to global uniformity of schooling? Chapters 5 and 6 discussed progressive and religious educational models that might be acting as countervailing influences to global educational uniformity. Also, civil society, as represented by international nongovernmental organizations (INGOs), might be countervailing powers to intergovernmental organizations (IGOs) like the World Bank and OECD. The complexity of the globalization of education is heightened by the findings of culturalists on how local communities and nations can change and adapt educational ideas in the global flow. Finally, as discussed in Chapter 7, the image of globalization becomes even more complex when global migration is included. Based on their past histories, nations are developing their own educational responses to multicultural and multilingual populations. Given all these factors, the globalization of education should be researched from a holistic and complex perspective with a consideration of the dynamic conflicts and intersections of the following major players: IGOs; global and local school leaders and citizens; media and popular culture; INGOs; multinational learning, publishing, and testing corporations; progressive and radical school agendas; religions; and the mass migration of the world's peoples.

Notes

1 Edgar Morin, *Seven Complex Lessons in Education for the Future* (Paris: UNESCO, 2008), p. 48.
2 Ibid., p. 75.
3 Ibid., pp. 20–21.
4 Ibid., p. 34.
5 Morin, *Seven Complex Lessons in Education for the Future*, pp. 21–23; and Joel Spring, *Wheels in the Head: Educational Philosophies of Authority, Freedom and Culture from Confucianism to Human Rights, Third Edition* (New York: Routledge, 2008).
6 Morin, *Seven Complex Lessons in Education for the Future*, p. 22.
7 David Baker and Gerald LeTendre, *National Differences, Global Similarities: World Culture and the Future of Schooling* (Palo Alto, CA: Stanford University Press, 2005), p. 174.
8 Eduardo Mendieta, "Society's Religion: The Rise of Social Theory, Globalization, and the Invention of Religion," in *Religions/Globalizations: Theories and Cases*, edited by Dwight N. Hopkins, Lois Ann Lorentzen, Eduardo Mendieta, and David Batstone (Durham, NC: Duke University Press, 2001), p. 47.
9 Nicholas Burbules and Carlos Torres, editors, *Globalization and Education: Critical Perspectives* (New York: Routledge, 2000); Michael Apple, Jane Kenway, and Michael Singh, editors, *Globalizing Education: Policies, Pedagogies, & Politics* (New York: Peter Lang, 2005); and Hugh Lauder, Phillip Brown, JoAnne Dillabough, and A.H. Halsey, *Education, Globalization & Social Change* (Oxford: Oxford University Press, 2006).
10 Michael Apple, "Are Markets in Education Democratic? Neoliberal Globalism, Vouchers, and the Politics of Choice," in *Globalizing Education*, pp. 209–231.
11 Ibid., p. 211.
12 Ibid., pp. 210–211.
13 Seyla Benhabib, "Multiculturalism and Gendered Citizenship" in *Education, Globalization & Social Change*, pp. 154–155.

INDEX

Lightning Source UK Ltd.
Milton Keynes UK